STUDIES IN HISTORY, ECONOMICS AND PUBLIC LAW

Edited by the

FACULTY OF POLITICAL SCIENCE
OF COLUMBIA UNIVERSITY

Number 207

THE INFLUENCE OF OVERSEA EXPANSION ON ENGLAND TO 1700

BY

JAMES E. GILLESPIE

THE INFLUENCE OF
OVERSEA EXPANSION
ON ENGLAND TO 1700

BY

JAMES E. GILLESPIE

OCTAGON BOOKS

A DIVISION OF FARRAR, STRAUS AND GIROUX

New York 1974

Reprinted 1974
by special arrangement with Columbia University Press

OCTAGON BOOKS
A DIVISION OF FARRAR, STRAUS & GIROUX, INC.
19 Union Square West
New York, N.Y. 10003

Library of Congress Cataloging in Publication Data

Gillespie, James Edward, 1887-
    The influence of oversea expansion on England to 1700.

    Reprint of the 1920 ed. published by Columbia University Press,
    New York, which was issued as no. 207 of Studies in history,
    economics, and public law.

    Thesis—Columbia University, 1920.
    Bibliography: p.

    1. Great Britain Colonies.   2. Imperial federation.
    I. Title.   II. Series: Columbia studies in the social sciences,
    no. 207.

JV1011.G52   1974   914.2'03   74-11125
ISBN 0-374-93079-1

Printed in USA by
Thomson-Shore, Inc.
Dexter, Michigan

CONTENTS

CHAPTER III

SOCIETY: MANNERS AND CUSTOMS (CONTINUED)

CHAPTER IV

COMMERCE

CHAPTER VII

MORALS AND RELIGION

CHAPTER VIII

THOUGHT

CHAPTER IX

THOUGHT (CONTINUED)

CHAPTER I

SOCIETY: RELIEF AND READJUSTMENT

As a result of oversea expansion during the sixteenth and seventeenth centuries England probably experienced more social relief and underwent a greater process of social readjustment than any other European country. Because of it the nation was enabled to pass through a critical period of its history with less injury and more benefit. England utilized in the colonies elements of the population which might have been of scant service at home. On the other hand, the strain to which it would have been subjected by adventurous, radical or criminal folk, otherwise denied an outlet for their activities or a chance for betterment abroad, would have been much greater.

As religious and political troubles became more intense during the Stuart régime, a noticeable exodus of the dissenting elements to America occurred.[1] Men who had independent ideas were thus enabled to enjoy them without disturbance to the state. At the same time they could maintain their connection with it and promote its commercial prosperity. The movement may be said to have started with the one hundred and ten Pilgrims whom the Mayflower carried to America in 1620.[2] Nine years later the migration was well under way when three hundred people went to

[1] It will be seen in another connection that many of the Puritan leaders came back from New England at the time of the Civil War. *Infra*, p. 343.

[2] *The Story of the Pilgrim Fathers 1606-1623*, edited by Edward Arber, p. 359.

Massachusetts Bay, and when in the next year, a fleet of fifteen vessels bore thither nine hundred and eighty Puritans. In 1637, as many as three thousand of them left for New England.[1] The following year the English authorities evidently began to experience some uneasiness regarding the social and economic effects of so large a migration, for Lord Maynard wrote to Archbishop Laud that he had been told of " the intention of divers clothiers of great trading to go suddenly into New England," and that he heard daily of " incredible numbers of persons of good abilities " who had sold their lands, " and are upon their departure thence." He declared further, that there was danger of various parishes becoming impoverished, because of the fact that so much grain was being carried away by the emigrants, and that fourteen ships in the Thames were getting ready for the voyage by Easter.[2] A number of years before this, Puritans had also gone to settle Providence Island in the West Indies, where Pym and other adventurers had aimed without success at founding an ideal community for the refuge of the oppressed.[3]

Members of other dissenting sects such as the Brownists, Quakers and Catholics, also left their native land to go to America. Calvert's first expedition to Maryland comprised three hundred people, of whom about one hundred and seventy-two were Catholics.[4] In 1681, Quakers from all parts of England hastened to join the expedition to Pennsylvania, and as many as three ships were sent. In one year

---

[1]Alexander Young, *Chronicles of the First Planters of the Colony of Massachusetts Bay 1623-1636*, p. 310.

[2]*Calendar of State Papers, Colonial Series, America and the West Indies*, vol. i, p. 266.

[3] Arthur P. Newton, *The Colonising Activities of the English Puritans*, p. 144.

[4]Henry Cabot Lodge, *A Short History of the English Colonies in America*, p. 97.

seven thousand settlers arrived at this colony.[1]   All the colonists, however, were not Quakers and they did not all come from England. Disbanded soldiers unable to settle down to a peaceful life, refugees of the weaker party driven from their homes, property owners dispossessed by the victor or ruined by war expenses, rebels or heretics who had to be disposed of at the conclusion of the struggle, were among the common social problems that European nations of the time had to meet as a result of the many civil and religious commotions. England's colonial enterprises were useful in helping to meet such conditions. Thus, when John Smith sought to find men for the Virginia colony, the English soldiers just home from the continental wars, with whom the city of London was filled, gladly welcomed the new adventure to America, and the nation was only too pleased to be rid of them.[2]

Sir Josiah Child, a seventeenth-century writer, famous for his work both as a pamphleteer and as governor of the East India Company, also mentions the large number of people ruined by the Civil War who left England for America, and attributes the growth of Virginia and Barbados chiefly to them. He declares that

the principal Growth and Encrease of the aforesaid Plantations of Virginia and Barbadoes happened in, or immediately after, our late Civil Wars, when the worsted party by the fate of War, being deprived of their Estates, and having some of them never been bred to labour, and others made unfit for it by the lazy habit of a Soldiers Life, there wanting Means to maintain them all abroad with his Majesty, many of them betook themselves to the aforesaid Plantations, . . . Another great swarm, or accession of the new Inhabitants to the afore-

[1] Lodge, *op. cit.*, pp. 212, 213.

[2] John Esten Cooke, *Virginia: a History of the People*, p. 14.

said Plantations, as also to New England, Jamaica and all
other his Majesties Plantations, in the West-Indies, ensued
upon his Majesties Restoration, when the former prevailing
party being by a Divine Hand of Providence brought under,
the Army disbanded, many dispossest of their pretended
Lands, Estates, etc. many became impoverished, destitute of
employment; and therefore such as could find no way of
living at home, and some which feared the re-establishment of
the Ecclesiastical Laws, under which they could not live, were
forced to transport themselves, or sell themselves for a few
years, to be transported to the Foreign English Plantations.
. . . .[1]

According to the laws of the time, furthermore, political
offenders were liable to the death penalty. The authorities
of the Commonwealth were the first to substitute banish-
ment for it. The settlement and development of the colonies
in America offered an opportunity to the government for
mitigating the punishment of such unfortunates, and for
enabling them to be of benefit to the nation in a new country
where they would no longer be dangerous to the old. Thus
after the capture of Drogheda, Ireland, by the Parliamentary
army in September 1649, the survivors of the executions that
followed were shipped across the Atlantic to be sold as servants. Moreover, " there remained behind, of necessity,
great numbers of widows and orphans and deserted wives
and families; and these the government proceeded to ship
wholesale to the West Indies—the boys for slaves, and the
women and girls for mistresses to the English sugar-
planters." [2]

[1] Josiah Child, *A New Discourse of Trade* (London, 1698), pp. 183, 184.

[2] Philip A. Bruce, *The Economic History of Virginia in the Seventeenth Century*, vol. i, p. 608; Charles George Walpole, *A Short History
of the Kingdom of Ireland from the Earliest Times to the Union with
Great Britain*, p. 19.

In 1653 as many as a hundred Irish Tories were sold as servants in Virginia.[1] Cromwell resorted to transportation likewise in the case of Scottish prisoners taken in the Preston campaign of 1648,[2] and after the battle of Dunbar in 1650, when between one hundred and fifty and three hundred were sent to New England,[3] and the next year a large number are said to have been deported after the battle of Worcester.[4] On several occasions, notably in consequence of the uprising in Scotland of 1678, and the Monmouth rebellion of 1685, this means of disposing of prisoners was employed.[5]

The Conventicle Act of 1664, which made anyone who attended a religious meeting not held in accordance with the practice of the English Church an offender against the law, created another class of political offenders which was usually sent to the colonies. In 1665, for example, as many as one

[1] Bruce, *op. cit.*, vol. i, p. 609.

[2] James Davie Butler, "British Convicts shipped to the American Colonies," in *The American Historical Review*, vol. ii, p. 13. These Scottish prisoners were to be shipped with "all the speed possible" in order to relieve the "several and respective counties of the Charge and Burden" of their support. The plantations were to be supplied first, and all who were not in demand there were to be sold to Venice. Some dealers in Bristol desired 500 of them. *Journals of the House of Commons*, vol. vi, p. 5.

[3] Butler, *op. cit.*, p. 13.

[4] Both Bruce and J. C. Ballagh think that about 1600 prisoners were sent to America at this time. Butler, on the other hand, says the number transported was much smaller than is generally stated. According to Samuel Rawson Gardiner, *History of the Commonwealth and Protectorate 1649-1660*, vol. i, p. 465, no proof is given that these political felons were sent at all. Bruce, vol. i, p. 608; James Curtis Ballagh, *White Servitude in the Colony of Virginia*, p. 35, in Johns Hopkins University Studies in Historical and Political Science, Baltimore, 1895; Butler, p. 13.

[5] Butler, *op. cit.*, p. 14. As many as 239 and others whose numbers are not given, were sent to Barbados after Monmouth's rebellion. *Acts of the Privy Council of England, Colonial Series*, vol. i, pp. 149, 651.

hundred and forty Quakers in Newgate and the Hartford jail were dispatched to the West Indies.[1]

However, transportation was found useful, not only in the cases of political offenses, but in that of actual criminals as well. Among the Acts of the Privy Council is one dated March 24, 1617, which reads as follows:

Whereas it hath pleased his Majestie oute of his singular Clemencie and mercy to take into his princely Consideration the wretched estate of divers of his Subjects who by the Lawes of the Realme are adjudged to dye for sondry offences thoughe heynous in themselves, yet not of the highest nature, soe as his Majestie both out of his gracious Clemencye, as also for diuerse weighty Considerations Could wishe they mighte be rather Corrected than destroyed, and that in theire punishmentes some of them might liue, and yealde a profitable Service to the Common wealth in partes abroad, where it shall bee founde fitt to imploye them, for which purpose his Majestie having directed his Commission under the greate Seale of England, to vs and the rest of his privey Counsell, gyving full power Warrent and Authoritye to us or and Sixe or more of vs whereof the Lord Chancelor or Lord Keeper of the Greate Seale, Lord Treasurer, Lord Privy Seall, and one principall Secretarye to be two, to Reprieve and stay from execution suche persons as now stand Convicted of any Robbery or felony (Willfull murther, Rape, witchcraft or Burglary onely excepted) who for strength of bodye or other abilityes shall be thought fitt to be imployed in forreine discoveryes or other Services beyond the seas. . . .[2]

Transportation appeared as a considerable mitigation of the severity of the law, especially when death was the penalty for over four hundred offenses and a code of laws was in force which in Cromwell's time sanctioned the execution of

[1] *Acts of P. C., Col. Series*, vol. i, pp. 393, 394, 402; Butler, p. 15.
[2] *Acts of P. C., Col. Series*, vol. i, p. 10.

3,000 persons for witchcraft alone.[1]   Judges who had been obliged against their will to decree death in many cases that they considered much too slight for such a penalty, now gladly availed themselves of the new manner of disposing of criminals. Throughout the seventeenth century many convicts were sent to the colonies where their labor was found very useful. So numerous had their class become in Virginia by the year 1670, that an order mentioning " the great number of felons and other desperate villains sent hither from the several prisons of England " and prohibiting their further importation, was issued by the General Court of Virginia.[2]   But this act like all others of a similar nature was annulled by the crown.[3]   Narcissus Luttrell in his diary, November 17, 1692, remarks that a ship lay at Leith, bound for Virginia, in which the magistrates were sending eighty disreputable women. All the American colonies outside of New England were penal settlements.[4]   Twenty thousand convicts were imported into Maryland alone before the American Revolution. Except for the possible fact that half of them came before 1750, there is no indication of how many of them arrived before the eighteenth century.[5]   Convicts also were greatly in demand as a labor supply

---

[1] John T. Scharf, *History of Maryland*, vol. i, p. 371.

[2] Butler, *op. cit.*, pp. 17, 18. In 1665 twenty-four convicts were shipped within two months' time to Virginia and Barbados. Eighteen were sent to the former colony in 1667. *Ibid.*, p. 17.

[3] Butler does not think the order of the Virginia Court had effect, and cites Luttrell as evidence. Bruce believes that during the first years following the Restoration the number of men and women of this character brought to Virginia was larger than it had been before. Ballagh, on the other hand, says that for the next half century Virginia had a respite from " Newgaters " and " Jail Birds." Butler, pp. 18, 19; Bruce, vol. i. pp. 604, 605; Ballagh, p. 37.

[4] Butler, *op. cit.*, 18, 19.

[5] *Ibid.*; Scharf, *op. cit.*, vol. i, p. 371.

throughout the English West Indies. In 1684 St. Kitts petitioned that 300 malefactors previously ordered for service on the plantations might be transported, so that they might strengthen the colony.[1]

Not only was a new method of dealing with criminals thus discovered and applied, but crime itself as a result of the opening of new fields of adventure, became less frequent. As one writer remarks:

There can be no doubt that the new discoveries led to new and more merciful punishments, and caused many men who would otherwise have found their way to the gallows, to seek a new home across the seas. The ultimate effect on a nation of withdrawing its most enterprising spirits can hardly be unmixed benefit; but if England showed less signs of turbulence in the eighteenth century than in the sixteenth, the emigrations of the seventeenth may fairly be assumed to have contributed something toward that result.[2]

From the latter part of the sixteenth century onward the proposal of colonizing America with England's poor and unemployed was vigorously agitated in numerous pamphlets and sermons written by prominent men of the day. Eventually the government, believing the plan a good one, took action upon the matter. On June 13, 1621, the statement is made in the Court Book of the Virginia Company, that it has just accepted a proposal made by Parliament to send paupers to Virginia. It as asserted in this connection that there has been " great complaynte of the multitude of poor people swarming in every city, town and parish." [3] This willingness of the Company was greeted by the House with

[1] *Acts of the P. C., Col. Series*, vol. ii, pp. 68, 69.

[2] Luke Owen Pike, *A History of Crime in England*, vol. ii, pp. 109, 110.

[3] *Records of the Virginia Company, Court Book 1619 to 1622*, edited by Susan Myra Kingsbury (Washington, 1906), vol. i, pp. 479, 489.

" a verie great and gratefull applause," although the parishes
themselves do not seem to have responded to any great extent to such an agency for relieving themselves of the " poore
with whome they (were) pestered." At any rate, a further
statement of the time, which says that the men recently
sent to the colonies were " choice spirits " drawn from all
parts of England, would lead to this conclusion.[1] It is
known that some had begun to be sent in 1617, even before
Parliament had made its proposal to the Company, and
that others were dispatched during 1619, 1622 and 1635
from Bridewell, where they were kept until a ship was ready
to take them. Their transportation expenses were generally
paid from municipal funds and collections, although in a
few cases the parochial officials themselves bore them.[2]

The vagrant and pauper adults dispatched to Virginia under this plan seem never to have been very many, for Governor Berkeley, in 1671, estimated the number of all the
servants in the colony at 6,000.[3] How many were sent to
the West Indies is difficult to determine. Some light on
the matter is afforded by the fact that in 1656 the Council
of State voted that 1,000 girls, and as many young men,
should be taken from Ireland and sent to Jamaica. In November of that year Cromwell ordered the Scotch government to apprehend "all known, idle, masterless robbers and
vagabonds, male and female," and transport them to
Jamaica.[4] Doubtless, taking into consideration all the English plantation colonies, many laborers of this sort went from
England during the century, especially since the demand for
labor was so great.

[1] Bruce, *op. cit.*, vol. i, p. 596.

[2] E. M. Leonard, *The Early History of the English Poor Relief*, pp.
229, 489; Edward D. Neill, *Virginia Vetusta, etc.*. p. 103.

[3] Bruce, *op. cit.*, vol. i, p. 610.

[4] Thomas Southey, *Chronological History of the West Indies*, vol.
ii, p. 11.

The authorities not merely strove to deport England's pauper and vagrant adults, but even used America [1] as a means of disposing of poor children. In 1619 London furnished 100 such children. In 1620 the Mayor declared that the city had agreed to provide 100 more, and to allow each five pounds for clothing and transportation. That they were sent may be inferred from a letter written by the Virginia Company in June, 1621, to the Aldermen of London thanking them for their " great forwardness " in aiding the plantation in this respect. That the youthful emigrants, also, were not to come merely from London is apparent from a motion made in 1620 by Sir Edwin Sandys, which was acted upon by the company. A committee was appointed to obtain from the justices of the peace in the shires of the kingdom such youths as were a burden upon their respective parishes. According to the policy that had already been inaugurated in the case of London, each of the parishes was to be asked to contribute five pounds sterling toward the equipment of every youth delivered by it.[2] The proposal seems to have been well received, for it is said that in one year alone, 1627, as many as 1,400 or 1,500 children, who had been gathered up in different parts of England, were

---

[1] Apparently children were deported from England as early as 1609, and according to *The Calendar of State Papers* their destination was the East Indies rather than America. It seems highly probable, however, that a mistake was made in the destination mentioned, or if this is correct, that they would be sold somewhere along the African coast to traders going to the West Indies, for white children would hardly be in demand in the Orient. The statement reads as follows: " Five caracks sailed on March 12/22, 1609 for the East Indies, laden with merchandise and carrying in place of soldiers, children and youths from the age of ten upward to the number of 1,500; in a few years they say these children will be able to do good service " . . *Cal. S. P.. Col. Series, East Indies* (1513-1616), p. 182.

[2] *Records of the Virginia Company*, vol. i, pp. 270, 293; Edward D. Neill, *The English Colonization of America during the Seventeenth Century*, pp. 159, 160; Bruce, vol. i, p. 592.

sent to Virginia.[1] Winthrop, in his *Journal*, mentions that on June 23, 1643, the " Seabright " arrived at Massachusetts Bay with twenty children. These, he observes, " with many more to come after, were sent by money given one fast day in London, and allowed by Parliament and the city for that purpose." [2]

The colonial demand for the labor of both children and adults became so great that it was the cause of one of the worst evils to which English society of that century was subject. Kidnapping or " spiriting," as it was called, began to be practiced during the reign of Charles I, and was continued throughout the Commonwealth Period, the reign of Charles II and into the eighteenth century. It is difficult to estimate its extent because, when successful it could rarely be proved, unless the victim was able to return to England.[3] In all parts of the land at the time, the expression "to spirit away " was commonly used, and " it was full of mysterious and terrifying significance to the popular mind." When the absence of any one could not be explained by his neighbors, he was said to have been " spirited away." The means employed by the kidnappers to gain possession of their victim were usually quite commonplace.

They played upon the ignorance of the simple minded, the restlessness of persons in the lower walks of life who were anxious for a change, the despair of those who were sunk in hopeless poverty, and the eagerness of those who had been guilty of infractions of the law to escape from the country.[4]

The persons who voluntarily made an agreement with the " spirits " were taken to some cook-shop in the neighbor-

[1] Edward D. Neill, *Virginia Carolorum*, p. 47.

[2] " Winthrop's Journal, 1630-1649," edited by J. K. Hosmer, vol. ii, p. 96, in *Original Narratives of Early American History*.

[3] Pike, *op. cit.*. vol. ii, p. 354; Ballagh, p. 38.

[4] Bruce, *op. cit.*, vol. i, p. 615.

hood of the wharves of one of the principal seaports, and here they were closely confined until sold to a merchant or ship-owner. These places became so notorious that warrants were frequently sued out, authorizing employers to search them for the recovery of their apprentices.[1]

Various classes of people made a comfortable living in this way. Ladies of the court, even the mayor of Bristol, were suspected of having profited from kidnapping.[2] Judge Jeffreys, when he investigated the matter at Bristol, found all the aldermen and justices concerned more or less in this form of evil doing, and the mayor himself was as badly involved as any of the other officials.[3] Sir Edward Hext, a justice of the peace of Somersetshire, wrote to the Privy Council that Owen Evans, messenger of the Chamber, had a false commission to seize maidens and send them to Virginia and the Bermudas. This " spirit's " conduct had caused such terror that no fewer than forty girls had fled from one parish, and their parents did not know where they were.[4] Bands of ruffians went sailing along the coasts, especially of Scotland and Ireland, picking up the people. Scarcely a ship departed from England for America that did not carry a number of abducted persons, or at least those who pretended that they had been stolen. By 1664 this evil practice had become so obnoxious that tumults frequently arose in the streets of London over some one who was accused of kidnapping.[5]

[1] Bruce, op. cit., vol. i, p. 615.

[2] Ballagh, op. cit., p. 38.

[3] William Hunt, Bristol, p. 142.

[4] Neill, The English Colonization of America during the Seventeenth Century, p. 160.

[5] Bruce, op. cit., vol. i, p. 617; James Rodway, The West Indies, p. 146; Ballagh, p. 39. For further accounts of kidnapping near London see The Middlesex County Records, edited by John C. Jeaffreson (London, 1888), vol. iii, pp. 100, 229, 253, 257, 259; vol. iv, pp. 70, 72, 79, 87, 245.

The Lord Mayor and Aldermen of London, and a number of merchants, planters and shipmasters, accordingly, petitioned the government to establish a registry office to put an end to kidnapping. This office was instituted in September 1664, with the object of registering all contracts of those who were taken as servants to the colonies. As this did not prevent the evil, in 1670 an act was passed making kidnapping a capital offense, but this also failed to accomplish its purpose. Ten years after the law was put into force, it was said that 10,000 persons were annually stolen away from the kingdom. An order of the Council, issued in 1682, reveals the prevalence of the evil in spite of all that had been done to eradicate it.[1]

Attention thus far has been confined to the relief that came to English society from emigration to the American colonies, and the evils incident to it. But there is another aspect of the matter which must be emphasized, namely the value of such possessions as a source of employment at home or on the seas. The growth of various English industries as a result of world commerce, such as the woolen, silk, cotton and hardware manufactures, mining, shipbuilding and even agriculture, resulted in the employment in England of ever increasing numbers of workmen. Sir Josiah Child estimates that during the second half of the seventeenth century, the plantation colonies alone gave employment to 200,000 persons in England. He explains this by saying that, as it was customary to give occupation to eight or ten negroes to every white man in the West India plantations " for Provisions, Cloaths and household-goods, Sea-men, and all others employed about Materials for Building, Fitting and Victualling of ships. Every Englishman in Barbadoes or Jamaica creates employment for four men at home."[2]

[1] Bruce, *op. cit.*, vol. i, p. 618; Ballagh, p. 39.
[2] Child, *op. cit.*, p. 188, *et seq.*

As early as 1605, when England had 250 ships in the New-foundland fisheries, they carried about 10,000 seamen and fishermen. Besides this, 20,000 other folk in the western part of England itself were kept busy equipping and supplying the fishing fleet, and were wholly dependent upon the trade for their living. In 1680, however, there were only about half as many persons engaged in the industry. In 1615, the Greenland fisheries are said to have employed 1,400 people and those of Iceland, 2,500.[1]

The trading voyages to the East, furthermore, provided work. As many as 2,500 seamen at one time manned the ships of the East India Company, and 120 factors or agents came to be kept in the East. As for those in impecunious circumstances "when all the other doors of charitie are shut, the East India gates stand wide open to receive the needy and the poore, giving them good entertainment, with two months wages before hand, to make their needfull provisions for the voyage." The Company, moreover, was very liberal in paying large sums of money for the relief of the seamen's widows and children. By 1628 the East India Company had at least 1,000 persons engaged in building and repairing its ships, and in making artillery and naval stores. Other laborers looked after the salt meat and other provisions for the voyage. Even the children might find work with the Company in picking oakum.[2]

The East Indies, as well as the American colonies, were

[1] *Cal. S. P. Col. Series, America and the West Indies* (*1513-1616*), p. 25; (*1681-1685*), p. 710; *Journals of the House of Commons*, vol. xi, p. 681; "The Trades Increase" (London, 1615), in *Harleian Miscellany*, vol. iii, pp. 301, 304.

[2] Edward Keble Chatterton, *The Old East Indiamen*, pp. 79. 86; A. Anderson, *Historical and Chronological Deduction of the Origin of Commerce*, vol. ii, p. 438; Thomas Mun, "A Discourse of Trade to the East Indies" in J. R. McCulloch, *A Select Collection of Early English Tracts on Commerce, etc.* (London, 1856), p. 35.

looked upon as affording an opportunity for the younger sons of the English landowning class who unfortunately, because of the custom of entail, were unprovided with means. The children of the clergy and other professional men were likewise now offered the chance for an independent life. Moreover, many of the young men, it is said, were sent as sailors or factors to India, in order that they might be gotten out of the way after disgracing the family.[1] The merchants too, took advantage of the openings for their sons in the colonies. Thus, Nicholas Ferrar, a prominent merchant adventurer of the seventeenth century, sent his son William to settle as a barrister in Virginia.[2]

In conclusion something must be said about the question whether emigration and oversea voyages tended materially to lessen or weaken the population of the mother country during the century under consideration. Both Child and Charles Davenant, the writer on economics, believed that the effect was slight. The former argues that " such as our employment is for People, so many will our people be." If the colonies were to draw away too many people, according to his reasoning, wages would be raised and that would bring foreigners into the country to take their places. After carefully studying the situation, he concluded that England had more people just before the Great Plague than previous to the occupation of New England, Virginia, Barbados and other colonies.[3] Davenant states that England did not lose in the seventeenth century more than 1,000 persons a year

[1] Hugh Edward Egerton, *The Origin and Growth of the English Colonies and of their System of Government.* p. 14; Chatterton, *op. cit.,* p. 86.

[2] Nicholas Ferrar is said to have regarded Virginia and Bermuda as " a project for the common good, for the employment of unsettled people, for estates to younger brothers." H. P. K. Skipton, *The Life and Times of Nicholas Ferrar,* pp. 61, 62.

[3] Child, *op. cit.,* p. 191.

to the American colonies above the number returning from them and the accessions to the nation from other European countries.[1] Undoubtedly England was deprived of some valuable men, especially among the religious and political refugees, but as Child points out, had it not been for the English possessions overseas, many of these emigrants would have gone to the continent. Besides, it must be remembered that, whatever the loss in this respect, there was a certain gain in another, since the country rid itself of large numbers of people whom it considered undesirable, and as already observed, gave them a chance to become successful in a new world. The balance, therefore, was on the whole favorable.

With those who met death upon the sea, or through privations endured in the colonies, the case was different. Some of the voyages to the East especially, were noted for their heavy mortality. On Henry Middleton's first voyage to the Orient the commander and all except ten of his original crew perished. Nicholas Downton took seventy sailors with him and brought back twenty. Captain Saris had ninety when he left England and returned with only twenty-two or twenty-three. Disease carried away about one hundred and thirty of the two hundred colonists who went with Francis Blackwell to Virginia.[2]

Although the actual loss in population was not considerable, a radical shifting of the centers of it took place. A pamphlet published in 1614, particularly mentions Colchester, Harwich, Orford, Aldborough, Dunwich, Warderswich, Southwold, Yarmouth, Blackley, Wells, Lynne and Boston as " reduced to an exceedingly poor and beggerly condition." [3] In other words, many ports on the eastern and

[1] Charles Davenant, *Political and Commercial Works*, vol. ii, p. 203.

[2] *Harleian Miscellany*, vol. iii, pp. 302, 303; Herbert L. Osgood, *The American Colonies in the Seventeenth Century*, vol. i, p. 105.

[3] Frederick Eden, *State of the Poor*, vol. i. p. 151.

southern coasts declined in importance, while those such as London, Yarmouth, Scarborough, Liverpool, Westchester, Bristol, Portsmouth, Lyme and Plymouth, which were directly in touch with the commerce then reaching out to the distant parts of the earth, kept increasing both in size and in wealth. Child, in fact, declares that the population of London and its neighborhood had doubled within sixty years.[1]

[1] Child, *op. cit.*, pp. 190, 191, 192.

CHAPTER II

SOCIETY: MANNERS AND CUSTOMS

Of all commodities gold was the one most eagerly sought by Europeans in their voyages to America and along the African coast. In its power of attraction the yellow metal made no discrimination among nationalities. The English felt it no less than the Spaniards. Each new voyage to the west tended to add fuel to the desire among them for wealth easily acquired. Thus, by the time that Frobisher had made his second journey, and had brought back some " black and glittering rock," the eagerness for riches had become so general that even the officers of state strove to become adventurers. Queen Elizabeth herself was keenly interested in the new enterprises, for she ordered Secretary Walsingham to write to the Lord Treasurer and the Lord Chamberlain, urging that a third voyage be undertaken.[1]

When settlements were made in Virginia, the English were still seeking gold. In a letter which the president and the council at Jamestown despatched to England by Newport, on his return in 1607, the London Company was urged to forward provisions with the utmost expedition, " lest the all devouring Spaniard lay his ravenous hands upon these gold-showing mountains." [2]

Captain Smith also reported that among the colonists of

---

[1] *Cal. of S. P., Col. Series America and W. I.*, vol. ii, p. xvi. Frobisher made three voyages between the years 1576 and 1578.

[2] Bruce, *op. cit.*, vol. i, p. 15.

this time, " there was no talk, no hope, no worke, but dig gold, wash gold, refine gold, loade gold." [1] The English however, were to be disappointed in their hopes of finding mines of the precious metals in America, and although the ships which traded along the African coast did actually bring back some gold dust, the amount was not considerable until well into the seventeenth century.[2] Their wealth in this respect was to come for awhile mainly through the plunder of Spanish and Portuguese galleons, and through systematic trade.

As will be shown more specifically in another connection,[3] it was the opening of the mines in Mexico and Peru and the development of the African trade which led to an immense increase in the world's supply of the precious metals. When gold and silver became relatively plentiful in England during the sixteenth and seventeenth centuries, large quantities were employed there as elsewhere for purely decorative purposes.[4] The costumes of civilians and military folk were adorned with a profusion of gold and silver lace and embroidery. Cloth of gold became the favorite fabric in English society. Gold was displayed on every rich material. Silver taffeta embroidered in gold, and a damask of crimson or yellow wrought with gold and trimmed with fur, were fashionable.[5]

The demand for silver plate became constantly greater until, toward the end of the reign of Charles II, the metal was used for many purposes. Found first in the residences

---

[1] John Smith, *The Generall Historie of Virginia, New England and the Summer Isles, etc.* (London, 1624), p. 53.

[2] *Infra*, p. 114.

[3] *Infra*, p. 162.

[4] One fifth of the supply was used in this manner. William Jacob, *An Historical Inquiry into the Production and Consumption of the Precious Metals*, vol. ii, p. 131.

[5] E. Aria, *Costume, Fanciful, Historical and Theatrical*, p. 49.

of princes, nobles and wealthy citizens, soon even tradesmen, clergy, lawyers and others of the middle rank of life possessed articles made of silver.   Eventually also, it came to be used in the manufacture of bedsteads, bath-tubs, braziers, mirror-frames, toilet-tables, toilet-sets, andirons, as well as commonly to be employed in table utensils.[1]

Another way in which the precious metals were utilized was in the making of rings, watches and neck-chains.   The curious custom of converting bullion into chains for personal adornment is exemplified by Sir Thomas Gresham, the bulk of whose wealth on his death in 1579 was found to consist of this kind of jewelery.   Indeed it was thought that no gentleman was properly equipped unless he wore at least one of these ornaments.[2]

On no article of luxury was the influence of the conquest of Mexico and Peru so visible as on gems.   " The dealers viewed with amazement the continual arrival of precious stones in fabulous quantities, and surpassing in size and beauty all they had hitherto known."   Immense amounts of emeralds, turquoises and opals came from Peru and Mexico, and vast numbers of pearls were brought from the West Indies.[3]   Many jewels also were among the spoils taken by English buccaneers from the Spaniards[4] and Portuguese, and still others came through legitimate trade.

On the other hand the voyages which the English made to the East in the seventeenth century were a most valuable

---

[1] Jacob, *op. cit.*, vol. ii, p. 128; James Jackson, *An Illustrated History of English Plate, Ecclesiastical and Secular*, vol. i, p. 220, *et seq.*

[2] H. Clifford Smith, *Jewelry*, p. 236, *et seq.*

[3] A. DeBarrera, *Gems and Jewels*, pp. 131, 220, 225.

[4] One Spanish ship captured by Sir Francis Drake was carrying four chests of pearls, each containing two bushels. W. B. Rye, *England as Seen by Foreigners in the Days of Elizabeth and James the First, etc.*, p. 89.

source of supply for jewels, especially for diamonds from India.[1] Indeed, ever since the discovery of a new route around the Cape of Good Hope, not only jewels, but other Oriental luxuries such as spices, dyes, perfumes, velvets, satins, cloth-of-gold and silk, which previously had been brought in smaller quantities at great cost, had fairly flooded the European markets and accordingly were sold at much lower prices than formerly. More than several caravans could carry were now taken in a single ship; and instead of several shiftings, the cargo was loaded only once. One million pounds of raw Persian silk, for example, sent by the old mode of conveyance would have cost £1,465,000, while the same quantity brought by the new route cost £511,458, or about one-third of the earlier sum.[2] Thus, the lower price of luxuries, the greater variety and attractiveness of the supply enhancing the desire for them, the increase in the amount and circulation of the precious metals, the extravagance naturally caused by sudden wealth, all contributed to make the period under consideration one in which great lavishness in dress and adornment was common.

At no time, in fact, had so many gems been used as personal ornaments. Queen Elizabeth, typical of her age, was extraordinarily fond of them, and wore them on every opportunity. " Her locks piled high in curls and puffs were surmounted by crowns of jewels, and her sleeves and skirts padded into diamond design traced with embroidery at every point held a pendent stone." [3]

---

[1] H. C. Smith, *op. cit.*, p. 278. In 1624, the East India Company ordered their agents in India to invest 10,000 or 20,000 rials yearly in diamonds. *The English Factories in India: a Calendar of Documents in the India Office, British Museum and Public Record Office* (1624-29), edited by William Foster, p. 25.

[2] David Macpherson, *The History of European Commerce with India, etc.*, p. 103.

[3] Aria, *op. cit.*, p. 54.

There is not a single portrait of her [said Horace Walpole] that one can call beautiful. The profusion of ornaments with which they are loaded are marks of her continual fondness for dress, while they entirely exclude all grace, and leave no more room for a painter's genius than if he had been employed to copy an Indian idol, totally composed of hands and necklaces. A pale Roman nose, a head of hair loaded with crowns and powdered with diamonds, a vast ruff, a vaster farthingale, a bushel of pearls, are features by which every body knows at once the pictures of Queen Elizabeth.[1]

Her surroundings were no less gorgeous than her attire. At Hampton Court the tapestries were of pure gold and fine silk; those in the queen's throne room were adorned with gold, pearls and precious stones. One table-cover alone was valued at over fifty thousand crowns. The royal throne was studded with very large diamonds, rubies and sapphires, " glittering among other precious stones and pearls as suns among stars." [2]

In England, furthermore, the splendor-loving sixteenth century far exceeded the Middle Ages in the use of the finger-ring. Pictures of the period represent persons with their hands heavily loaded with rings. Every finger-joint up to the nail was covered with them and they were worn even upon the knuckles. Due to the projection of the rings' bezels, it would have been impossible to wear gloves, if the custom of placing the rings outside the gloves, as well as the ugly fashion of slitting their fingers, had not furnished a solution of the difficulty. In Lucas Cranach's portrait of a lady, in the National Gallery, rings are worn both over and beneath the gloves, and every finger and the thumbs are adorned with two or three. Men's gloves were also slashed to show their rings.[3]

[1] H. C. Smith, *op. cit.*, p. 214.
[2] Rye, *op. cit.*, p. 18; H. D. Traill, *Social England*, vol. iii, p. 393.
[3] H. C. Smith, *op. cit.*, p. 258, *et seq.*

The custom of wearing earrings, doubtless in imitation of Oriental peoples,[1] furthermore, became popular during this period. "Another sorte of dissolute minions and wanton Sempronians (for I can term them no better)," remarks Philip Stubbes the satirist, " are so far bewitched, as they are not ashamed to make holes in their eares, where-at they hang rings, and other Jewels of gold and precious stones."[2] If anything the men were more addicted to this form of display than the women. Both Sir Walter Raleigh and King Charles I wore earrings. This ornament vanished for a time during the Protectorate.[3]

Not only were the Tudor courtier's eyes dazzled by the splendor of fine jewelry, but his sense of smell was likewise treated to more elaborate and costly perfumes than had before been known in England. Indeed, so backward had society been in this respect that it was said that the English could not make any costly wash or perfume until about the fourteenth and fifteenth year of Elizabeth's reign, and the custom of using them had not been generally adopted until her time.[4] The chief odors were strong ones such as those derived from musk, civet and ambergris, all of which were brought from the Orient by the English and other nationalities, and the material last named was found also in Bermuda

[1] " There is a certen kinde of people in the Orientall parte of the World . . . that, having plentie of precious Stones and Margarits amongst them, they cut and launce their skinnes and fleshe, setting therein these precious Stones . . . " *Philip Stubbes' Anatomy of the Abuses in England in Shakespere's Youth, A. D. 1583, pt. i, collated with other editions in 1583, 1585 and 1595*, edited by F. J. Furniwell (The New Shakespere Society Publications Series), vi, nos. 4 and 6, p. 70.

[2] *Ibid.*

[3] H. C. Smith, *op. cit.*, p. 235.

[4] Arnold J. Cooley, *The Toilet and Cosmetic Arts in Ancient and Modern Times, etc.*, p. 68; Eugene Rimmel, *The Book of Perfumes*, p. 201.

and other parts of the New World.[1] A ball of perfumed
paste, called pomander or " pomme d'ambre " carried in the
pocket, held in the hand, or hung around the neck, enjoyed
special favor in Elizabethan society, both with the object of
preventing infection and for the agreeable odor of the rose-
water, labdanum, benzoin, storax,[2] ambergris, civet and
musk in which it was steeped.[3] These perfumes were also
lavished upon such articles as gloves, leather jerkins and
cloaks and even shoes, while the floors of apartments and
churches received their share.[4] Delicate scents were introduced into soap[5] and found their way to the fashionable
toilet. Thus a writer of the time instructs the servants to

> Bring, oh bring the essence pot,
> Amber, musk, and bergamot,
> Eau de chipre, eau de luce,
> Sanspareil and citron juice.[6]

One may easily imagine the variegated colors of the rich
silks and velvets, the flashing jewels, the scent of rare
Oriental perfumes, the gleam of gold which appeared on the
gay social butterflies suddenly arisen from the somber Eng-

---

[1] Rimmel, *op. cit.*, pp. 204, 242, 243, 246, 247; *A Calendar of the Court
Minutes of the East India Company* (*1640-43*), p. 6, mentions musk as
imported from India in 1640; Samuel Purchas, *Purchas His Pilgrimes,*
etc., vol. xix, pp. 179, 203, mentions ambergris as found in Bermuda.
Flowers such as the tuberose and hyacinth introduced from the Orient
before the eighteenth century were valuable for perfume. Spices such
as cinnamon, cloves and mace were also used. Rimmel, pp. 251, 253, 256.

[2] Benzoin came from the East Indies, while storax was common in the
Levant, and came to be cultivated in England and France, John C.
Sawer, *Odorographia*, vol. i, pp. 232, 241.

[3] Rimmel, *op. cit.*, p. 202.

[4] *Ibid.*, pp. 202, 204, 206; Cooley, *op. cit.*, pp. 68, 69.

[5] Cinnamon, cloves and sassafras were used in soap, Rimmel, pp. 256,
257. See *infra*, p. 70 for amount of sassafras introduced and its other
uses.

[6] Cooley, *op. cit.*, p. 69, *note.*

lish chrysalis. These signs of extravagance were not to be
seen alone among the dignitaries of the land and those able to
bear such expense, but every one was permitted " to flaunt
it out in what apparell he lust himself, or can get by aine
kind of means." This made it very hard to know the noble
or official from the man who was " both base by byrthe,
meane by estate and servyle by calling." [1] The costumes in
fact, were so extravagant that they called forth from William Harrison, another contemporary author, the remark:

It is a world to see the costliness and the curiositie; the excess
and the varietie; and finally the ficklenesse and the follie, that
is in all degrees; in so much that nothing is more constant in
England than inconstancie of attire.[2]

By the middle of the seventeenth century, moreover, new
kinds of cloth imported from the East came into vogue, and
became really cheaper than the ordinary English woolen
goods. As early as 1590 cotton cloth of native manufacture
had been brought to London from Benin on the coast of
Guinea.[3] India, however, was the great source of this cheap
but serviceable commodity. Large quantities of it were
imported into England during the seventeenth century.
Calico, named after Calicut, is especially mentioned among
the cotton textiles from the East, but muslins, chintzes and
ginghams were also introduced and the etymology of their
names attests their Oriental origin.

Several illustrations of the popularity of cotton cloth
may be cited. A pamphlet written in 1678 states that
" painted and Indian-stained and striped calico," twelve
pence cheaper than " perpetuana or shalloon," was employed

[1] Stubbes, *op. cit.*, pt. i, p. 34.

[2] William Harrison, *Description of England*, edited by F. J. Furniwell
(London, 1877), pt. i, bk. ii, p. 168, *et seq.*

[3] Macpherson, *Annals of Commerce, etc.*, vol. ii, p. 108.

to line men's coats, while a " Bengale " brought from India, was much favored for linings of coats and for petticoats, because it was thinner and cooler in summer than English goods.[1]   East India muslins had also become very fashionable, and had in a great measure supplanted French cambrics, Silesian lawns, and the linens of the Netherlands and Germany.[2]   Defoe, writing of the popularity that cotton cloth had attained in England during the later seventeenth century, tells how :

The general fansie of the people runs upon East India goods to that degree, that the chints and painted calicoes, which before were only made use of for carpets, quilts etc., and to clothe children and ordinary people, became now the dress of our ladies; and such is the power of a mode as we saw our persons of quality dressed in Indian carpets, which but a few years before their chambermaids would have thought too ordinary for them: the chints was advanced from lying upon their floors to their backs, from the foot-cloth to the petticoat; and even the queen herself at this time was pleased to appear in China and Japan, I mean China, silks and calico.   Nor was this all, but it crept into our houses, our closets, and bed-chambers; curtains, cushions, chairs, and at last beds themselves, were nothing but callicoes or Indian stuffs; and in short, almost everything that used to be made of wool or silk, relating either to the dress of the women or the furniture of our houses, was supplied by the Indian trade.[3]

In fact the use of cotton goods had become so general that in 1700 the woolen manufacturers secured the prohibition of all importations of them, except in the unfinished stage.[4]

[1] *The Ancient Trades Decayed and Repaired Again* (1678), pp. 16, 17.

[2] Macpherson, *The History of the European Commerce with India, etc.*, p. 136.

[3] Edward Baines, *History of the Cotton Manufacture in Great Britain*, pp. 78, 79.

[4] *11 and 12 William III*, Cap. 10 (1700).

However, it was not only the importations of cotton goods manufactured in the Orient which reduced the price of the textiles in common use, but the raw cotton imported first from the Levant and later from India and the West Indies [1] was mixed with flax in the manufacture of linens and thus furnished a cheaper class of goods. This tended to promote the custom of wearing underclothing among the masses and thus resulted in a marked improvement in personal cleanliness and health. [2]

A number of foodstuffs introduced from beyond the seas, which were destined to be of increasing importance to the English as well as to other Europeans, now call for attention. It is fitting that among these the potato should first be mentioned, as there is no better known, or more highly valued, vegetable used today by the white race than this gift of the New World.

So far as investigations have shown, the batata, the sweet or as it is sometimes called the Spanish potato, was the only kind imported into England prior to 1586. [3] It was known there for some time before the white or Irish potato, and quite naturally came to be thought of as the commoner of the two. Before 1586 many batatas are said to have been brought to England from Spain and the Canaries, where the cultivation of the tubers had been introduced from Spanish America soon after 1510. [4] However, Sir John Hawkins, the English navigator, evidently considered them in 1565

[1] *Infra*, pp. 110, 117, 135.

[2] Cooley, *op. cit.*, p. 70.

[3] T. N. Brushfield, "Raleghana," pt. ii, p. 7, reprinted from the *Transactions of the Devonshire Association for the Advancement of Science, Literature, and Art*, 1899, vol. xxx, pp. 158, 197.

[4] Ernest Roze, *Histoire de la pomme de terre*, p. 73; Ludwig Reinhardt, *Kulturgeschichte der Nusspflanzen*, Bd. iv, pt. i, p. 361, *et seq.*

to be of sufficient novelty and value for him to bring home some of them on his return from the New World.   He also favored his fellow countrymen with an interesting account of the appearance and virtues of batatas.   He judged them to be "the most delicate rootes that may be eaten," far superior to parsnips and carrots.   He declared that they resembled apples in taste, but were " more delicious than any sweet apple sugred." [1]   Sir Francis Drake is likewise said to have brought over potatoes, in all probability the sweet variety, from Peru or elsewhere in South America in 1580.[2]

It was due to that interesting expedition fathered by Raleigh, and led by Ralph Lane, which went to colonize Roanoke Island off the coast of North Carolina, that the white potato came to England.   In 1586 Sir Francis Drake stopped at the colony on his way back to England from the West Indies, and found the colonists so anxious to return home that he took them all on board.   Lane before embarking was careful to make a collection of the native products of the new land, among which were white potatoes and tobacco.   These samples upon his arrival in England were delivered to Raleigh.[3]

The first white potatoes to be cultivated in the British Isles were planted in Ireland through the instrumentality of Raleigh,[4] or by an ancestor of Sir Robert Southwell,[5] President of the Royal Society.   They were used as a food by the Irish long before their value was generally known in England.[6]   Thus from the locality of their first extensive

[1] Richard Hakluyt, *The Principal Navigations, etc.* (Glasgow MCMIV), vol. x, p. 27.

[2] Louis von Stieglitz-Mannichwald, *Die Einführung der Kartoffel in Europa seit 300 Jahren*, p. 15.

[3] Roze, *op. cit.*, pp. 63, 71.

[4] Henry Phillips, *History of Cultivated Vegetables*, vol. ii, p. 81.

[5] Roze, *op. cit.*, p. 72.

[6] Phillips, *op. cit.*, p. 80.

cultivation and use, they came to be known as "Irish" potatoes.

Opinions in England regarding potatoes differed. Early in the seventeenth century they were grown in the gardens of the nobility and herbalists as curious exotics. By some people they were considered unfit to eat, or at least inferior to carrots and radishes. Others deemed them altogether poisonous on account of their being a species of nightshade, and therefore injurious in effect.[1]

The prominent herbalists of the period, on the contrary, extol their virtues and tell of attractive ways to prepare them. Thus Gerard, writing in 1597, says of white potatoes, or "potato's of Virginia" as they were then called, that they were " a food, as also a meat for pleasure " which might be " roasted in the embers, or boiled and eaten with oile, vinegar and pepper, or dressed some other way by the hand of a skillful cooke." In the case of sweet potatoes he furnished the following information:

Of these roots may be made conserves no less toothsome, wholesome, and dainty, than of the flesh of Quinces; and likewise those comfortable and delicate meats called in shops, Morselli, Placentulae, and divers other such like.

These roots may serve as a ground or foundation whereon the cunning Confectioner or Sugar Baker may worke and frame many comfortable delicate Conserves and restorative sweet-meats.

They are used to be roasted in the ashes. Some when they be so roasted, infuse and sop them in wine: and others to give them greater grace in eating, do boil them with prunes and so eat them: likewise others dresse them (being first roasted) with oile, vinegar, and salt, every man according to his owne taste and liking.[2]

[1] Phillips, *op. cit.*, p. 86, *et seq.*
[2] John Gerard, *Herball, etc.* (London, 1636), p. 926, *et seq.*

John Parkinson, the herbalist, in 1629, gives a quite similar account of the use of sweet potatoes, as follows:

The Spanish Potato's are roasted under the embers, and being pared or peeled and sliced, are put into sacke with a little sugar, or without, and is delicate to be eaten.

They are used to be baked with Marrow, Sugar, Spice, and other things in Pyes, which are a daintie and costly dish for the table.

The confit-makers preserve them, and candy them as divers other things, and so ordered, is very delicate, fit to accompany such other banqueting dishes.[1]

Of the white potatoes he writes: " The Virginia Potato's, being dressed after all these waies before specified, maketh almost as delicate meate as the former [ie sweet potatoes]." Sir William Monson, another contemporary author, mentions a further use of potatoes—their employment in brewing " a delicate kind of Drink." [2]

In spite of the praise of the herbalists, potatoes were slow in gaining popular favor, partly because of prejudice, partly because of their scarcity and high price which rendered them a luxury to such people as really did want to use them. In 1619 they are enumerated among the different articles destined for the royal table, but the quantity was very small. At a meeting of the Royal Society, held in March 1663, there was read a letter from Mr. Buckland, a gentleman of Somerset, recommending the cultivation of the potato in all parts of the country as a means of preventing famine. In consequence of a favorable report on this communication,

[1] Joh.₁ Parkinson, *Paradisi in Sole Paradisus Terrestris, or The Garden of Pleasant Flowers.* Faithfully reprinted from the edition of 1629 (London, 1904), p. 518.

[2] *Ibid.*, p. 518.

[3] "Naval Tracts" in John Churchill, *Voyages* (1704), vol. iv, p. 452.

several members of the Society were asked to cultivate the plant.[1] Yet whatever their value potatoes were not much used. In horticultural works, published toward the end of the seventeenth century, a hundred years after the introduction of the tubers, they were scarcely spoken of except with disdain. " They are extensively used in Ireland and in America for food," writes one contemporary, " and could be advantageously cultivated for the poor." " I have not learned that the attempt has yet been made to cultivate them," adds another; " perhaps because one cannot obtain large quantities of them to feed pigs or other animals." Evelyn, the diarist, seems to have had some prejudice against potatoes, for he says, in 1699, that they should be planted in the poorest earth and that their stock would not soon be diminished.[2]

" Potatoes of Canada," a species of artichoke, appear to have been used during the sixteenth and seventeenth centuries in somewhat the same manner as potatoes. Gerard says that the Englishmen during his time received them from Peru, Brazil and Canada; but at the period he was writing there was little need to import them, as so many were then growing in English gardens. He gives the following account of their use:

These roots are dressed divers wayes, some boile them in water, and after stew them with sacke and butter, adding a little ginger. Others bake them in pies, putting [in] Marrow, Dates, Ginger, Raisons of the sun, Sacke, etc.[3]

Parkinson says of them: " by reason of their great increasing " they had become so common at London, that even the lowest ranks of society commenced to despise them, although

[1] Roze, *op. cit.*, p. 75.

[2] *Ibid.*, p. 76.

[3] Gerard, *op.* cit., p. 753.

when they were first introduced, they were "dainties for a Queene."

Being put into seething water [he adds], they are soone boyled tender, which after they bee peeled, sliced and stewed with butter, and a little wine, was a dish for a Queene, beeing as pleasant as the bottome of an Artichoke : but the too frequent use, especially being so plentifull and cheape, hath rather bred a loathing than a liking of them.[1]

The tomato, or love-apple, as it was then called, was a native of South America, and in all probability of Mexico, from which it was brought by the Spaniards to Europe. It was cultivated in England as early as 1596.[2] Parkinson states that the English only had the tomato in their garden for curiosity, "and for the amorous aspect."[3] So commonly used today. it does not appear to have been employed at all as food during the period under consideration.

Maize, or Indian ccrn, was long known as "Turkey corn" or "Turkey wheat", indicative of the common belief of the time that things strange or outlandish came from Turkey. First brought to Spain by Columbus, from the beginning of the sixteenth century it was sown in Spanish, Italian, German and English gardens, and soon the plant was cultivated on a larger scale in the fields.[4] Colonists returning to England from America doubtless helped to promote the use of the new grain, but it never became especially popular there. Gerard says of it :

Wee have as yet no certaine proofe or experience concerning

---

[1] Parkinson, *op. cit.*, p. 518.

[2] Henry Phillips, *Pomarium Britannicum*, p. 225; William Aiton, *Hortus Kewensis*, vol. i, p. 399.

[3] Parkinson, *op. cit.*, p. 379.

[4] Gerard, *op. cit.*, p. 82; Victor Hahn, *The Wanderings of Plants and Animals from their First Home*, p. 384.

the vertues of this kinde of Corne; although the barbarous
Indians, which know no better, are constrained to make a
vertue of necessitie, and thinke it a good food: whereas we
may easily judge, that it nourisheth but little, and is of hard
and evill digestion, a more convenient food for swine than for
men.[1]

Parkinson confirms the unfavorable impression by saying:
" Many doe condemne this Maiz to be as dry and of as little
nourishment as Millet or Panicke." [2]   Sir Francis Bacon, on
the contrary, thought maize had " an excellent spirit of nourishment," but it had to be " thoroughly boiled, and made into
a maiz-cream like a barley-cream." [3]

The discovery of America, also, was largely responsible
for the fact that sugar became a commodity of ordinary
use.   The cultivation of sugar-cane had been an important
industry in Sicily during the fifteenth century.   From there
the plant was taken to the Canary and Madeira Islands, and
finally came in the early sixteenth century from the former
to Brazil.   About the same time its cultivation began to assume importance in the Spanish colony of Hispaniola or
Santo Domingo, spreading thence to several other islands
in the West Indies.[4]   During the seventeenth century the
English raised it on large plantations in their West India
colonies, especially Barbados, and exported it to England
and other parts of Europe.   Thus, although it was not of
American origin, it came to be considered as one of the principal products of the New World.

Sugar was first used as a medicine,[5] and the belief in this

---

[1] Gerard, *op. cit.*, p. 83.

[2] John Parkinson, *Theatrum Botanicum, etc.* (London, 1640), p. 1139.

[3] *The Works of Francis Bacon* (Cambridge, 1863), vol. iv, p. 190.

[4] George Thomas Surface, *The Story of Sugar*, p. 17.

[5] Phillips, *History of Cultivated Vegetables*, vol. ii, p. 244.

aspect of its virtues appears to have lingered long in the minds of the people. Gerard declares that: "It drieth and cleanseth the stomacke, maketh smooth the roughness of the breast and lungs, cleareth the voice, and putteth away hoarsenesse, the cough, and all sournesse and bitternesse." [1] Lignon, a historian of Barbados in 1659 remarks that: ". . . As this plant has a faculty, to preserve all fruits, that grow in the world, from corruption and putrefaction; so it has a virtue, being rightfully applied, to preserve us men in our healths and fortunes too." He further relates how Doctor Butler "one of the most learned and famous Physitians that this Nation, or the world ever bred" used to say that:

> "If Sugar can preserve both Pears and Plumbs,
> Why can it not preserve as well our Lungs?"

That sugar might have the same effect upon himself, the worthy doctor always drank much of the best refined sugar in his claret wine.[2] To sugar was ascribed the virtue of preventing worms, and even the plague had never been known in a country where it composed a material part of the people's diet.[3] Nearly 300 medicines of the time had sugar as an ingredient.[4]

Honey had been commonly used as the national sweet, but during the sixteenth and seventeenth centuries, when sugar began to reach England in greater amounts, it largely replaced the former commodity. Thus Sir Francis Bacon, in 1627, remarks: "Sugar hath put down the use of honey: insomuch as we have lost those observations and prepara-

[1] Gerard, *op. cit.*, p. 38.

[2] Richard Lignon, *A True and Exact History of the Island of Barbados*, p. 96.

[3] Phillips, *op. cit.*, vol. ii, p. 250.

[4] John Oldmixon, *The British Empire in America*, etc. (London, 1708), vol. ii, p. 153.

tions of honey which the ancients had, when it was more in price." [1]   Sugar or honey was taken as a luxury with everything, with roast meat, with wines, and in the form of sweetmeats, " so that the teeth of most people were black in consequence." [2]   According to Gerard, sugar was used in making " infinite confections, confectures, Syrups and such like, as also [in] preserving and conserving of sundry fruits, herbes, and floures, as Roses, Violets, Rosemary floures, and such like " . . . which were called " Sugar Roset, Sugar Violet . . . " etc. [3]   The introduction of the new beverages, tea, coffee and chocolate, doubtless had much to do with promoting the general use of sugar. [4]

Molasses or treacle, from the sugar refineries in the West Indies and England, came to be valued in the latter for its " excellent Use in Medicines " as well as in fermented liquors and other drinks, in which it was preferred to the " Sweets of Malt." [5]   From molasses, as will be shown below, came a new drink called " rum."

The English voyagers to tropical and semi-tropical countries, furthermore, would have supplied England with many new and delicious fruits, if some way of keeping them on the long homeward voyages had been discovered.   Travelers gave glowing accounts of the great variety of fruits discovered and eaten, but their fellow countrymen had no knowledge of them other than hearsay.   The seamen of those days faring to distant lands enjoyed, for example, the banana, that delicate fruit like " meal and butter," with a smell comparable to that of roses, and with leaves large enough to have clothed our first ancestors, thus appearing

[1] *The Works of Francis Bacon*, vol. v, p. 88.
[2] Walter Besant, *London in the Time of the Tudors*, p. 293.
[3] Gerard, *op. cit.*, vol. ii, p. 245.
[4] Phillips, *op. cit.*, vol. ii, p. 245.
    Oldmixon, *op. cit.*, vol. ii, p. 153.

to resemble the " forbidden fruit;"[1] or again, the plantain of the West Indies which might be " relished like a Windsor pear," and "melts in one's mouth."[2] Some fruits, however, which otherwise could not have been seen in England at all, much less used, were brought to that country in the form of seeds, plants, shrubs or trees, which with careful nursing in greenhouses and botanical gardens were kept alive, and in some cases bore fruit. Such were the papaw tree, a native of both Indies introduced in 1690,[3] and the custard apples or sour-sops, first cultivated respectively in 1656 and 1690.[4] The Virginia raspberry grown in the Chelsea Garden before 1696,[5] and the "American date" or persimmon, brought also from North America in 1629,[6] may be mentioned as examples of the more hardy fruit-bearing shrubs and trees which did not need so much attention.

The " China " orange-tree, a native of the Orient, was introduced before 1595 by Sir Francis Carew from Portugal, whither it had found its way from the East as early as 1547, while the lemon-tree, a product of India, was cultivated in the Oxford Garden in 1648. Regarding the use of the fruit, Evelyn notes in his diary, September 25, 1679 : " Mr. Slingsby and Sig. Verris came to dine with me, to whom I gave China oranges off my owne trees, as good, I think, as were ever eaten."[7] John Rea, the botanist, on

---

[1] Purchas, *op. cit.*, vol. vi, p. 331; Thomas Astley, *A New General Collection of Voyages and Travels* (London, 1745), vol. i, p. 561.

[2] Astley, *op. cit.*, vol. i, p. 538; John Harris, *A Complete Collection of Voyages and Travels* (London, 1705), vol. i, p. 408.

[3] Aiton, *op. cit.*, vol. v, p. 400.

[4] *Ibid.*, vol. iii, p. 334.

[5] *Ibid.*, vol. iii, p. 268.

[6] *Ibid.*, vol. v, p. 478.

[7] *Ibid.*, vol. iv, pp. 419, 420; Evelyn says that at the Carew's estate there were " large and goodly [orange] trees laiden with fruite," John Evelyn, *Memoirs* (edited by W. Bray), vol. iv, p. 254.

the contrary, writing in 1676, said that the fruit of the orange trees in England never came to maturity because of the cold English climate.[1]   It appears quite evident, therefore, that although occasionally the fortunate gardener succeeded in getting fruit, this was not usually the case.   A few oranges and lemons doubtless reached England from Spain or Portugal,[2] but none could have lasted through the long voyage from Bermuda or the West Indies.

The one fruit that survived the voyage from America was the pineapple; but even this could not have been brought except a few times, for John Oldmixon, who wrote in 1708 a history of the British Empire in America, remarks that " It would never endure bringing to England, tho frequent Trials had been made to do it." [3]   Except once, no mention is made of a pineapple in England prior to 1657, when Cromwell received a present of one.[4]   Evelyn, writing in 1661, tells of having seen another of " Ye famous Queen pine " variety, which had recently been brought from Barbados and presented to Charles II.[5]   Seven years later he mentions a different kind, the " King pine," and relates how, " standing by His Maty at dinner in the presence, there was of that rare fruit call'd the King-pine, growing in Barbados and ye West Indies (the first of them I had ever seen)," and how His Majesty having cut it up, was pleased to give him a piece, " off his owne plate " to taste.   In his opinion, it fell short of " those ravishing varieties of deliciousness describ'd in Captain Lignon's *History*, and others; but possibly it might, or certainly was much impair'd in com-

---

[1] John Rea, *Flora* (London, 1676), p. 15.

[2] Evelyn, *Memoirs*, vol. iv, p. 254.

[3] Oldmixon, vol. ii, p. 99.

[4] Henry Phillips, *Pomarium Britannicum*, p. 292; *infra*, p. 52.

[5] *Memoirs*, vol. ii, p. 174.

ing so far." He admits, however, that it had "a gratefull acidity, but tastes more like ye quince and mellon than any other fruit."[1] It was from these pineapples that the king's gardener raised the first to be grown in England. As hothouses were not in use at the time, further experiments along this line probably failed.[2]

In two other cases pineapples appear to have been introduced during the century, once before 1625, from America, and again by the Earl of Portland, from Holland in 1690. The plants of the latter consignment were set out in Sir Mathew Decker's garden at Richmond, in Surrey.[3] The writer of a tract printed in 1684 and entitled, *Friendly Advice to the Gentlemen Planters of the East and West Indies*, has left an interesting account of the earlier instance. He says:

When some of them, by great care, and the favour of a speedy voyage, were brought into England (for very rarely can they be preserved so long) and presented to King James, he was so ravisht with its charming deliciousness, that he said, "It was not fit to be tasted by a Subject, but only proper to Regale the Gusto of Princes inured to the highest delicacies."

Further on the author remarks that it "makes a good breakfast or supper with the help of Bread." Presumably it was only good in its raw state, for nature had "already cook't it to the sublimest Perfection, it being the best and most fragrant fruit the West Indies do bring forth."[4]

[1] *Memoirs*, vol. ii, p. 304.

[2] Phillips, *Pomarium Britannicum*, p. 294.

[3] *Ibid.*, p. 294; Philotheos Physiologus, *Friendly Advice to the Gentlemen Planters of the East and West Indies* (London, 1684), p. 4. The introduction of the pineapple before 1625 may probably be assumed, as Physiologus, writing in 1684, the year before James the Second's accession to the throne, mentions the fact that pineapples were presented to King James.

[4] Philotheos Physiologus, *op. cit.*, p. 4.

Lignon, who has already been mentioned in connection with the introduction of sugar, remarks:

I must name the Pine, for in that single name, all that is excellent in a superlative degree, for beauty and taste, is totally and summarily included. . . . The rinde being taken off, we lay the fruit in a dish, and cut it in slices, halfe an inch thick; and as the knife goes in, there issues out of the pores of the fruit, a liquor, cleer as Rockwater, neer about six spoonfulls, which is eaten with a spoon; and as you taste it, you find it in a high degree delicious, but so milde, as you can distinguish no taste at all; but when you bite a piece of the fruit, it is so violently sharp, as you would think it would fetch all the skin off your mouth; but, before your tongue have made a second triall upon your palat, you shall perceive such a sweetnesse to follow, as perfectly to cure that vigorous sharpnesse; and between these two extreams, of sharp and sweet, lies the relish and flaver of all fruits that are excellent; and those tastes will change and flow so fast upon your palat, as your fancy can hardly keep way with them, to distinguish one from the other: and this at least to a tenth examination, for so long the Eccho will last. This fruit within, is neer of the colour of an Apricot not full ripe, and eats crispe and short as that does; but it is full of pores, and those of such formes and colours, as 'tis a very beautiful sight to look on, and invites the appetite beyond measure.[1]

Thus to the travelers of the time the pineapple was the "Prince of Fruits." Some said it had the taste of "all Fruits;" others that it tasted like "claret wine and strawberries" or "ripe strawberries and cream." Its "fine smell like an apricot "could be smelt far off.[2]

The peanut or groundnut, so commonly used today, was first brought to England from America and Africa during

[1] Lignon, *op. cit.*, p. 82, *et seq.*
[2] Astley, *op. cit.*, vol. ii, p. 338; Purchas, *op. cit.*, vol. vi, p. 333.

the centuries under discussion.[1] Parkinson gives the following account of it:

There is growing in sundry places in Brassil and in America also, neare the River Maranona a certaine fruit or Pease breeding under the ground like as puffes doe, without either leafe or roote as it is sayed, but they are no bigger than great Pease, and inclosed in a small grayish thicke and short cod, very like a small Pescod, with one or two Pease therein, of a pale reddish colour, on the outside and white within, tasting like unto an Almond, which will rattle being shaked in the skinne, growing many together and tyed by small strings. The fruits are eaten as junkets with great delight, for their pleasant tastes sake eyther fresh or dryed, but a little tosted make them rellish much better, and are served to the table of the better sort as an after course, and doe dry and strengthen the stomacke very much, but taken too liberally breed headache and heavinesse.[2]

Of special interest were the new beverages introduced into the British Isles during the seventeenth century. The earliest mention made of tea by an Englishman is that contained in a letter sent June 27, 1615, by Wickham, agent of the East India Company at Firando, Japan, to Eaton, another officer of the company resident at Macao, China, asking for " a pot of the best Cha." The date of the herb's appearance in Europe is uncertain; nor is it known whether Portugal or Holland was the first nation to bring the plant over.[3]

Small quantities of tea were imported into England as early as 1640.[4] The earliest mention of its use is contained

[1] Alphonse de Candolle, *Origin of Cultivated Plants, etc.*, p. 412; Parkinson, *Theatrum Botanicum, etc.*, p. 1619.

[2] *Theatrum Botanicum*, p. 1619.

[3] Joseph M. Walsh, *Tea, its History and Mystery*, pp. 16, 17, 19.

[4] *Ibid.*, p. 19.

in a copy of the *Mercurius Politicus*, dated September 30, 1658, reading as follows: " That excellent, and by all Physicians approved, China drink, called by the Chineans Tcha, by other nations Tay, alias Tee, is sold at the Sultaness Head Coffee-House, in Sweeting's Rents, by the Royal Exchange, London." [1] A handbill of 1660, bearing the title, *An Exact Description of the Culture, Qualities and Virtues of the Leaf Tea*, and written by Thomas Garway or Garraway, a tobacco merchant and dealer in tea and coffee at wholesale and retail in Exchange Alley near the Exchange in London, is a further evidence as to the date of its coming into use.[2] On September 25, 1660, Pepys records in his diary having sent for a cup of tea, a drink which he had never tasted before.[3] That tea was beginning to be known in England by this time, is proved also by an act of Parliament, in 1660, placing a duty of eight pence on each gallon of tea sold in the taverns.[4] A rare manuscript which escaped the fire in the Tower of London asserts that an English ship unloaded tea at that city in 1661.[5] The only authority who assigns a date later than 1660 for the earliest introduction of tea in large quantities is Dr. Johnson, who gives the Earls of Arlington and Ossory the credit of having brought the first cargo to England in 1666. This shipment is said to have been made from Holland.[6]

No authentic document indicates the quantity of tea imported between 1652 and 1669, the date of the arrival in London of the first cargo of the leaf tea transported by the

---

[1] Robert Chambers, *Book of Days*, vol. ii, p. 666.

[2] J. G. Houssaye. *Monographie du Thé*, p. 9.

[3] *The Diary of Samuel Pepys*, September 25, 1660, edited by Henry B. Wheatley (London, 1893), vol. vi, p. 376.

[4] *12 Car. II*, ch. 23.

[5] Houssaye, *op. cit.*, p. 9, *et seq.*

[6] Chambers, *op. cit.*, vol. ii, p. 666.

East India Company.   The Company it seems, had ordered
their agents " to send home by their ships one hundred
pounds weight of the best tey " that they could get.[1]   That
the factors exceeded their instructions is evident from all
accounts, but there appears to be some difference of opinion
as to just how large the shipment was.   Two prominent
authorities upon the subject state the quantity as 143 pounds
and eight ounces.[2]   The figures of the annual importations
of the commodity vary so appreciably that it is difficult to
estimate just how large the consumption of tea was during
the period under review.[3]   However, it is quite evident
that there was no regular popular demand for the commodity
until the following century.

Indeed, the price of tea was so high that only the wealthy
could afford to use it.   In 1660 it was advertised at from
sixteen to fifty shillings a pound.[4]   In 1664 the East
India Company made the king a present of two pounds of
it, costing the donor forty shillings a pound.   This was
procured in Europe.[5]   Five years later the price had risen to
from fifty to sixty shillings, gross weight, a pound.[6]   Phillips gives sixty shillings as the average price, and says that
it continued at that high rate almost to the end of the
century.[7]

At first tea served only " as a regalia in high treatments
and entertainments," and was presented " to princes and
grandees." [8]   It was a curious foreign drink, prepared very

[1] Phillips, *History of Cultivated Vegetables*, vol. ii, p. 291.

[2] Houssaye, *op. cit.*, pp. 12, 21; William Milburn, *Oriental Commerce*,
vol. ii, p. 531.

[3] *Infra*, p. 119.

[4] Chambers, *op. cit.*, vol. ii, p. 667.

[5] Walsh, *op. cit.*, p. 22.

[6] Houssaye, *op. cit.*, p. 11.

[7] Phillips, *History of Cultivated Vegetables*, vol. ii, p. 293.

[8] Chambers, *op. cit.*, vol. ii, p. 666.

carefully according to rule, and swallowed with a certain amount of anxiety as to the possible consequences. Precautions were for long taken against any evil effects which might result. Certain ladies of London, indeed, are said to have taken brandy after their tea as a corrective.[1]

Like so many other new commodities, tea was thought valuable as a medicine. On June 29, 1667, Pepys enters in his diary the fact that he found his wife making tea, "a drink which Mr. Pelling, the potticary, tells her is good for the cold and defluxions."[2] According to Garraway's handbill mentioned above:

The quality is moderately hot, proper for winter or summer. The drink is declared to be most wholesome, preserving in perfect health until extreme old age. The particular virtues are these. It maketh the body active and lusty. It helpeth the headache, giddiness and heaviness thereof. It removeth the obstructions of the spleen. It is very good against the stone and gravel. . . . It taketh away the difficulty of breathing, opening obstructions. It is good against lippitude distillations, and cleareth the sight. It removeth lassitude, and cleanseth and purifieth adust humours and a hot liver. It is good against crudities, strengthening the weakness of the stomach, causing good appetite and digestion, and particularly for men of corpulent body, and such as are great eaters of flesh. It vanquisheth heavy dreams, easeth the brain, and strengtheneth the memory. It overcometh superfluous sleep, and prevents sleepiness in general, a draught of the infusion being taken; so that, without trouble, whole nights may be spent in study without hurt to the body. It prevents and cures agues, surfeits, and fevers by infusing a fit quantity of the leaf, thereby provoking a most gentle vomit and breathing of the pores, and hath been given with wonderful success. It (being pre-

---

[1] Walter Besant, *London in the Time of the Stuarts*, p. 292, *et seq.*
[2] *Pepys' Diary*, vol. vi, p. 376.

pared and drunk with milk and water) strengtheneth the in-
ward parts and prevents consumptions. . . . It is good for
colds, dropsies and scurvies, and expelleth infection. . . . And
that the virtue and excellence of the leaf and drink are many
and great, is evident and manifest by the high esteem and use
of it, (especially of late years), by the physicians and knowing
men in France, Italy, Holland, and other parts of Christendom. . . . [1]

Tea was thought particularly beneficial as a stimulant for
literary men. As one writer observes:

The introduction of tea, as a beverage of a man of letters is
a curious circumstance in intellectual history, and I think the
literary tribe are much indebted to those who familiarized
them with the cup that cheers but does not inebriate.[2]

Waller, the poet, tells of its virtues in this respect as follows:

> The Muses' friend, Tea, does our fancy aid,
> Repress the vapors which the head invade;
> And keeps that palace of the soul serene;
> Fit on her birthday to salute the Queen.[3]

Tea-drinking was opposed on the grounds that it took
men away from the pipe and the bottle, and brought together men and women, and afforded them an opportunity
for vice and evil doing. It was justly thought to be too
costly; while its effects were believed to be detrimental to
men's strength and women's beauty. A learned physician,
in fact, writing at the close of the century, declared that tea
and coffee " are permitted by God's Providence for lessening
the number of mankind by shortening life, as a kind of
silent plague." [4]   Up to 1700, therefore, tea showed few,

---

[1] Chambers, *op. cit.*, vol. ii, p. 666.

[2] Phillips, *History of Cultivated Vegetables*, vol. ii, p. 304, *et seq.*

[3] Chambers, *op. cit.*, vol. ii, p. 666.

[4] Besant, *London in the Time of the Stuarts*, p. 294.

if any, signs of becoming the Englishman's national drink and the adjunct of his social amenities.

Coffee began to be used generally in western Asia toward the middle of the sixteenth century. The first coffee-house in Europe was established at Constantinople in 1554. Not until the middle of the following century was the beverage introduced among Christian nations.[1]

Among the English travelers who called attention to the use of coffee was William Finch, who, describing a visit to Sierra Leone in 1607, observes: " Their best entertainment is a China dish of Coho, a black, bitterish drink made of a berry like a bayberry, brought from Mecca, supped off hot, good for the head and stomache." [2] So, too, Sir Thomas Herbert, speaking of a journey made in 1626 through Persia, tells of coffee, or " coho," a drink " as black as Soot, wholsome as they say, but not toothsome; if supped hot it comforts the brain, expels melancholy and Sleep, purges Choler, lightens the spirits, and begets an excellent concoction, and by custom becomes delicious ". . . .[3] Coffee appears to have created enough interest by this time for Sir Francis Bacon to take notice of it in his *Natural History*, published the year following Herbert's journey. He sums up the knowledge which the English possessed of it as follows:

They have in Turkey a drink called coffa, made of a berry of the same name, as black as soot, and of a strong scent, but not aromatical; which they take, beaten into powder, in water, as hot as they can drink it: and they take it, and sit at it in their coffa-houses, which are like our taverns. This drink comforteth the brain and heart, and helpeth digestion.[4]

[1] Francis B. Thurber, *Coffee from Plantation to Cup*, p. 54.

[2] Purchas, *op. cit.*, vol. iv, p. 18.

[3] Harris, *op. cit.*, vol. i, p. 454.

[4] *Works*, vol. v, p. 27.

Ten years later, Evelyn remarks in his diary:

There came in my tyme to the Coll': one Nathaniel Conopios out of Greece, from Cyrill the Patriarch of Constantinople, who returning many years after was made (as I understand) Bishop of Smyrna. He was the first I ever saw drink coffee, wch custom came not into England till 30 years after.[1]

A coffee-house, probably the first one in England, was opened at Oxford in 1650, by one Jacob, a Jew.[2] Daniel Edwards, a member of the Turkey Company, is said to have brought coffee to London in 1652, and his servant, Pasqua Rossée, opened the first coffee-house there. Edwards, it seems, set his servant up in business as a consequence of the large number of people who wanted to try the taste of coffee. His house was so thronged with friends and visitors who came to sample the new drink, that he had to relieve himself in that fashion from annoyance.[3]

In London coffee readily won favor. It is suggested that one reason why the English received it so favorably at the time was that, neither at home or in the colonies had they any good or cheap wines, but had to import them from other nations. By the use of the new stimulant not only the English stomach, but English pride was gratified; for England always disliked commercial dependence upon its neighbors, and in this case was independent of them.[4] Indeed the sale of coffee increased so rapidly that by an act

[1] *Memoirs*, vol. i, p. 13, *et seq.*

[2] Phillips, *Pomarium Britannicum*, p. 106.

[3] Houssaye, *op. cit.*, p. 9; Aubrey differs from the majority of writers in saying that the first vendor of coffee in London was one Bowman, coachman to a Turkey merchant named Hodges. He had a coffee-house in St. Michael's Alley, Cornhill in 1625. John Aubrey, *Letters Written by Eminent Persons ... Lives of Eminent Men* (London, 1813), vol. ii, pt. i, p. 244.

[4] Thurber, *op. cit.*, p. 57.

of 1663 for the collection of excise, express provision was made for licensing all coffee-houses.[1] Ray, the botanist, in his *History of Plants,* written in 1688, estimated that these houses in London alone were as numerous as in Cairo itself. Many others also were scattered through all the important English towns. For more than fifty years after its introduction Arabia furnished the entire supply of coffee.[2]

At the time Rossée's coffee-house was opened, coffee sold from about 80 to 100 shillings a pound, but the prices soon fell.[3] According to " The Kingdom's Intelligencer " for 1662, the price of coffee-powder at "The Great Turk" coffee-house ranged from four shillings to six shillings eight pence a pound, while that pounded in a mortar cost two shillings.[4]

Coffee, like tea, won renown for its supposed medicinal virtues. Rossée's handbill first advertising the drink is interesting in this connection:

The grain or berry called coffee, groweth upon little trees only in the deserts of Arabia. It is brought from thence, and drunk generally throughout all the Grand Seignour's dominions. It is a simple, innocent thing, composed into a drink, by being dried in an oven, and ground to powder, and boiled up with spring water, and about half a pint of it to be drunk fasting an hour before, and not eating an hour after, and to be taken as hot as possibly can be endured; the which will never fetch the skin off the mouth, or raise any blisters by reason of that heat.

The Turks' drink at meals and other times is usually water,

[1] *15 Car. II, Cap. ii, Sec. 15.*

[2] Thurber, *op. cit.*, pp. 57, 58.

[3] Joseph M. Walsh, *Coffee, its History, Classification and Description,* p. 11.

[4] George Roberts, *The Social History of the People of the Southern Counties of England,* p. 447.

and their diet consists much of fruit; the crudities whereof are very much corrected by this drink.

The quality of this drink is cold and dry; and though it be drier, yet it never heats, nor inflames more than hot posset. It so incloseth the orifice of the stomach, and fortifies the heat within that it is very good to help digestion; and therefore of great use to be taken about three or four o'clock afternoon, as well as in the morning. It much quickens the spirits, and makes the heart lightsome; it is good against sore eyes, and the better if you hold your head over it and take in the steam that way. It suppresseth fumes exceedingly, and therefore is good against the headache, and will very much stop any defluxion of rheums, that distil from the head upon the stomach, and so prevent and help consumptions and the cough of the lungs.

It is excellent to prevent and cure the dropsy, gout, and scurvy. It is known by experience to be better than any other drying drink for people in years, or children that have any running humours upon them, as the kings evil, etc. It is a most excellent remedy against the spleen, hypochondriac winds, and the like. It will prevent drowsiness, and make one fit for business, if one have occasion to watch, and therefore, you are not to drink of it after supper, unless you intend to be watchful, for it will hinder sleep for three or four hours.

It is observed that in Turkey, where this is generally drunk, that they are not troubled with the stone, gout, dropsy, or scurvy, and that their skins are exceeding clear and white. It is neither laxative nor restringent.[1]

A doggerel poem of 1665, one of the earliest on the subject, and called " The character of a Coffee-house," also calls attention to the stimulating power of coffee:

> " More, it has such reviving power
> 'Twill keep a man awake an houre,
> Nay, make his eyes wide open stare
> Both Sermon time and all the prayer." [2]

[1] Chambers, *op. cit.*, vol. i, pp. 170-171.
[2] Besant, *London in the Time of the Stuarts*, p. 295.

Regarding the medicinal work of the beverage, it says:

> " But if you ask, what good does Coffee?
> He'll answer, Sir, don't think I scoff yee,
> If I affirm there's no disease
> Men have, that drink it, but find ease."

In the same connection Sir Henry Blunt, the traveler, speaking of the use of coffee among the Turks, declared that when one of them was sick he fasted and took coffee, and if that were of no avail, " makes his will and thinks of no other physick." [1] Coffee, furthermore, was so valued as a preventive of the plague that it was asserted that, if its qualities had been fully known in 1665, Dr. Hodges and other learned men of that time would have recommended it. In Gideon Harvey's *Advice Against the Plague,* published in that year, the value of coffee as a prophylactic was strongly emphasized.[2]

As a medicine, coffee was sometimes combined with other ingredients. A concoction called " Electuary of Cophy " was made in the following manner:

Take equal quantity of butter and sallet-oil, melt them well together, but not boyle them; then stir them well that they may incorporate together; then melt therewith three times as much honey and stir well together; then add thereunto powder of Turkish Cophie to make it a thick Electuary.

Another mixture included oatmeal, powdered coffee, a pint of ale or any wine, ginger, honey or sugar to please the taste. To these ingredients butter and spice might be added.[3]

As coffee had its admirers, so also it had its detractors.

---

[1] Edward Forbes Robinson, *The Early History of Coffee-houses in England*, p. 62.

[2] *Ibid.*, p. 58.

[3] *Ibid.*, p. 59, *et seq.*

The following lines from a broadside against the beverage, which refer to Rossée and his first coffee-house afford an idea of how far satire might go in this direction:

> A coachman was the first (here) coffee made,
> And ever since the rest drive cn the trade:
> *'Me no good Engalash!* and sure enough,
> He played the quack to salve his Stygian stuff;
> *'Ver boon for de stomack, de cough, de phthisick,*
> And I believe him, for it looks like physic.
> Coffee a crust is charred into a coal,
> The smell and taste of the mock china bowl;
> Where huff and puff, they labour out their lungs,
> Lest Dives-like, they should bewail their tongues.
> And yet they tell ye that it will not burn,
> Though on the jury blisters you return;
> Whose furious heat does make the waters rise,
> And still through the alembics of your eyes.
> Dread and desire, you fall to't snap by snap,
> As hungry dogs do scalding porridge lap.
> But to cure drunkards it has got great fame;
> Posset or porridge, will't not do the same?
> Confusion hurries all into one scene,
> Like Noah's ark the clean and the unclean.
> And now, alas! the drench has credit got,
> And he's no gentleman that drinks it not;
> That such a dwarf should rise to such a stature!
> But custom is but a remove from Nature.
> A little dish and a large coffee-house,
> What is it but a mountain and a mouse? [1]

How the use of coffee influenced social life in England is revealed by the importance attained by the coffee-house. Usually the floor space of the coffee-house was separated into high-backed little boxes, resembling old-fashioned pews. The visitor had to pay a penny for admittance, and two pence more if he wished a cup of coffee or tea. Regular patrons had their allotted seats and could smoke and write letters. Their mail could be sent to their favorite coffee-

---

[1] Chambers, *op. cit.*, vol. i, p. 171.

house, where it might be looked over at leisure.[1] In the
coffee-house, therefore, one may see the origin of the modern club, and it came to represent an even more important
place in the society of this time than the latter does today,
especially as some of these houses welcomed all ranks of
society. Foreigners remarked that this institution was a
unique feature of London society and distinguished it from
that of other cities. It was the " Londoner's home," and a
stranger who wished to find a gentleman usually inquired
which coffee-house he frequented, rather than his place of
residence.[2]

One of the chief characteristics of coffee-house society
was its cosmopolitanism. As Macaulay remarks:

Nobody was excluded these places who laid down his penny
at the bar. Yet every rank and profession, and every shade
of religious and political opinion, had its own head quarters.
. . . There were coffee-houses where the first medical men
might be consulted.

Radcliffe, who, in the year 1685, rose to the largest practice
in London, came daily, at the hour when the Exchange was
full, from his house in Bow Street, then a fashionable part of
the capital, to Garraway's and was to be found, surrounded by
surgeons and apothecaries, at a particular table. There were
Puritan coffee-houses where no oath was heard, and where
lank haired men discussed election and reprobation through
their noses; Jew coffee-houses, where dark-eyed money chang-
ers from Venice and from Amsterdam greeted each other;
and Popish coffee-houses where, as good Protestants believed,
Jesuits planned, over their cups, another great fire, and cast
silver bullets to shoot the king.[3]

[1] A. W. Jarvis, " Old London Coffee-houses " in *The English Illustrated Magazine*, vol. xxiii, p. 107.

[2] Thomas Babington Macaulay, *History of England from the Accession of James the Second* (London, 1899), vol. i, p. 340.

[3] *Ibid.*, vol. i, pp. 340, 341.

Among the frequenters of " Wills, the great resort of the men of letters, might be seen " earls in stars and garters, clergymen in cassocks and bands, pert Templars, sheepish lads from the universities, translators and indexmakers in ragged coats of frieze." [1] "Man's" the fop's coffee-house, " was among the more exclusive houses for fashion and dress." The society here included fops, dandies, " place-hunters," " bribe-lovers," " writers of wicked broadsides," " Puritan-haters," " French agents " and " mysterious messengers " who had secret conferences in side rooms reserved for their use. At " Jonathan's " were promoters, lawyers, cattle-drovers, Nonconformist divines, bishops, ship-captains, booksellers' hacks, Jews and an occasional wealthy merchant. The " Grecian " catered to the learned and was the favorite resort of the fellows of the Royal Society.[2]

All sorts of conversation both useful and foolish, as well as the transaction of much business, took place in the coffee-houses. In them, according to Jarvis

Clergymen discussed the latest ecclesiastical items, and good churchmen talked of the last remarkable sermon; the gossip retailed the latest witticism or court scandal; literary coteries debated on books; and fops anxiously considered the newest fashionable folly. They served, too, as consulting-rooms for physicians and lawyers. Business men came thither, and over a dish of coffee many a good stroke of work was done; anxious underwriters learnt of the safety of some long overdue vessel, and gathered hints of risks for future guidance. Above all else they were the meeting-places of politicians of all shades of opinion. Here the last news-sheets and pamphlets might be consulted, and the doings and misdoings of the Government discussed.[3]

[1] Macaulay, *op. cit.*, vol. i, pp. 340, 341.

[2] Jarvis, *op. cit.*, pp. 109, 110, 112.

[3] *Ibid.*, p. 107.

The coffee-house, in fact, became a highly important institution. As Macaulay says, when parliament had not been summoned for years and even the city council no longer expressed the popular opinion, before public meetings, harangues, and resolutions were common and the modern newspaper existed, coffee-houses became the chief places for venting the peoples' views on the questions of the day.[1] The government soon realized this fact, especially as they proved a center for plots and schemes. Accordingly the authorities attempted to handle the situation roughly, by suppressing coffee-houses as " seminaries of sedition." It was said that the effect of this order was to paralyze all social life in London, and raised such a storm of protests that the obnoxious regulation was immediately withdrawn.[2]

In order to understand how important these centers of information were, one has only to picture how eager for news and gossip people in an age devoid of real newspapers would be. Every man of the upper and middle classes went daily to his coffee-house to learn the news and discuss it. Each coffee-house had one or more orators to whose eloquence the crowd listened with admiration. Pepys makes frequent mention in his diary of the discussion which embraced everything, from the newest inventions, the Roman Empire, the form of the Turkish government, travel in the Orient, trade and business, the Dutch war, music, character, waking and dreaming, and the art of memory, to such sensational topics as a burglar's last speech before execution, the story of a fire, the comet, and gossip concerning a rich widow.[4] A broadside song, published in 1667, quite cor-

[1] Macaulay, *op. cit.*, vol. i, p. 339.

[2] Jarvis, *op. cit.*, p. 108.

[3] Macaulay, vol. i, p. 339.

[4] *Diary*, vol. iii, pp. 217, 305, 319, 366; vol. iv, pp. 1, 10, 19, 22, 25, 28, 52, 58, 87, 90, 155, 230, 242, 246, 248, 277, 287, 324.

rectly represents the pulsing intellectual life found in the coffee-house as follows:

> You that delight in wit and mirth,
> And long to hear such news
> As come from all the parts of earth,
> Dutch, Danes, and Turks, and Jews,
> I'll send you to a rendezvous,
> Where it is smoking new;
> Go hear it at a coffee-house.
> It cannot but be true.
>
> There battles and sea-fights are fought,
> And bloody plots displayed;
> They know more things than ere was thought,
> Or ever was betrayed:
> No money in the minting-house
> Is half so bright and new;
> And, coming from the coffee-house.
> It cannot but be true.
>
> There's nothing done in all the world,
> From Monarch to the mouse,
> But every day or night 'tis hurled
> Into the coffee-house.
> What Lily, or what Booker can
> By art not bring about,
> At coffee-house you'll find a man
> Can quickly find it out.
>
> They know all that is good or hurt,
> To bless ye, or to save ye;
> There is the college, and the court,
> The country, camp, and navy;
> So great a university,
> I think there ne'er was any,
> In which you may a scholar be
> For spending of a penny.
>
> A merchant's prentice there shall show
> You all and every thing
> What hath been done, and is to do,
> 'Twixt Holland and the king;
> What articles of peace will be
> He can precisely shew;
> What will be good for them or we
> He perfectly doth know.

The drinking there of chocolate
Can make a fool a Sophy;
'Tis thought the Turkish Mahomet
Was first inspired with coffee,
By which his powers did over flow
The land of Palestine;
Then let us to the coffee-house go,
'Tis cheaper far than wine.

You shall know there what fashions are,
How periwigs are curled;
And for a penny you shall hear
All novells in the world.
Both old and young, and great and small,
And rich and poor, you'll see;
Therefore let's to the coffee all,
Come all away with me.[1]

The knowledge of cocoa or cacao as an article of diet dates from the time of Columbus, who took home samples of it. Cocoa and chocolate were first obtained on a considerable scale from Mexico.[2] Here the natives were accustomed to prepare a drink called " chocolatl," consisting of a little vanilla, maize and allspice mingled with cacao, and taken cold.[3] The Spaniards were the first to adopt the custom of serving chocolate hot.[4]

The earliest intimation of the introduction of cocoa into England is contained in a notice in the *Public Advertiser* of June 16, 1657, more than one hundred and thirty years after its appearance in Spain. This notice announces that " in Bishopsgate street, in Queens Head alley, at a Frenchman's house, is an excellent West India drink called choco-

[1] " News from the Coffee-House, or The Newsmongers Hall " (London, 1667), in Chambers, *op. cit.*, vol. i, p. 172.

[2] Richard Cadbury, *Cocoa, all about it*, p. 38, *et seq.*

[3] Alexander von Humboldt, " Essai Politique sur le Royaume de la Nouvelle Espagne " in *Oeuvres* (Paris, 1811), vol. iii, p. 194.

[4] J. M. Bigbee, *Cocoa and Chocolate*, pp. 26, 34.

late, to be sold, where you may have it ready at any time; and also unmade, at reasonable rates." [1]

After the Restoration, there were shops in London for the sale of chocolate at ten or fifteen shillings a pound. The custom of using chocolate was deemed a token of elegant and fashionable taste.[2]   According to a book written in the time of Charles II entitled *The Indian Nectar,* the best kind of chocolate could be purchased of one Mortimer, " an honest though poor man, living in East Smithfield," for six shillings eight pence per pound, and commoner sorts for about half that price.[3]   By 1668, there were as many as forty-seven cocoa-walks in Jamaica, yielding annually 188,000 pounds of nuts which supplied the English market.[4]

Other beverages of less importance might be mentioned in passing.   Sassafras chips, boiled down into a kind of tea and mixed with milk and sugar, were sold as a drink in London coffee-houses during the seventeenth century.[5] Because of its agreeable taste, the mixture may have been taken in place of the cinnamon-water, which some considered necessary to counteract the supposed evil effects of tea and coffee.[6]   About sassafras Gerard says: " It has as sweet a smell as cinnamon, and it imitates it in colour and sharpness of taste and pleasantness of smell.   It procureth the same works and effects as cinnamon doth." [7]   Shiploads of it were early sent home from America.   As early as

---

[1] Bigbee, *op. cit.,* p. 39.

[2] Cadbury, *op. cit.,* p. 46.

[3] Bigbee, *op. cit.,* p. 40.

[4] Ellen D. Ellis, *An Introduction to the History of Sugar as a Commodity* (Bryn Mawr College Monographs), p. 90.

[5] Robinson, *op. cit.,* p. 120 *note.*

[6] Besant, *London in the Time of the Stuarts,* p. 296.

[7] Gerard, *Herball,* p. 341.

1602, Gosnold mentions taking a cargo of sassafras on board on his homeward voyage, and asserts that roots were then worth three shillings a pound and £336 a ton.[1] From this early importation one might infer that sassafras was valued chiefly for its medical qualities. Later it was served like tea in the coffee-houses and was used, as has been noticed above, to perfume soap.[2]

Large quantities of lime juice were shipped home, during the seventeenth century, from English colonies in the West Indies. Oldmixon, the historian, writing in 1708, says of it:

The Juice of this Fruit, since Punch has been such a fashionable Drink in England, has sold in great Quantities at good Rates, and is now a staple Commodity, some Tuns of it having been imported at London, and other Ports of England and Ireland, in a Year.[3]

Citron-water was also sent to England from Barbados. According to the author just mentioned:

With the Rind of this Fruit the Ladies of Barbadoes make the finest Cordial in the World; that which is imported for Sale is not so good as what they keep for their Closets; which, they taking Care to have all the Ingredients good, is infinitely above the choicest Waters at Phillips's; and the L'eau de Barbade, as the nice People affect to call their Citron Water, would without doubt be esteem'd more than any of his costly Cordials, did it not come from our own Plantation.[4]

An interesting question to consider in connection with the new non-intoxicating beverages is, whether they had

[1] Purchas, *op. cit.*, vol. xviii, p. 319.

[2] *Supra*, p. 38.

[3] Oldmixon, *op. cit.*, vol. ii, p. 92.

[4] *Ibid.*, vol. ii, p. 91.

any influence toward promoting temperance. On this point Raynal, the French philosopher, writing of tea toward the close of the eighteenth century, declared " that it contributed more to the sobriety of the nation [England] than the severest laws, the most eloquent harangues of Christian orators or the best treatises of morality." [1] Tea at all events was regarded as an antidote against intemperance. Among the upper classes it tended toward inducing the gentlemen to leave the bottle for the polite society of females. In the lower classes it often kept the father home from the ale house to enjoy a cup of tea with his family. [2]

The introduction of coffee, too, may be regarded as a step toward refinement and temperance. The coffee-houses provided places for the public to meet away from the taverns. As a contemporary expressed it:

Whereas formerly apprentices and clerks with others used to take their morning draught in ale, beer or wine, which by the dizziness they caused in the brain made many unfit for business, they use now to play the good-fellows in this wakeful and civil drink, coffee. [3]

It was argued, furthermore, that commercial matters could not properly be conducted in an ale-house where the continual sipping, " though never so warily," went to the head, but if people might be induced " to play the goodfellows in this wholesome, wakeful, innocent drink, coffee, they would find it do no less good to their bodies. and much more, promote their business and employments." [4]

<hr>

[1] G. T. F. Raynall, *A Philosophical and Political History of the Settlements and Trade of the Europeans in the East and West Indies*, vol. i, p. 500.

[2] Phillips, *History of Cultivated Vegetables*, vol. ii, p. 307.

[3] Robinson, *op. cit.*, pp. 116, 117, 130.

[4] *Ibid.*

Coffee-houses, in fact, were one of the means by which the middle classes of society were enabled to pass with less harm to themselves through the period of the Restoration when dissipation was so common in England. To break off habits of intemperance and find a substitute for too much wine and other intoxicating liquors, Pepys sent for a cup of tea. He then tried chocolate and also orange juice mixed with sugar. It was just at this time also that he frequented coffee-houses.[1] Besides being substituted for intoxicating drinks, coffee, it was claimed, counteracted their effects. Many people went to the coffee-house from the tavern just before the nine o'clock closing hour. Some of the coffee-house keepers advertised for this kind of trade. One notice read: "Art thou surfeited with gluttony or drunkenness, then let this be thy common drink."[2]

At least one intoxicating drink, rum or rumbullion, was manufactured in the West Indies[3] and shipped to England as a finished product, or perhaps more frequently it came from molasses made in English sugar refineries.[4] This new beverage was much in demand to take the place of brandy, as it was considered more healthful. Brandy drinkers, some thought, did not live long, "Whereas the Rum Drinkers hold it to a good old age."[5] Others contended that rum was "a hot, hellish, and terrible liquor."[6] In all probability it was first commonly used in the colonies and by sailors on their long voyages. Mixed with other ingre-

---

[1] Robinson, *op. cit.*, p. 135.

[2] *Ibid.*, p. 64.

[3] "The chief fudling they make in the island is Rumbullion, alias Kill-Divil, and this is made of sugar canes distilled." MSS. description of Barbados (1651) in *The Academy*, September 5, 1885, p. 155.

[4] Oldmixon, *op. cit.*, vol. i, p. xxiii; vol. ii, p. 152.

[5] *Ibid.*, vol. ii, pp. 99, 152, 153, 155.

[6] Edward R. Emerson, *Beverages, Past and Present*, vol. ii, p. 410.

dients, it was drunk in England under the name of "Bristol milk.[1]"

Before closing this account of the new beverages, some mention should be made of the large quantities of spices used in English drinks, after the supply of this commodity became more plentiful upon the opening of direct trade with the East Indies. Thus, "aqua mirabilis," or wonderful water, consumed in large quantities by people of the time, was a mixture of spirits of wine with cloves, galangals, cubebs, mace, cardamoms, nutmegs and ginger. "Spiritus pimento" was a compound of wine, honey and spices. Spiced ale also enjoyed great popularity. The rule appears to have been that the more spice a drink contained, the better chance it had for meeting with general approval.[2]

[1] Oldmixon, *op. cit.*, vol. ii, p. 272.

[2] *Ibid.*

CHAPTER III

SOCIETY: MANNERS AND CUSTOMS (CONTINUED)

NONE of the new commodities came to be better known, or seems to have had more medical virtues attributed to it, than tobacco. Among the Indians in nearly every part of America the custom of smoking had been an ancient practice[1], and was destined to find emulators among the Europeans. As early as the middle of the sixteenth century the tobacco plant was grown in Spain. From there its cultivation and use spread to Portugal, France, Italy and other countries. Although the potato had been discovered practically at the same time as tobacco, the cultivation in Europe of the latter preceded that of the former by more than a hundred and twenty years.[2]

The English appear to have been much behind the other European nations in the introduction of the new herb, as they were with most of the other new products. Nevertheless to England belongs the distinction of making the custom of smoking popular and disseminating it in Europe. Who was the first to carry it to England, and when, is uncertain. Some hold that Sir John Hawkins brought it over from Florida as early as 1565. Others are inclined to award the honor to Sir Francis Drake; and there is little doubt that during his voyages he and his crew smoked the herb,

[1] Friedrich Tiedemann, *Geschichte des Tabaks*, p. 45.

[2] E. R. Billings, *Tobacco: its History, Varieties, Culture, Manufacture and Commerce, etc.*, p. 80, *et seq.*

which had been presented to him by the California Indians as a sacrifice to a supposed deity.[1] Doubtless the sailors of Hawkins', Drake's and Grenville's expeditions were the first people to smoke tobacco in England.[2] It was, however, through Ralph Lane and Thomas Hariot, the governor and the historian of Raleigh's unsuccessful colony on Roanoke Island, off the Carolina coast, that tobacco in any considerable quantity was brought to England. When the disappointed colonists returned to the mother land in 1586, aboard the ships of Sir Francis Drake, the implements and materials for smoking were taken with them. Both Lane and Hariot, as well as the other colonists, had acquired the habit of using tobacco from the Indians during their sojourn of twelve months in America.[3] As Hariot says: " We ourselves, during the time we were there, used to sucke it after their maner, as also since our returne, and have found many rare and wonderfull experiments of the vertues thereof." [4]

Englishmen early took tobacco to appease their hunger and relieve their privations during the expeditions to the New World. Thus at first its use was confined to sailors and travelers who resorted to it from necessity rather than from pleasure.[5] On the continent of Europe tobacco had been employed as a remedy for many diseases.[6] Now that Hariot and Lane enjoyed their pipes as a luxury in Virginia and through them and the other colonists the habit was made known in England, the custom of smoking soon became

[1] W. A. Penn, *The Soverane Herbe: A History of Tobacco*, p. 14, *et seq.*
[2] *Ibid.*, p. 17.
[3] *Ibid.*, p. 15, *et seq.*
[4] Hakluyt, *op. cit.*, vol. viii, p. 364.
[5] Penn, *op. cit.*, p. 25.
[6] Brushfield, *Raleghana*, pt. ii, p. 40.

common there.   Sir Walter Raleigh, as patron of the
Roanoke colony, took especial interest in its products, and
was among the first to learn the new art.   Tobacco is said
to have become such a necessity with him that he " tooke a
pipe of tobacco a little before he went to the scaffold." [1]
Largely through his influence, smoking came into vogue
at court, and " some of the great ladies, as well as noblemen
therein would not scruple to take a pipe sometimes very
sociably."   Prynne, the famous Puritan inveigher against
the stage, declares that in his time ladies at the theatre were
sometimes offered the tobacco pipe as a refreshment instead of apples.[2]   Raleigh, indeed, often gave entertainments to his friends, in which the fare consisted of pipes of
tobacco and ale seasoned with nutmegs.   This appears to
have been the origin of " smoking parties," [3] and the fore-
runner of the present " smoker."   The practice in time became such a necessity for fashionable society that, however
careless the London gallant was in paying most of his
debts, he took care to keep his credit good with the tobacco
merchant.[4]   For some time the extremely high price of the
herb prevented its use by the poorer classes; yet the Wilt-
shire records give an instance of an ordinary villager using
tobacco in 1613.[5]

King James I, in his *A counter blaste to Tobacco,* comments in the following manner upon the increasing ad-
diction to the weed:

[1] William Stith, *The History of the First Discovery and Settlement ol
Virginia* (London, 1753), p. 21.

[2] Brushfield, *op. cit.,* p. 38; F. W. Fairholt, *Tobacco: Its History and
Associations, etc.,* p. 67.

[3] Besant, *London in the Time of the Tudors,* p. 285.

[4] Billings, *op. cit.,* p. 91.

[5] George Louis Beer, *The Origins of the British Colonial System,
1578-1660,* p. 79.

The public use whereof, at all times, and in all places, hath now so farre prevailed, as divers men very sound both in judgement, and complexion, have bene at last forced to take it also without desire, partly because they were ashamed to seeme singular, (like the two Philosophers that were forced to duck themselves in that raine water, and so become fools as well as the rest of the people) and partly, to be as one that was content to eat Garlicke (which hee did not love) that he might not be troubled with the smell of it, in the breath of his fellowes. And is it not a great vanitie, that a man cannot heartily welcome his friend now, but straight they must bee in hand with Tobacco? No, it is become, in place of a cure, a point of good fellowship, and he that will refuse to take a pipe of Tobacco among his fellowes, (though by his own election he would rather feele the savour of a Sinke) is accounted peevish and no good company, even as they doe with tippling in the cold Easterne countries.[1]

The use of tobacco became so extensive that Barnaby Rich, in his *Honestie of this Age,* written in 1614, says:

There is not so base a groome that comes into an ale-house to call for his pott, but he must have his pipe of tobacco; for it is a commodity that is nowe as vendible in every taverne, wine, and ale-house, as eyther wine, ale, or beare; and for apothecaries' shops, grocers' shops, chandlers' shops, are (almost) never without company, that from morning till night are still taking of tobacco. What a number are there besides, that doe keepe houses, set open shoppes, that have no other trade to live by, but by the selling of tobacco.[2]

In the year the pamphlet just quoted was published there were said to be in London alone 7000 shops selling tobacco; while the year before it was asserted that England spent

[1] James I, "A counter blaste to Tobacco" (London, 1604), in *English Reprints*, no. 19, edited by Edward Arber, p. iii, *et seq.*
[2] Fairholt, *op. cit.*, p. 75.

yearly £200,000, or even more, on tobacco.[1]   According to the customs' records, the average quantity of tobacco imported into England during the seven years ending September 29, 1621, was 142,085 pounds.   It was generally admitted, however, that as much again was smuggled in.[2] It was estimated in 1621, also, that England consumed daily 1000 pounds of tobacco.[3]   By 1659 the tobacco habit appears to have taken such a hold upon the people that Regidius Everaerdts, in a pamphlet published in that year, says: "Were the planting and traffick of Tobacco now hindred, millions of the Nations, in all probability must perish for want of food, their whole livelihood almost depending upon it.   So many Druggists, Grocers, Tobaccoshops, Taverns, Inns, Ale-houses, Victuallers, Carriers, Cutters and Dryers of Tobacco, pipe-makers, and the like, that deal in it, will prove no less."[4]   Twelve years later smoking had become so necessary to many people, both men and women, that some   even could not be separated from their pipes upon retiring for the night.   Jorevin de Rochefort, who published at the time an account of his travels in England, remarks on this point:

I have known several who, not content with smoking in the day, went to bed with pipes in their mouths, and others who

[1] Beer, *The Origins of the British Colonial System,* 1578-1660, p. 78, *et seq.*

[2] *Ibid.*   Penn estimates that about 1611 the annual consumption of tobacco in England was nearly 1,000,000 pounds, or six ounces per head of the population.   He bases this calculation on a statement of Stith's that the importation of the commodity from Virginia amounted in that year to 142,085 pounds, or one-sixth of the previous annual supply. Penn, *op. cit.,* p. 207.

[3] *Journals of the House of Commons,* vol. i, p. 579.

[4] Regidius Everaerdts, *Panacea, or The Universal Medicine; being a Discovery of the Wonderfull Vertues of Tobacco, etc.* (London, 1659), *dedicatory epistle,* p. A 3.

have risen in the night to light their pipes, to take tobacco with as much pleasure as they would have received in drinking either Greek or Alicant wine.[1]

The first dealers in the herb were the apothecaries. They kept the tobacco " in fine lily pots that open'd smell like conserve of roses, or French beans," [2] and always had ready their " Winchester pipes," " maple cutting-blocks," juniper-wood charcoal-fires, and silver tongs with which to hand the hot charcoal to their customers.[3] The apothecaries not only sold tobacco, but they were also required to be masters of the art of smoking. They, as well as some of the cavaliers and old sailors or soldiers, became veritable professors of it. Each smoking-master had his own special feat to perform. Some taught their pupils to exhale the smoke in little globes and rings; others to discharge the smoke evenly in a certain number of seconds, neither more or less.[4] The method of exhaling the smoke from the nostrils was the fashionable and practically the only known mode of smoking, and it was recommended by doctors for discharging " rheums and great defluxions " from the head.[5]

Some smokers appear to have carried large quantities of tobacco about with them. For instance, Sir Walter Raleigh's tobacco-box contained a receiver of glass or metal which might hold from half a pound to a pound. In this box were also carried from six to eight pipes. The rich at first used small silver pipes; while the poor, when by chance they

[1] Penn, *op. cit.*, p. 79.

[2] " The Alchemist," act i, sc. i, in *The Works of Ben Jonson* (London, 1816), vol. iv, p. 38.

[3] Billings, *op. cit.*, p. 95.

[4] *Ibid.*; Penn, *op. cit.*, p. 62, *et seq.*

[5] Penn, *op. cit.*, p. 66.

obtained the herb, had to be content with a walnut shell
and a straw. These Elizabethan pipes were so small that
now when they are dug up in Ireland the poor call them
" fairy pipes." [1] Such as were made of silver and other
metals, though not easily broken, were found inconvenient,
as they soon became dirty and were hard to clean. Accordingly they began to be made of clay. During the early
days one pipe had to suffice for several persons, and was
handed around the table, Indian fashion. Some landladies
even hired out pipes at three pence the pipeful. [2]

Naturally opinions differed in regard to the use of tobacco. At first the English were convinced from the accounts of the Indians [3] and the tales of the Spaniards that
the plant possessed miraculous healing power. It was
called by the latter " hierba panacea," " hierba santa,"
" divine tobacco " etc. [4] Josselyn, a contemporary author,
writing in the latter part of the seventeenth century, gives
in the following account an excellent summary of the many
qualities which it was long believed to possess:

The vertues of Tobacco are these, it helps digestion, the
Gout, Tooth-ache, prevents infection by scents, it heats the
cold, cools them that sweat, feedeth the hungry, spent spirits
restoreth, purgeth the stomach, killeth nits and lice; the juice
of the green leaf healeth green wounds, although poisoned;
the Syrup for many diseases, the smoak for the Phthisick,

[1] Billings, *op. cit.*, p. 95; Aubrey, *op. cit.*, vol. ii, pt. ii, p. 512.

[2] Thomas Fuller, *The History of the Worthies of England*, vol. iii,
p. 315; Aubrey, *Letters Written by Eminent Persons in the Seventeenth
and Eighteenth Centuries, etc.*, vol. ii, pt. ii, p. 512; *English Reprints;*
No. 19, p. 87.

[3] Drake and his men are reported to have followed the example of the
Indians and used the herb first as a remedy for indigestion. Chewing
tobacco was also practiced by sailors as a cure and preventive of scurvy.
Penn, *op. cit.*, p. 28.

[4] Fairholt, *op. cit.*, p. 46, *et seq.*

cough of the lungs, distillations of Rheume, and all diseases of a cold and moist cause, good for all bodies cold and moist taken upon an empty stomach, taken upon a full stomach it precipitates digestion, immoderately taken it dryeth the body, enflameth the bloud, hurteth the brain; weakens the eyes and the sinews.[1]

The following prescription for using tobacco as a remedy was advocated by William Barclay in a tract called *Nepenthes, or the Virtues of Tobacco,* published in 1614:

To the cure and preservation of an armie of maladies, Tabacco must be used after this maner. Take of leaf Tabacco as much as being folded together, may make a round ball of such bignesse that it may fill the patients mouth, and inclyne his face downward towards the ground, keeping the mouth open, not moving any whit with his tongue, except now and then to waken the medicament, there shall flow such a flood of water from his brain and his stomacke, and from all parts of his body that it shall be a wonder. This he must do fasting in the morning, and if it be for preservation, and the body very cacochyme, or full of evil humours, he must take it once a weeke, otherwise once a month: But if it bee to cure the Epilepsie or Hydropsie once every day. . . . Thus much for the use of Tobacco in substance. As concerning the smoke, it may be taken more frequently, and for the said effects, but always fasting, and with an empty stomach.[2]

Another physician of the time, a Dr. Gardiner, prescribed " tobacco gruel," " tobacco wine," also tobacco made up into a kind of soup, or syrup, with sufficient sugar. The patient was advised to drink the decoction hot.

[1] John Josselyn, *An Account of Two Voyages Made during the Years 1638, 1663 to New England* (London, 1675), vol. i, p. 61.

[2] *English Reprints,* No. 19, p. 115.

The antiseptic properties of tobacco were recognized by
Thomas Willis, physician to Charles the Second. He recommended it to keep people from becoming infected with
the plague, and many during the time that it was raging had
recourse to the herb as a protective against the dread disease.[1] Pepys says he bought some tobacco " to smell and
to chaw," and this took away his apprehension.[2] Indeed,
the Great Plague of 1665 did much to popularize and
establish the use of tobacco in England. From the large
number of pipes belonging to this period which may be seen
in London, it would appear that almost every person who
ventured from home sought the protection of tobacco.[3]
Such people as doctors, nurses and the collectors and buriers
of the dead smoked with this end in view.[4] At Derby
" the market-people having their mouths primed with
tobacco as a preservative, brought their provisions." [5]

Even the school children at this critical time were compelled to smoke. Thomas Hearne, the historical antiquary,
under the date of January 21, 1721, states:

I have been told that in the last great plague at London, none
that kept tobaconists shops had the plague. It is certain, that
smoking it was looked upon as a most excellent preservative,
in so much, that even children were obliged to smoak. And I
remember, that I heard formerly Tom Rogers, who was yeoman beadle, say, that when he was that year, when the plague
raged, a school boy at Eaton, all the boys at that school were
obliged to smoak in the school every morning, and that he was
never whipped so much in his life as he was one morning for
not smoaking.[6]

[1] E. V. Heward, *St. Nicotine of the Peace-Pipe*, p. 84.
[2] *Diary*, vol. vi, p. 401.
[3] Brushfield, *op. cit.*, p. 36.
[4] Penn, *op. cit.*, p. 78.
[5] Brushfield, p. 36.
[6] *Ibid.*

This custom of smoking at school appears to have been continued, probably due to its good effects as a prophylactic, for de Rochefort observed in 1671 that

When the children went to school they carried in their satchel with their books a pipe of tobacco which their mother took care to fill early in the morning, it serving them instead of breakfast, and that at the accustomed hour every one laid aside his book to light his pipe, the master smoking with them and teaching them how to hold their pipes, and draw in the tobacco, thus accustoming them to it from their youths, believing it absolutely necessary for a man's health.[1]

Tobacco was thought to be very stimulating and helpful to literary men. It was said by one contemporary that it was " a good Companion to one that converseth with dead Men; for if one hath been poring long upon a book, or is toil'd with pen, and stupify'd with study, it quickeneth him, and dispels those Clouds that usually o'erset the Brain." [2] Another, in a poem published in 1651 called *Hymnus Tabaci*, describes most graphically the effects it was supposed to have upon the mind:

> So sovereign, if diffused, is the smell,
> It doth Contagion from bad aires expell.
> The heavy head it hath a power to rear,
> And with smart sneezings makes the nostrils clear.
> Once turn'd to airy vapour by the flame,
> Big with that active salt, whose pride does aim
> At heavenly Towers, it climbes the Capitoll,
> Where like a Goddesse sits the humane soul;
> There gives supplies to the exhausted brain,
> And makes the drowsie minds grow quick again.
> Thou glory of the Earth, a gift from Heaven,
> Most happy plant, who wer't not only given
> T'refresh the Pesants limbs, whom toyl and sweat
> Have weary made, or kill the love of meat;

[1] Penn, p. 79.

[2] Besant, *London in the Time of the Stuarts*, p. 296.

Nor yet t'infuse without the help of food
Into decayed Nerves new strength, new bloud;
But hast a nobler office; thou art Eyes
To the dark mind, a Lantern to the wise,
When e're a sudden night the brains possesse
By too much cockering of the Genius:
Or when the tired understanding brings
Forth only shadows of disjoynted things,
Unapt to frame Ideas that are cleare,
Or being fram'd, unapt to keep them there.
For thou no sooner arm'd with light doest come,
But (like a shining Taper into a room
Obscure before) all things turn clear and bright;
The black Clouds fly, and Cares that fast do bite;
Th' inventing Power shines forth, and now descries
The worlds large Fabrick to the mentall eyes.
Th' eternall Species now do naked stand
In comely order rank'd by Nature's hand,
And all the notions of th' inlightned brain
Do now return to their true shapes again.[1]

It is said that Hobbes, the philosopher, soon after dinner retired to his study, and had his candle with ten or twelve pipes of tobacco laid before him. Then shutting his door, he fell to smoking, thinking and writing for several hours. In the morning he prepared for the day's work by filling ten or twelve pipes with tobacco, and laying them ready for use. Other eminent English authors such as Shakespeare, Marlowe, Fletcher, and Beaumont made extensive use of tobacco while at their daily task. Ben Jonson, even while writing his satire on the herb, sought inspiration from it.[2] Bacon from personal experience declared that tobacco " hath power to lighten the body and shake off uneasiness." [3]

The idea first inspired by the Indians that tobacco pro-

---

[1] Raphael Thorius, *Hymnus Tabaci: a Poem in honour of Tobacco,* translated by Peter Hausted (London, 1651), p. 27.

[2] For an example of Jonson's satire on tobacco see *infra,* p. 86.

[3] Chambers, *op. cit.,* vol. ii, p. 655; Penn, p. 238.

moted endurance, and gave strength at times of strenuous endeavor is well expressed in the dedicatory epistle of Everaerdt's *Panacea*, published in 1659:

Sea-men will be supplied with it for their long voyages: Souldiers cannot [but] want it when they keep guards all night, or are upon other hard duties in cold and tempestuous weather: Farmers, Plough-men, Porters, and almost all labouring men plead for it, saying they find great refreshment by it, and very many would as soon part with their necessary food as they would be totally deprived of the use of Tobacco. The Nobility and Gentry, who find no fault with it, but that it is too common amongst the Vulgar, do ordinarily make it the complement of all their entertainment, and oft-times all their entertainment besides is but a complement. Scholars use it much, and many grave and great men take Tobacco to make them more serviceable in their callings.[1]

On the other hand great was the opposition to the use of tobacco, as can be seen in the frequent references to its evils in plays, poems, treatises and even sometimes in the debates of the House of Commons. Thus Ben Jonson satirically remarks:

Ods me, I marle what pleasure or felicity they have in taking this roguish tobacco. It's good for nothing but to choke a man, and fill him full of smoke and embers: there were four died out of one house last week with taking of it, and two more the bell went for yesternight.[2]

That people actually believed in the power of tobacco to discolor part of the body is seen in a pamphlet written by one John Deacon in 1616. In the introduction to the readers it says:

[1] Everaerdt, *op. cit., Dedicatory Epistle*, p. A 3.

[2] "Everyman in His Humour," act iii, sc. ii, in *The Works of Ben Jonson* (1816), vol. i, p. 34.

If thy mind be still a mammering doubt, whether the venim-
ous condition of these poysonsome fumes be so pestiferous as
this present Discourse doth seeme to purport, then turn thy
present thoughts (I pray thee) towards the untimely deaths
of sundry such excellent personages as (tampering too much
therewith) have (even now of late) not onley bene sodainly
surprised by an unnatural death, but (which more is) their
dead bodies being opened, had all their entrails as black as a
coale, and the very fat in their bodies resembling (in all outward appearance) the perfect colour of rustie, or reesed
bacon. . . . [1]

Tobias Venner, who wrote a treatise in 1621 upon the subject, was equally convinced of the evils of smoking:

As touching the temperature and faculties of it, it is hot and
drie in the third degree, and hath a deleteriall, or venomous
quality, as I suppose; for it being taken into the body, it tor-
tureth & disturbeth the same with violent ejections both upward and downeward, astonisheth the spirites, stupifieth and
benummeth the senses and all the members.[2]

But it was King James I who gave free play to his feelings upon the matter, and indulged his love of showy
writing, in his *A counter blaste to Tobacco,* already quoted.
He declared that tobacco was first used by the Indians as
an antidote against the smallpox, and inquired whether
Englishmen should debase themselves so far as to imitate
beastly Indians.   Attacking the assertion that tobacco drove
" rheumes and distillations " from the head and stomach, he
illustrated his arguments from astronomy:

For even as the smoakie vapours sucked up by the Sunne, and

---

[1] John Deacon, *Tobacco Tortured or The Filthie Fume of Tobacco
Refined* (London, 1616), *introduction,* p. A.

[2] Tobias Venner, *A Briefe and accurate Treatise, concerning the
taking of the fume of Tobacco, etc.* (London, 1621), p. B.

staid in the lowest and colde Region of the ayre, are there contracted into cloudes and turned into raine and such other watery Meteors: So this stinking smoake being sucked up by the Nose, and imprisoned in the colde and moyst braines, is by their colde and wett facultie, turned and cast foorth againe in waterie distillations, and so are you made free and purged of nothing, but that wherewith you willfully burdened your-selves. . . . [1]

More forcefully and picturesquely still did he condemn the noxious weed in *A Collection of Witty Apothegms* at-tributed to him. Here he said that tobacco was like hell, for

It had, by allusion, in it all the parts and vices of the world whereby hell may be gained; to wit: First, It was a smoke; so are the vanities of this world. Secondly, It delighteth them who take it; so do the pleasures of the world delight the men of the world. Thirdly, It maketh men drunken and light in the head; so do the vanities of the world, men are drunken therewith. Fourthly, He that taketh tobacco saith he cannot leave it, it doth bewitch him: even so the pleasures of the world make men loath to leave them, they are for the most part so in-chanted with them: and further, besides all this, It is like hell in the very substance of it, for it is a stinking loathsome thing; and so is hell.[2]

For a time considerable governmental opposition was shown toward smoking. This took the form of restraint through the imposition of heavy duties. In consequence of these high imposts the importation of tobacco from Virginia during James the First's reign was reduced about five sixths. Efforts were then made to cultivate the plant in England

[1] *English Reprints*, no. 19, p. 104.
[2] Fairholt, p. 82, *et seq.*

itself, but were speedily checked. Thereupon since the law related to Virginia tobacco only, a large supply was imported from Spain and Holland. At last the Virginia planters appealed to the throne, and in 1624 an act was passed lessening the duty. The king, however, had a further act passed forbidding anyone to deal in tobacco without letters patent from himself. This is said to have ruined many dealers. The governmental opposition to tobacco continued through the reigns of the Stuarts, and also during the Protectorate. With William III opposition of the sort ceased, as well as interference with the sale or use of tobacco.[1]

Another narcotic brought to England from overseas was opium; but no indication is given that it came to be used in any quantity during the period under discussion. As early as 1616 one of the East India Company's factors wrote that he intended to send a small quantity of opium annually to England. The first order given by the Company for the importation of the narcotic was in 1682. It is stated that up to 1786 the amount came to only 750 pounds a year.[2]

The influence of oversea commodities is visible in many other respects. From the trade with the East came many kinds of bric-a-brac, china and other articles for the decoration of English homes and the usages of polite society. As Sydney, in his *Social Life in England from the Restoration to the Revolution,* remarks:

The silks, the chintzes, the porcelain, the lacquerware and the

[1] Henry J. Meller, *Nicotina or the Smoker's and Snuff-taker's Companion, etc.,* p. 38, *et seq.*; Penn, *op. cit.,* p. 207, *et seq.*

[2] *Letters Received by the East India Company from its Servants in the East; transcribed from the Original Correspondence Series of the India Office Records* (1616), edited by William Foster, p. 299; George C. M. Birdwood, *Report on the Old Records of the India Office,* p. 226.

toys of China excited the deepest admiration in the minds of the English people, and so great was the eagerness with which such articles were sought after, that it was nothing uncommon for fashionable beaux and belles, so soon as they learned the tidings that the India ships had arrived in the River Thames, straightway to take the boat at the Temple Stairs for Blackwall, and there to make numerous purchases on board the vessels.[1]

Chinaware came more and more into favor, especially after the Revolution of 1688. According to Macaulay, Queen Mary

had acquired at the Hague a taste for the porcelain of China, and amused herself by forming at Hampton a vast collection of hideous images, and of vases on which houses, trees, bridges, and mandarins were depicted in outrageous defiance of all the laws of perspective. The fashion—a frivolous and unelegant fashion, it must be owned — was thus set by the amiable Queen and spread fast and wide. In a few years almost every great house in the kingdom contained a museum of these grotesque baubles. Even statesmen and generals were not ashamed to be renowned as judges of teapots and dragons; and satirists long continued to repeat that a fine lady valued her mottled green pottery quite as much as she valued her monkey, and much more than she valued her husband.[2]

Oriental cabinets and screens were also in demand. Evelyn mentions going to see a Mr. Bohun, " whose whole house is a cabinet of all elegancies, especially Indian; in the hall are contrivances of Japan skreens instead of wainscot." The landscapes of the screens represented " the manner of living, and country of the Chinese." [3] In another place

---

[1] William C. Sydney, *Social Life in England from the Restoration to the Revolution,* 1660-1690, p. 27.

[2] *History of England, etc.,* vol. iii, p. 63.

[3] *Memoirs,* vol. iii, p. 69.

Evelyn says "the Queen brought over with her from Portugal such Indian cabinets as had never before been seen here." [1]

Interest was taken during the later Tudor and the Stuart period in surrounding English mansions with beautiful flower-gardens, shrubs and ornamental trees; while greenhouses were erected to shelter the rare tropical exotics that could not stand the colder climate. Perhaps nowhere was the great influence of oversea enterprise shown more clearly than in the extensive additions made to English floriculture. The new flowering plants and shrubs were usually brought over in the form of seeds, bulbs or roots. Occasionally a plant might be preserved and kept from dying on the long voyages home, but usually insufficient care was taken, and too little was really known about horticulture to make these attempts successful. Persia, Constantinople and the Levant in general appear to have been the first great centers from which flowering plants were imported. English traders, merchants and factors were most zealous in the collection of every possible variety of flora with which they might meet in their journeys. As early as 1561 Anthony Jenkins is supposed to have brought back from Persia the bulbs and seeds of many plants, among them a new kind of hyacinth. [2] Parkinson and other contemporary writers mention no fewer than thirteen varieties of this beautiful flower, besides several species of musk-grape flower, about twelve or thirteen varieties of daffodils, four or five of tulips, four of fleur-de-lys, four of anemones, the Persian iris, the cloth-of-gold and the common yellow crocus, rose campions of violet, white and blue shades, the crimson-flowered Turkish peony, the common laurel, the deep red corn-flag,

---

[1] *Memoirs*, vol. ii, p. 192.

Henry Phillips, *Flora Historica*, vol. ii, p. 132.

the great star flower of Arabia, the double yellow rose, five varieties of crowfoot or ranunculus, the "corona imperialis" lily, with orange-colored flowers striped with purple lines, the white lily of Constantinople, the copper-colored day lily, the martagon lily and the Persian lily of a " dead or over-worne purplish color." [1]   The Persian lily, it seems, was first carried from Persia to Constantinople, and thence sent to England by " the Turkie merchants, and in speciall, by the procurement of Mr. Nicholas Lete, a worthy merchant and a lover of all fair flowers." [2]   Lord Zouch, also was responsible for the introduction of at least some of these flowers, including one variety of hyacinth and the cloth-of-gold crocus.[3]

Of the many varieties of Oriental hyacinths and musk-grape flowers Gerard remarks: " These plants came from the Thracian Bosphorus, out of Asia, and from about Constantinople, and by the means of Friends have been brought into these parts of Europe, whereof our London gardens are possessed." [4]   According to the same authority, " the double white daffodil of Constantinople " was sent into England unto the right honorable the Lord Treasurer, among other bulbed flowers." [5]   Bacon, who held that office at the time, is said to have had some specimens of Asian crowfoot forwarded to him.   These " came from Asia in and about Constantinople " and on the " further side of the Bosphorus," whence plants were brought " at divers times, and by divers persons, but they suffered them to lie in a

---

[1] Parkinson, *Paradisus, etc.*, pp. 27, 28, 30, 39, 51-54, 65, 86, 112-128, 134-135, 163-166, 172, 179-191, 207-213, 222-223, 343, 420; Aiton, *op. cit.*, vol. ii, pp. 240, 242, 305.

[2] Parkinson, *op. cit.*, p. 30.

[3] *Ibid.*, p. 128.

[4] Gerard, *op. cit.*, p. 120.

[5] *Ibid.*, p. 127.

box so long," that when they were received " they were as
dry as ginger." Thereupon he procured fresh plants from
Turkey, but upon their arrival they were as dry as the
others had been.[1] This probably accounts for Bacon's
giving such careful directions in his *Natural History* about
the proper way of transporting plants on long journeys.[2]

The voyages to the East Indies, moreover, resulted in
bringing to England the tri-colored amaranthus, the gloriosa
lily, the oleander, the tuberose, Job's-tears, the double
flowered changeable rose hibiscus, and seven other varieties
of this flower, including those of the purple, red, white and
striped kinds, certain species of cannas, and the great
flowered double Arabian or Tuscan, as well as the Spanish,
jasmine.[3] The common hollyhock from China and the
white lilac from Persia, both introduced in 1597, the red
and yellow crown fritillay, cultivated in 1596, and the blue
lilac in 1640, also from Persia, may have been carried to
England through the Levant.[4] About thirty-five other
plants were introduced from the East Indies before 1700.[5]

From the Cape of Good Hope the great and small honey-
flower, the African lady-smock, the marsh-marigold, several
varieties of everlasting, the salmon-colored haemanthus or
blood-flower, the African blue lily, the sea daffodil of Africa,
reddish blue in color, and the star-flower of Ethiopia were
taken to England during the seventeenth century.[6]   About

---

[1] Gerard, *op. cit.*, p. 960.

[2] *The Works of Francis Bacon*, vol. iv, p. 437.

[3] Aiton, *op. cit.*, vol. i, pp. 1, 16, 18; vol. ii, pp. 68, 248; vol. iv, 226-230;
vol. v, pp. 236, 271; J. C. Loudon, *An Encyclopaedia of Plants, etc.*,
p. 254.

[4] Aiton, *op. cit.*, vol. i, p. 24; vol. ii, p. 244; vol. iv, p. 209.

[5] *Ibid., passim.*

[6] *Ibid.*, vol. ii, pp. 207, 221; vol. iv, pp. 69, 102; vol. v, pp. 152, 167, 223;
Parkinson, *Paradisus*, pp. 98, 138.

eighteen other varieties of plants came from this region.[1]
The Earl of Portland was among the prominent persons
interested in the importations.

Of still more interest are the great numbers of flowering
plants, shrubs and trees which were brought over from
America during the sixteenth and seventeenth centuries.
Such men as John Parkinson, the first to cultivate about
forty trees and shrubs from America, the two Tradescants,
one the gardener of Charles I and the other a collector and
publisher of a catalogue of plants from Virginia, Henry
Compton, Bishop of London, John Banister, the Virginia
missionary, and the Dutchess of Beaufort, besides many
travelers and colonists, were directly responsible for the
introduction of the American flora that added so much to
the beauty of English gardens.[2]

Among the flowers that England gained from the New
World up to 1700, some of those from North America may
be mentioned. They included the atamasco lily, the
martagon Virginia lily, with its large yellow flowers tipped
with red, and the deep-colored Canadian lilies, the yellow
flowered dog-tooth violet, three varieties of Solomon's seals,
the purple side-saddle flower, the Virginia guelder-rose,
the Canadian columbine, the bell-flower, several varieties of
coreopsis, two varieties of meadow rue, eight varieties of
starwort, ten varieties of golden-rod, the double-flowered
annual sunflower, the tree primrose, with its pale yellow
flowers, the scarlet and blue cardinal flowers or lobelias, the
purple and crimson monardas, the common acacia, the
purple, double white, red and bluish Virginia daffodils, the
Virginia spider-wort, with its deep blue flowers touched with
red, the Michaelmas daisy or aster, the single and double

---

[1] Aiton, *op. cit., passim.*

[2] W. J. Bean, *Trees and Shrubs hardy in the British Isles*, vol. i,
p. 4, *et seq.*

flowered French marigolds and the double-flowered African marigold from Mexico, and seven species of lobelia. From the West Indies and South America were procured the common annual sunflower, three varieties of passion flower, the Jacobea lily, four varieties of the "marvel of Peru," the blue, white and bluish purple starry hyacinths, and the Indian autumn daffodil with its red flowers.[1] About eighty other plants also were derived from America.[2]

Several beautiful flowering vines from the New World, which now cling to the garden-walls and arbor-trellises of English gardens, deserve a little fuller treatment. The most attractive of them were the marcoc, or Virginian clematis or climber, its white blossoms spotted with peach color, "the surpassing delight of all flowers."[3] the great and small trumpet honeysuckles from Virginia, with their orange-scarlet flowers,[4] and the convolvulus major, or morning-glory. Seeds of the last-named came by way of Italy before 1629 to beautify English parterres. Its graceful shaped corollas displayed the "most beautiful shades of violet, reddish purple, and lilac," which were sometimes "delicately shaped, and at others, striped, so as to form a star."[5]

The nasturtium, Indian cress, or "yellow larke's heel" as it was called, Parkinson thought to be a flower of "so great beauty and sweetness withall, that my Garden of delight cannot bee unfurnished of it." He further states that the flower

---

[1] Aiton, *op. cit.*, vol. i, pp. 50, 51, 330, 352, 358, 359, 377, 378, 382; vol. iv, p. 323; Rea, *op. cit.*, pp. 34, 41, 73, 74, 76, 79; Phillips, *Flora Historica*, vol. ii, pp. 338, 414; Parkinson, *Paradisus, etc.*, pp. 98, 264; Gerard, *op. cit.*, pp. 49, 343.

[2] Aiton, *passim*.

[3] Rea, *op. cit.*, p. 34.

[4] Aiton, *op. cit.*, p. 377, *et seq.*

[5] Phillips, *Flora Historica*, vol. ii, p. 145.

hath a fine small scent, very pleasing, which being placed in the middle of Carnations or Gilloflowers (for they are in flower at the same time) make a delicate Tuffimussie, as they call it, or Nosegay, both for sight and scent. This goodly plant was first found in the West Indies, from whence all other parts have received it. It is now very familiar in most Gardens of any curiosity.[1]

The arbor-vitae, or tree of life, with its yellow flowers on evergreen stalks, first came from " that part of America which the French doe inhabite, about the river Canada, which is at the back of Virginia northward." From France, to which it was first taken, it spread so extensively that " few gardens of respect either in France, Germany, the Low Countries or England " were without it.[2]

The sunflower, which delighted many an English gardener's heart with its showy petals, was used by the Incas of Peru in their religious services in honor of the sun-god. It is said that the virgins in the Temple of the Sun wore sunflowers of pure gold carefully copied from nature. The first mention of the flower in England was made by Gerard, in 1596, under the name of " The Flower of the Sunne or the Marigold of Peru." He states that it grew to a height of fourteen feet, in his garden and produced flowers that measured sixteen inches across.[3]

Two other American flowers which added greatly to the beauty of English gardens were the Indian canna, or Indian flowering-reed, and the " marvel of Peru." The former had red flowers with yellowish spots. " We preserve them with great care in our gardens, for the beautifull aspect of their flowers, " writes Parkinson. The " marvel of Peru "

---

[1] Parkinson, *Paradisus*, p. 280, *et seq.*

[2] *Ibid.*, p. 436.

[3] Phillips, *Flora Historica*, vol. ii, p. 369; Gerard, *op. cit.*, p. 752.

was said to yield five or six varieties of beautiful flowers, such as " pure white, pure yellow, pure red, white and red spotted, red and yellow spotted and pale purple or peach color.[1]

English green-houses and orangeries became quite a feature of the country gentleman's estate during the seventeenth century. Evelyn, in 1658, tells of going to Bedington, " that ancient seate of the Carews, a fine old hall, but a scambling house," famous for the first orange gardens in England. Here he saw " over-growne trees, planted in ye ground, and secur'd in winter with a wooden tabernacle and stoves."[2] Orange trees were grown for " the beauty of the evergreen leaves, and sweet smelling flowers."[3] Here, too, might be found the aloe which Bradley, the horticulturist, thought was " the most beautiful Tribe of Plants belonging to the Green-House." He says that the most common kinds were brought from America, but that the greatest varieties of them came from Africa, chiefly from the Cape of Good Hope.[4] Here, too, was the sensitive plant or mimosa, brought from Brazil in 1648, which long proved such a curiosity.[5]

The great number of exotic trees from the East, but more especially from America, may well have served as a background for English parterres and landscapes. From the Levant before 1700 came the Oriental plane, the Aleppo pine, the cedar of Lebanon, the hazelnut and the common horsechestnut; while from the East Indies and eastern Asia were

[1] Parkinson, pp. 364-366, 376.

[2] *Memoirs*, vol. ii, p. 136.

[3] Rea, *op. cit.*, p. 15.

[4] Richard Bradley, *New Improvements of Planting and Gardening* (London, 1718), pt. ii, p. 367.

[5] Aiton, *op. cit.*, vol. v, p. 455.

brought the Portugal cypress, the variegated mountain ebony, the nickertree, the tamarind, the cocoanut, the Bengal fig-tree, the common walnut from Persia, and the white mulberry from China.   The Cape of Good Hope furnished at least one familiar tree, the smooth ironwood.[1]   Many of these trees got no further than the botanical gardens, as they were not sufficiently adapted to the English climate to become common.

The case was quite different with American trees, for the majority of them could flourish in England.   John Tradescant, but especially John Banister and Bishop Compton, were responsible for the great number of trees brought to England.   Among the trees of American origin imported before 1700, were the balm-of-Gilead fir, the long-leaved deciduous cypress, the Tacamahac poplar, the Virginia red cedar or juniper tree, the red mulberry, the scarlet oak, the black walnut, the shell-bark walnut, the white hickory, the dwarf chestnut, the blue-berried dogwood, the sassafras tree, the common tulip tree, the evergreen swamp magnolia, the Virginia sumach, the scarlet-flowered maple, the American date or persimmon, the locust, the ash-leaved maple, the scarlet haw, the American plane, the cockspur thorn, the balsam poplar, the ironwood and the butternut tree.[2] Others less well known, such as the nettle tree, the Virginia hop-hornbeam, the liquidamber and the spindle tree, from North America, and the physic-nut and sponge trees from South America and the West Indies, might also be mentioned.[3]

[1] Aiton, *op. cit.*, vol. ii, pp. 13, 22, 32, 335; vol. iv, p. 134; vol. v, pp. 266, 279, 295, 304, 305, 316, 321, 323, 484.

[2] Aiton, *op. cit.*, vol. i, 262; vol. ii, pp. 162, 430; vol. iii, p. 330; vol. v, pp. 266, 292, 296-7, 298, 319, 323, 414, 424, 446, 449, 471, 478; Bean, *op. cit.*, vol. i, pp. 423, 664; vol. ii, pp. 4, 94, 211, 307, 412, 501.

[3] Aiton, *op. cit.*, vol. ii, p. 29; vol. v, pp. 302, 305-6, 329, 450, 471.

A number of other commodities introduced at this time, which will be dealt with in later chapters, were: fish and fish-oil, naval supplies, cedar, mahogany, furs from America, raw silk, saltpeter, and Oriental varnishes from the East, ivory from Africa and dyes from both hemispheres.

CHAPTER IV

COMMERCE

WITH the age of discovery a great revolution took place in the world's commerce. Trade that had kept to inland seas, the rivers and coasts, and overland between Europe and Asia, became oceanic and world-wide. In the process the western seaboard countries assumed the leadership, and launched forth with their exploring and trafficking far away from all known lands into the most distant reaches of the ocean; they attained and developed new regions and viewed for the first time directly the far distant sumptuous East.

To understand how these long voyages came to be possible, one should not only read of the exploits and daring of the seamen of that age, but also note the achievements of the students. Though bold adventures had to be undertaken with an equipment that to the present-day mind would seem utterly crude, the steady advance of commerce could only be possible as improvements were made in the instruments and in the knowledge of navigation. Indeed the influence was reciprocal; as the one tended to promote study and invention in the aid of navigation, so the other gave the mariner and merchant the chance to better his fortunes. By the seventeenth century, at all events, conditions had so changed that the coasts in many cases came to be feared more than the former perils of the great ocean. As a contemporary expressed it: " Our course and passage is throw the great Ocean, where is no feare of Rockes or

Flattes, nor subject to the streights and restraints of for-
raine Princes. . . ." [1]

That there were many dangers to be encountered, however, is perfectly evident, but a bold race of navigators
was being created by the life at sea, and the increased
knowledge of nautical science inspired men with more confidence in their own powers of understanding and master-
ing the waters. Moreover, many instruments such as
octants, quadrants, sextants, chronometers and reflectors,
to measure time, longitude, latitude and altitude were discovered.[2]   By the end of the sixteenth century and the
beginning of the next, the telescope, the log-line, the Mercator's chart, and other helpful aids to navigation were already in use by mariners.[3] These instrumentalities proved
of inestimable value to the sailor, enabling him to venture
far from land without fear of disaster.

This general background provided, one may now proceed
to trace the effect of activities in America and the East upon
English commerce. Before the sixteenth century the insignificant trade of England had moved in a groove.

The wine brigs made annual voyages to Bordeaux and Cadiz;
the hoys plied with such regularity as the winds allowed them
between the Scheldt and the Thames; summer after summer
the Iceland fleet went north for cod and the ling which were
the food of winter fasting days; the boats of Yarmouth and

---

[1] "Nova Britannia Offering Most Excellent Fruits by Planting in
Virginia, printed for Samuel Macham, etc." (London, 1609), p. 10, in
Peter Force, *Tracts, etc.*, vol. i.

[2] H. Scherer, *Histoire de commerce de toutes les nations*, vol. ii, p. 6.

[3] Other instruments such as the celestial and terrestrial globes, a universal horologe for knowing the hours of the day in every latitude, and a
nocturne labe for telling the hour of the night came into use on the
ships of this period. E. Keble Chatterton, *Ships and Ways of Other
Days*, p. 212.

Rye, Southampton, Pool, Brixham, Dartmouth, Plymouth, and Fowie fished the channel.[1]

Such was the commerce of England before it embarked on oversea ventures.

Following the voyages of the Cabots the Newfoundland fisheries were opened to many English fishing ships. Under Henry VIII a " tall and goodly ship " first sailed for the coast of Guinea and there carried on trade for negroes, gold dust and ivory, whence crossing to Brazil, much of the cargo was advantageously disposed of. Meanwhile the quest of the northwest and the northeast passages and the fisheries continued giving employment and training to numerous seamen. Many Protestant west-country gentlemen, who, driven by the Marian persecutions, had taken to the Channel and plundered impartially all shipping in the " narrow seas," soon discovered the Spaniard's weakness at sea, and were thrilled by the grim attractions of a lawless buccaneering life. So profitable did ventures of the sort become that during the Elizabethan period many were induced to sail across the seas to West-Indian waters, and in the case of Drake, to circumnavigate the globe. Voyages, also, were undertaken to America and the East which resulted in the organization and promotion of numerous trading companies, such as the Cathay, the Levant, the Barbary, the African, and finally with the closing years of the century, the East India Company, destined to be the greatest of them all. This, briefly, is the story of the expansion of English commerce until the seventeenth century is reached.

As the century advanced a number of important fields of endeavor were developed, such as the fishing trade with

[1] A. Froude, *History of England from the Fall of Wolsey to the Death of Elizabeth*, vol. viii, p. 2, *et seq.*

Newfoundland and New England, the tobacco trade with Virginia, Maryland and Bermuda, the fur trade mainly with New England and the Hudson Bay region, that in forest products with many of the continental colonies, the trade in sugar and other commodities from the West Indies, the transportation of colonists, the trade in slaves, gold dust, ivory and dyes with the coast of Africa, and the trade in Eastern wares carried on by the Levant and East India Companies. It now remains to be seen what importance each of them had, and in conclusion to observe the extent of the national trade up to 1700.

Before the discovery of America the English had shared in the fisheries in the North Sea and around Iceland. When the Cabots made their voyages to America and discovered Newfoundland which they reported to be rich in fish, a new opportunity for extending trade was afforded. The earliest narrative in the reign of Elizabeth about Newfoundland is contained in a letter of Anthony Parkhurst to Richard Hakluyt, the geographer, written in 1578. In it he declared that there were more than 100 Spanish vessels, 50 Portuguese, 150 French and Breton, but only 50 English at the fisheries.[1] For twenty years before Gilbert's voyage at least 50 English boats were actually engaged in the transatlantic fisheries, while merchantmen from London, Southampton and other ports also took part in the traffic as freighters or " sack ships." [2]

[1] Hakluyt, *op. cit.*, vol. viii, p. 10, *et seq.* 33 Henry VIII, C, xi shows that fishing was going on in Newfoundland during Henry's reign. Act 2nd and 3rd Edward VI, Cap. vi., A. D. 1548, speaks of merchants and fishermen as having " used and practiced the Adventures and Journeys into Iceland, New Foundland, Ireland and other places commodious for Fishing and the getting of fish." D. W. Prowse, *A History of Newfoundland*, pp. 33, 53.

[2] Prowse, *op. cit.*, p. 58.

In 1615, an anonymous author in a pamphlet called *The Trades Increase* asserted that the Greenland whale fisheries employed 15 ships manned by 1400 men, those around Iceland 120 ships and barks with 2500 men, and those off Newfoundland 250 ships "from all parts" with 1500 men.[1] Captain Richard Whitbourne, in his tract, *A Discourse and Discovery of Newfoundland,* published in 1620, corroborates and adds to this information. He says that there were in Newfoundland during 1615 as many as 250 English vessels of a total tonnage of more than 15,000. Every one of them carried 120,000 fish and five tons of train-oil. At £4 a thousand the value of the fish would amount to £120,000, and the 1250 tons of train-oil, at £12 a ton, would sell for £15,000, or £135,000 in all. Besides, at least forty other ships went to Newfoundland simply to load the fish and train-oil.[2] According to the *Calendar of State Papers* there were 97 ships fishing in the English ports of Newfoundland in 1680 alone. These totaled 9,305 tons burden and carried 3,922 men.[8] What made the trade especially important was the fact that through the "sack ships" it was carried on extensively with the countries of southern Europe. After the Reformation the English did not demand the quantities of fish which they formerly had done; consequently a ready market was found for this commodity in the Catholic countries of Spain and Portugal. Here the fish was exchanged for fruits, wines and other commodities.

The fishing trade with New England naturally was of later development, and much of it was soon diverted to supplying the West Indies. As early as 1620 there were

[1] *Harleian Miscellany,* vol. iii, pp. 295, 301, 304.

[2] Richard Whitbourne, *A Discourse and Discovery of Newfoundland, etc.* (London, 1620), pp. 12, 46.

[8] *Cal. S. P. Col. Series, America and W. I.* (1677-1680), p. 643.

six or seven ships that went from the west of England to fish on the New England coast. By the next year there were ten or twelve. By 1624 the number had increased to about fifty,[1] and in 1640 it was reported that 300,000 dried fish were exported.[2] In 1635 more than forty vessels were so engaged.[3]

By far the most valuable trade with the southern group of continental colonies in North America was that in tobacco. It became the staple commodity in Virginia and Maryland. Its exportation to England increased from 20,000 pounds in 1619 to 1,300,000 in 1641,[4] and by 1668 the annual imports of this herb from all the English colonies, including the West Indies, was 9,026,046 pounds.[5] Two hundred ships a year were freighted with tobacco from the Chesapeake Bay region. Fifty vessels from Virginia and Maryland were to be seen in Bristol harbor during the same period, while other ports had eight or ten.[6]

Compared with other forms of commerce the English fur-trade was not very extensive during the seventeenth century. When settlements began to be formed in America it was only natural that hopes should be entertained of a

---

[1] Young, *op. cit.*, p. 5.

[2] William B. Weeden, *Economic and Social History of New England*, vol. i, p. 141.

[3] *Ibid.*, p. 128.

[4]

1619 ...... 20,000 pounds	1628 50,000	pounds
1620 ...... 40,000 "	1639 1,500,000	"
1621 ...... 50,000 "	1640 1,300,000	"
1622 ...... 60,000 "	1641 1,300,000	"

Beer, *The Commercial Policy of England towards the American Colonies*, p. 26.

[5] Beer, *The Old Colonial System* (1660-1754), vol. i, p. 40.

[6] Oldmixon, *op. cit.*, vol. i, p. 317. Though Oldmixon gives no definite date, it is probable that he refers to the latter part of the preceding century, as he does in the case of the statistics about sugar.

great traffic in peltry. As a matter of fact, both the Dutch in New Netherlands and the French in New France surpassed the English in this regard. There appears to have been some dealing in furs with New England, but the chief activities centered about Hudson Bay. In 1671 it was announced that " on the 5th of December ensuing there will be sold in the Great Hall of this place, London, 3,000 weight of beaver skins belonging to the Governor and Company of Merchants Adventurers trading into Hudson's Bay." This was the first official sale held by the Company, founded in the previous year.[1] At first not more than three ships were engaged in the trade at the same time.[2] In 1679, however, the Company's vessels brought home cargoes totaling 10,500 beaver skins, 1,100 marten, 200 otter, 700 elk, and many smaller furs such as muskrat and ermine.[3] That the traffic kept increasing is shown by the fact that fifteen years after the founding of the Hudson's Bay Company it had trading posts at five different places in northern Canada.[4] This business, as will be shown in another connection,[5] proved profitable since a large number of furs could be obtained with a small quantity of merchandise.[6] As time went on, the English began not only supplying themselves with furs,

[1] Beckles Willson, *The Great Company*, p. 60, *et seq.*

[2] George Bryce, *The Remarkable History of the Hudson's Bay Company, etc.*, p. 20.

[3] Agnes C. Laut, *The Conquest of the Great Northwest*, vol. i, p. 162; see *infra*, p. 146, for an account of English goods exported by the Hudson's Bay Company.

[4] Bryce, *op. cit.*, p. 21.

[5] *Infra*, p. 169.

[6] Twelve beaver skins for a large gun, ten for a medium-sized one, and eight for the smallest weapon, a beaver for half a pound of powder, a beaver for four pounds of shot, a beaver for half a pound of beads, are fair examples of this trade. Bryce, *op. cit.*, p. 21.

but they also sent agents to Holland and Russia to seek new markets.[1]

From the first discoveries in America hopes were entertained that the new lands with their dense woods, would furnish the naval stores required by English ships. It was thought very important that this import should be developed since England was rapidly losing her forests, and it soon became difficult to find lumber or masts suitable for shipbuilding. In the tract called *The Trades Increase* a great complaint is raised against cutting down so many large trees to build the East India ships of 1000 tons burden: " Our woods are extraordinarily cut down, in regard to the greatness of the shipping, which doth as it were devour our timber." It is further stated that since the East India Company began to build their ships " of so great burden," the exhaustion of timber had been such that its value was five shillings more a load than formerly.[2]

As soon as Russia was " discovered " by Chancellor and Willoughby in the middle of the sixteenth century, large quantities of hemp, wax, cordage and other naval supplies were imported from this country. In 1595, the sale of Russian cordage by the Muscovy Company amounted to £6,000; while in 1597 the government ordered £10,000 worth for the next year.[3] Other naval supplies such as tar, masts and lumber were brought from Scandinavia. As the demand for their products increased, the northern nations began to raise the prices; besides they always sent their products to England in their own ships and charged heavy freights. This made the English more anxious than

---

[1] Bryce, *op. cit.*, p. 24.

[2] *Harleian Miscellany*, vol. iii, p. 297.

[3] A. J. Gerson, *The Organization and Early History of the Muscovy Company*, p. 71 in University of Pennsylvania Studies in the History of English Commerce in the Tudor Period.

ever to develop American sources of supply. Contemporary interest in this matter is well illustrated by a tract called *Nova Britannia Offering most Excellent Fruits by Planting in Virginia,* in which the anonymous author states that

the expense and waste of woode, will be no hurt, but great service to that country [America]; the great superfluity whereof, the continually cutting downe, in manie hundred yeares, will not be able to overcome, whereby will likewise grow a greater benefite to this land, [England] in preserving, our woodes and tymber at home, so infinitely and without measure upon these occasions cut downe. . . . [1]

It was not, however, until the latter part of the seventeenth century that naval stores in any quantity were exported from America. Then the amount was far from sufficient and the quality was not of the best, while the prices, if anything, were higher than those which were paid to the Scandinavians and Russians.[2] The Carolinas [3] and the New England colonies were the chief centers of this trade. Fine masts were sent from Piscataqua, and in time the " mast ships," as the swiftest vessels, came to carry the mails. When the Massachusetts government wished to conciliate the king and obtain new favors, it often sent a load of masts which was always a very acceptable present.[4]

[1] " Nova Britannia, etc.," p. 16, in Force, *Tracts, etc.,* vol. i.

[2] *Cal. S. P. Col. Series, America and the W. I.* (1693-1696), p. 263.

[3] John Lawson in his *History of Carolina* says that "none of our continent plantations are to be compared to Carolina for affording such vast quantities of naval stores; such as pitch, tar, turpentine, rosin, masts, yards, planks, boards, timber, pipestaves, lumber, hemp, flax," etc. Anderson, *Commerce,* vol. iii, p. 29.

[4] Some large specimens presented to the king cost Massachusetts £1600. In 1666 Pepys speaks of a present from Massachusetts of a shipload of masts sent to the king. In 1665, seven or eight ships and a large supply of masts were at Piscataqua. Weeden, *op. cit.,* vol. i, p. 243, *et seq.*

During the seventeenth century the plantations in the West Indies were of immense commercial value to England. The article of supreme importance was sugar, and its products, rum and molasses. For a time the Dutch had control of this lucrative traffic throughout Europe. The English, however, were destined to become dominant in the cultivation and refining of sugar, and by the latter part of the century through the cheapness of this product they had gained possession of the northern European markets. They succeeded in expanding the trade more than all the other nations that had hitherto dealt in sugar, and even sent that commodity into the Levant, to the very region from which it had formerly been imported.[1] The leadership was maintained until it passed to the French, who because of the amount of land available in their West Indian colonies for producing a greater quantity of the commodity, and their cheaper processes of refining carried on there. lowered the price of sugar.

By 1675, the English trade in sugar was so extensive that it employed 400 vessels averaging 150 tons burden.[2] About the same time as many as 30,000 hogsheads were annually taken over from the West Indies. Approximately half of the quantity this represents was consumed in England and the remainder exported to other countries. Its value was estimated at £250,000. Together with other commodities from the West Indies, such as ginger, cotton and molasses, the total exports from this area to England reached £350,000.[3] From December 15, 1697, to Septem-

---

[1] John Campbell, *Considerations on the Nature of the Sugar Trade*, p. 10; Ellis, *op. cit.*, p. 5.

[2] William Reed, *The History of Sugar*, p. 7; Oldmixon, *op. cit.*, vol. ii, p. 162.

[3] Oldmixon, *op. cit.*, vol. ii, p. 168. By 1678 the yearly trade of the Leeward Islands in sugar. tobacco and indigo required 200 ships to carry

ber 29, 1700, Jamaica exported to England 32,438 hogsheads and 980 barrels of sugar; while Barbados, from March 25, 1698 to March 25, 1700 sent 33,788 hogsheads, 7940 barrels and 2646 tierces [1] of sugar to England.

By the end of the seventeenth century much dyeing material was sent from the West Indies. Jamaica especially came to be well known for this trade. It obtained much of its supply from the Bay of Campeche, although it was said that there was an abundance of fustic, redwood and logwood upon the island.[2] Indigo appears to have been found and exported to England from nearly every English colony in the West Indies, and Jamaica produced more of it than any other settlement.[3] In 1662-1663 as much as 140 hundred-weight of indigo and 4,334 hundred-weight of fustic came from the American colonies.[4] Logwood, which formerly was bought from the Spaniards at £100 a ton, was by the beginning of the eighteenth century imported at the rate of £15 a ton in amounts as large as 1000 tons a year.[5] 7,500 bags of cotton-wool, 2,000 hundred-weight of ginger, 1,200 hundred-

it. *Cal. S. P. Col. Series, American and the W. I.* (1677-1680), p. 222. From April 1678 to October 14, 1679, 51 ships, 39 of which were English built, and twelve foreign were at Barbados. *Ibid.*, p. 435. During the seven years and nine months from June 25, 1671 to March 25, 1679, 7,637¼ tons of sugar, 44¾ of cacao, 305 of indigo, 177 of ginger, 2,357 of fustic, 5119 of logwood, 43¾ of tobacco and 134½ of pimento, 38,587 hides and 866 bags of cotton were exported from Jamaica alone During 1678, 47 ships were laden for England at Port Royal in that island. *Ibid.*, p. 344.

[1] A tierce equals 42 gallons.

[2] Oldmixon, *op. cit.*, vol. ii, pp. 334, 344.

[3] *Ibid.*, vol. ii, pp. 163, 180, 192.

[4] Beer, *The Old Colonial System* (1660-1754), vol. i, p. 40. Dalby Thomas gives the amount of indigo imported from the West Indies in 1690 at 50,000 pounds yearly. *Harleian Miscellany*, vol. ix, p. 412.

[5] Oldmixon, *op. cit.*, vol. i, p. xxiii.

weight of calico, 1,088 hundred-weight of lignum vitae, 2,896 pounds of tortoise shell and 144 hundred-weight of granadilla were sent from the West Indies to the mother country in 1662-1663.[1] Considerable tobacco was also grown and exported from the island colonies.[2] Mahogany, too, was an article of trade from this part of the world, for English log-cutters established themselves in Honduras after 1655, and soon several hundred traders were engaged in cutting down and exporting its rich timber to England.[3]

Something should be said, also, of the benefit to English commerce from the transportation of the colonists and their personal effects. By 1640 it was estimated that 20,000 people had been carried to New England. About 200 ships were engaged in this work. The fare was five pounds a person and four pounds a ton was charged for freight. At this rate it is estimated that their transportation together with their movables cost £95,000 and that £12,000 was paid to transfer their cattle to America.[4]

The income from this same source must have been considerable likewise in the case of emigration to other parts of America. Thus between 1606 and 1625, 5,649 emigrants left England for Virginia,[5] and the statistician, Davenant, towards the close of the seventeenth century, estimates that

[1] Beer, *The Old Colonial System* (1660-1754), vol. i, p. 400. One thousand tons of cotton and 4,000 tons of ginger are said to have been imported in 1690. *Harleian Miscellany*, vol. ix, p. 412.

[2] *Supra*, p. 110.

[3] A. Wyatt Tilby, "Britain in the Tropics 1527-1910," *The English People Overseas*, vol. iv, pp. 9, 10.

[4] Daniel Neal, *History of New England*, vol. i, p. 193; Young, *op. cit.*, p. 117.

[5] Edward Channing, *History of the United States*, vol. i, p. 204. Chalmers estimates the cost of transporting settlers to Virginia before 1625, at £150,000; but apparently he bases this figure on the transportation of 9,000 settlers. George Chalmers, *Political Annals of the Present United Colonies, etc.*, bk. i, p. 69.

for many years about 1,800 annually left England for the West Indies,[1] which at the prevailing rate of transportation for persons, and their necessary baggage and supplies for settling must have been quite an amount.

Oversea expansion, of course, was directly responsible for one of the most evil kinds of business the world has ever known, viz. the negro slave trade, and England was destined to become the chief slavemonger. Its share began in 1562, when Sir John Hawkins sailing with three ships to the coast of Sierra Leone, captured or bought 300 negroes and took them to Santo Domingo where he sold them at great profit. Several other lucrative voyages were undertaken by Hawkins who was the only Englishman to have success in the traffic for nearly a hundred years. During the sixteenth century it was still a Portuguese monopoly, but after 1600 it fell for awhile under Dutch control. It was the Dutch who introduced the first negroes into Virginia in 1619, and who furnished Barbados and other islands in the West Indies with the large supply they needed for the sugar industry.[2]

The first attempt which the English made to establish a regular trade to the African coast occurred in 1618, when an exclusive charter for this trade was granted by James I to Sir Robert Rich and other London merchants. A second charter to last for thirty-one years and providing for exclusive monopoly of the trade was granted in 1631. Ports and warehouses were erected on the African coast, but due largely to the competition of private adventurers and interlopers of all nations, especially the Dutch who had forced the trade open, the enterprise did not succeed.[3]

---

[1] Davenant, *op. cit.*, vol. ii, p. 7.

[2] Channing, *op. cit.*, vol. i, pp. 118, 214.

[3] W. O. Blake, *The History of Slavery and the Slave Trade, Ancient and Modern*, p. 107.

After 1660, the English undertook to wrest from the Dutch the control of the traffic in slaves which yielded such alluring profits. In 1662 the Duke of York and Prince Rupert became interested in it, and as a consequence a third attempt was made to start a joint-stock company with exclusive rights, and accordingly all except the trade carried on by the Company was forbidden. Due to constant conflicts with the Dutch, the merchants in this African trade suffered serious losses both in shipping and stations. The Company was reconstructed in 1672.[1] It undertook to supply the English plantations with 3,000 negroes annually.[2] Stations were erected along the African coast and the traffic began to prove very important. In the year 1674 fifteen ships were sent there, six of which carried about 2,000 negroes to Barbados. The next year twenty vessels were despatched to Africa, and eight bore away 3,000 negroes to that island. These latter sold at £15 a head.[3] During this year and part of the next four ships with 1,660 blacks went to Jamaica. In 1676, it was stated that the planters there owed the Company £25,000 for slaves, and had ordered 1,540 more.[4] Those sent over between 1674 and 1675 and part of the following year, for the four colonies of Barbados, Nevis, Jamaica and Virginia, are said to have numbered 7,025.[5] In the nine years from 1680 to 1688, as many as 60,783 slaves were shipped from Africa. During this time 28 ships a year were employed by the Company in their business.[6]

---

[1] Beer, *The Old Colonial System*, 1660-1754, vol. i, pp. 325, 327.

[2] Blake, *op. cit.*, p. 107.

[3] *Cal. S. P. Col. Series, America and the West Indies* (*1675-76*), p. 388.

[4] *Ibid.*, p. 503.

   Ibid., pp. 202, 388.

[6] Beer, *The Old Colonial System*, 1660-1754, vol. i, p. 344; William Wood, *A Survey of Trade* (London, 1719), p. 185. Wood says that

At this point further mention should be made of the earlier trade to Guinea for gold and ivory. Reference to English trading expeditions thither appear as early as 1555, when gold was secured there, as well as in 1556, 1557 and in subsequent years. In 1555 alone 400 pounds of gold dust and 150 "elephant's teeth" are spoken of. The quantity of gold at all events was sufficient to arouse and maintain interest in the prospect of obtaining that precious commodity.[1]   The East India Company, appreciating the value that a supply would have for their Indian commerce, obtained a charter in 1651, which permitted them to trade with the Guinea coast. They sent factors there and exchanged English goods with the natives for gold dust.[2]   In 1673 as many as 50,000 guineas were coined from this gold.[3]   According to a report of the Royal African Company made in 1696, the value of the precious metal which had been brought in their ships for that year to England

46,396 negroes were delivered to the English plantation colonies between the years 1680 and 1689. Bryan Edwards gives 140,000 as the number of colored slaves imported by the Company during the period from 1680 to 1700. He also says 160,000 more were acquired by private individuals. Bryan Edwards, *The History Civil and Commercial of the British Colonies in the West Indies*, vol. ii, p. 52. These figures appear altogether too large. Woodward states that in 1680 four or five thousand were imported annually. He thinks the yearly number exported in 1700 was perhaps 25,000. W. H. Woodward, *A Short History of the Expansion of the British Empire*, p. 172.

[1] Hakluyt, *op. cit.*, vol. vi, pp. 163, 173, 209, 220, 244, 245.

[2] Cunningham, *The Growth of English Industry and Commerce in Modern Times*, pt. i, p. 273.

[3] Blake, *op. cit.*, p. 107. In the tract called "Reflections upon the Constitution and Management of the Trade to Africa" (1709), p. 6. Brit. Mus. 712. m. (19), quoted in Cunningham, *op. cit.*, pt. i, p. 274, it is stated that such "quantities of Gold Dust (were brought) from the Coast of Africa, that they frequently Coin'd Thirty, Forty or Fifty Thousand Guineas at a time, with the Elephant upon them, for a Mark of Distinction."

was 12,144 pounds, 18 shillings and 4 pence, while at Barbados they had 12,172 pounds, 4 shillings and 6 pence more.[1] That much of the African gold was turned into English guineas is evident from the common application of this term to gold coins.

The traffic carried on with " the Dark Continent " was on the whole very highly thought of at the time in England, as it afforded a good market for English cloth, supplied labor to the American plantations and procured commodities like gold, ivory and dyes.[2] English goods could be sent to Africa where they could be largely exchanged for slaves. These were taken to the West Indies and sold for sugar, which in turn was sent to England or re-exported thence to other European countries. Slaves not thus disposed of to English planters were sold to foreign purchasers, and money or sugar was given in payment. The trade, in fact, was so lucrative that it was termed " England's silver-mine." Out of the several transactions described the profit ranged from one hundred to three hundred per cent.[3]

The Levant or Turkey Company was the first of the English mercantile organizations to carry on trade with the East in silks, spices, drugs and the like. In 1553 Anthony Jenkinson was successful in obtaining concessions in Turkey, and in 1581 Elizabeth granted a monopoly to him and his associates which was to last for seven years. Occasional voyages thereafter were undertaken. When the Turkey Company was reconstructed, regular trade was established between England and the domains of the Sultan. It was

[1] *Journals of the House of Commons*, vol. xi, p. 628.

[2] *Ibid.*, vol. xi, p. 68.

[3] Davenant, *op. cit.*, vol. ii, p. 15; John Carey, *Discourse on Trade, etc.* (London, 1745), p. 53.

looked upon much more favorably than the activities of the East India Company, as it did not involve the export of so much bullion, while at the same time it called for the shipment of large quantities of English manufactures.[1]

The East India trade, nevertheless, came to be the most important. Up to July, 1620, 79 ships had been sent to India. Of these, 34 had returned richly laden, 6 had been captured by the Dutch and 21 were still in the Indies. During the twenty years of the Company's existence it had already brought merchandise to the value of £356,288 to England, and had besides £484,088 worth of goods stored in the Indies ready to transport.[2] In 1626 the total value of the shipments home was estimated at £360,000; while it was reported in 1630 that the Company's ships that had recently returned brought a cargo worth £543,000.[3] An anonymous writer, probably Child, gives the total value of the imports from India for the year 1674-1675 as £1,050,-000. Of this amount £6,000 is assigned to pepper, £30,000 to saltpetre, £30,000 also to raw and wrought silk, £160,000 to calico, £15,000 to indigo and drugs, all of which was consumed at home. This left goods valued at £809,000 for exportation to foreign countries. At this date thirty to thirty-five ships averaging from 300 to 600 tons burden were annually employed.[4]

A more specific statement of the amounts of the various commodities imported in the Eastern trade may not be out

[1] Cunningham, *op. cit.*, pt. i, p. 250. See *infra*, p. 134 for figures of exports to the Levant.

[2] Thomas Mun, "A Discourse of Trade from England into the East Indies," in McCulloch, *Collection* (1856), p. 31.

[3] *Cal. S. P. Col. Series, E. I.* (1625-1629), pp. 284, 615, 616; (1630-1634), p. xi.

[4] Macpherson, *The History of European Commerce with India*, p. 133, *et seq.*

of place at this juncture. From 1664 to 1670 as many as 9,426,387 pounds of pepper, or a yearly average of 1,346,-669 pounds, were brought to England.[1] By the conditions of its charter the East India Company was to furnish 500 tons of saltpetre to the crown. In 1698 they had £1,300,-000 worth of this commodity on hand.[2] In 1617, 500 bales of silk were shipped from Persia.[3] Four years later, Mun, an English merchant of the time, estimates the importations of this article of trade at 107,140 pounds.[4] Seven hundred bales of silk were bought in 1625, and it was found difficult to sell so large a quantity.[5] At that time 600 bales would have sufficed for the home market, and 2,000 bales would have been all they were sure of selling in other countries.[6] Later the importations appear to have fallen off, as in 1641, 300 bales are given as the annual shipment.[7] Mun, in 1628, estimated the yearly importation of calicoes at 50,000 pieces.[8] In 1630, two of the company's ships, the " Discovery " and the " Reformation," were loaded with 579 bales of calico and 250 bales of cotton yarn and 22 bales of cotton wool. At this time the company advised its agents to send 600 or 700 bales of cotton yarn annually, but no cotton wool except when there was space in the vessels' hold which might be filled.[9] As

---

[1] Milburn, *op. cit.*, vol. i, p. 286.

[2] *Journals of the House of Commons*, vol. ii, p. 390.

[3] *Cal. S. P. Col. Series, E. I.* (1617-1621), p. 46.

[4] Milburn, *op. cit.*, vol. ii, p. 247.

[5] *Cal. S. P. Col. Series E. I.* (1625-1629), p 9.

[6] *Calendar of Venetian State Papers* (1625-1626), p. 502, *et seq.*

[7] Henry Robinson, *England's Safety in Trades Encrease* (London, 1641), p. 15.

[8] Milburn, *op. cit.*, vol. ii, p. 230.

[9] *The English Factories in India, etc.* (1630-1633), pp. 19, 127.

much as 200,000 pounds of indigo came from the East during the year 1620.[1]

Other commodities, such as carpets and quilts, sugar, gum-lac, precious jewels, ebony,[2] perfumes, drugs and tea, formed part of the English East India trade. Of these carpets and quilts are upon several occasions mentioned as having been taken in small quantities.[3] Sugar evidently did not prove a very profitable article of Oriental commerce, for after the company's agents had bought some of it and sent it home they were ordered not to purchase any more.[4] The West Indies, as has been seen, proved to be the most fruitful source of supply for this valuable commodity and destroyed all competition from other parts of the world. Gum-lac, used as a varnish, came in large quantities from India. In 1630, as many as 20 bales were imported, and as much as three or four tons were ordered for future shipment.[5] The factors in India received directions in 1624 to invest 10,000 or 20,000 rials annually in diamonds.[6] Many of these were in all probability traded for other goods as they were in great demand with the natives.

Soon after the East India Company imported its first tea [7] it was given a monopoly of the new commodity on condition that it keep one year's supply on hand in its warehouses. Besides it had to bring the tea to London, and

---

[1] Milburn, *op. cit.*, vol. ii, p. 213.

[2] *The English Factories in India, etc.* (1624-1629), p. 39.

[3] *Letters Received by the East India Company from its Servants in the East* (1616), pp. 299, 303. In 1630 the agents were instructed not to send any more quilts and carpets until ordered to do so. *The English Factories in India* (1630-1633), p. 9.

[4] *The English Factories in India* (1630-1633), p. 19.

[5] *Ibid.*, pp. 9, 19.

[6] *Ibid.* (1624-1629), p. 25.

[7] *Supra,* p. 54.

offer it at quarterly public sales at the rate of a penny a
pound in advance of the gross cost, the price being determined by adding to the rate at which it was bought in
China, the freight charges, insurance, interest on capital
and other charges.[1] The number of pounds of tea imported
during the latter part of the century varied greatly from
year to year. Thus while in 1678 as much as 4,717 pounds
were taken to England, by the very next year the amount
had fallen to 197 pounds. In 1681 none is mentioned, and
in the following year only 70 pounds, which appeared to
satisfy the demand until 1685, when the large amount of
12,070 pounds reached London. However, by 1689 such
large importations as 25,300 pounds, and in 1690 the still
larger amount of 41,471 pounds were made. The last five
years of the century furnish such varying figures as
13,270, 22,416, 21,302, and 13,221 pounds.[2]

The following table taken from Charles Whitworth's
State of Trade of Great Britain summarizes the extent of
England's oversea commerce at the close of the seventeenth
century, and affords a striking contrast to the situation two
hundred years before.[3]

TRADE OF GREAT BRITAIN WITH EAST INDIES:

Imports	Exports
1697 ...... £262,837. 9s. 5d.	£ 67,094. 16s. 6d.
1698 ...... £356,509. 7s. 7d.	£451,195. 16s. 2d.
1699 ...... £717,695. 4s. 5½d.	£156,908. 13s. 11½d.

[1] Walsh, *Tea, its History and Mystery*, p. 23.

[2] Milburn, *op. cit.*, vol. ii, p. 532.

[3] *Supra*, p. 101.

TRADE OF GREAT BRITAIN WITH AFRICA:

Imports	Exports
1697 ...... £ 6,615. 16s. 8d.	£13,435. 16s. 10d.
1698 ...... £ 2,496. 6s. 8d.	£70,587. 17s. 4d.
1699 ...... £19,225. 18s. 7½d.	£96,295. 5s. 8¾d.

TRADE OF GREAT BRITAIN WITH BARBADOS:

Imports	Exports
1697 ...... £196,532. 18s. 5d.	£ 77,465. 8s. 1d.
1698 ...... £308,090. 10s. 9d.	£146,851. — 4d.
1699 ...... £273,947. 15s. 5d.	£150,532. 7s. 5¼d.

TRADE OF GREAT BRITAIN WITH JAMAICA:

Imports	Exports
1697 ...... £ 70,000. 6s.	£ 40,726. 7s. 8d.
1698 ...... £189,567. 10s. 4d.	£120,777. 15s. 4d.
1699 ...... £174,845. —s. 8½d.	£136,733. 6s. 1d.

TRADE OF GREAT BRITAIN WITH MONTSERRAT:

Imports	Exports
1697 ...... £14,699. 14s. 3d.	£3,532. 10s. —.
1698 ...... £24,422. 2s. 6d.	£3,372. 12s. 8d.
1699 ...... £23,163. 9s. 6d.	£7,162. 14s. 2¼d.

TRADE OF GREAT BRITAIN WITH NEVIS:

Imports	Exports
1697 ...... £17,096. 13s. 3d.	£13,043. — 8d.
1698 ...... £54,748. 16s. 8d.	£14,550. 13s. 7d.
1699 ...... £ 4,857. 17s. 6¼d.	£16,480. 6s. 4¾d.

TRADE OF GREAT BRITAIN WITH NEW PROVIDENCE:

Imports	Exports
1697 .... £708. 4s. 9d.	£1,422. 15s. 4d.
1698 .... £184. 14s. 10d.	—— — —
1699 .... —— — —	£ 305. 4s. —

TRADE OF GREAT BRITAIN WITH BERMUDA:

Imports	Exports
1697 ...... £ 20. 6s. 3d.	£ 626. 16s. —
1698 ...... £ 2,926. 8s. 11d.	£3,971. 10s. —
1699 ...... £ 300. 10s. 1½d.	£1,430. 13s. 11d.

TRADE OF GREAT BRITAIN WITH VIRGINIA AND MARYLAND:

	Imports	Exports
1697	£227,756. 11s. 4d.	£ 58,796. 10s. 11d.
1698	£174,053. 4s. 5d.	£310,135. — —
1699	£198,115. 16s. 10d.	£205,078 — 8½d.

TRADE OF GREAT BRITAIN WITH CAROLINA:

	Imports	Exports
1697	£12,374. 5s. 3d.	£ 5,289 19s. 1d.
1698	£ 9,265. 7s. 6d.	£18,462. 13s. 1d.
1699	£12,327. 1s. 9¾d.	£11,401. 18s. 5½d.

TRADE OF GREAT BRITAIN WITH NEW YORK:

	Imports	Exports
1697	£10,093. 16s. 10d.	£ 4,579. 3s. 5d.
1698	£ 8,763. 13s. 8d.	£25,279. 14s. 1d.
1699	£16,818. 18s. 10½d.	£42,792. 1s. 1d.

TRADE OF GREAT BRITAIN WITH NEW ENGLAND:

	Imports	Exports
1697	£26,282. 2s. 3d.	£ 68,468. 17s. 9d.
1699	£31,254. 18s. 10d.	£ 13,517. 1s. 10d.
1699	£26,660. 16s. 8d.	£127,279. 19s. 2½d.

TRADE OF GREAT BRITAIN WITH HUDSON BAY:

	Imports	Exports
1697	£1,995. 1s. —	£1,291. 19s. 7d.
1698	£8,031. 11s. 4d.	£2,853. 8s. 6d.
1699	£4,235. 5s. ¼d.	£943. 15s. 7¼d.

TRADE OF GREAT BRITAIN WITH NEWFOUNDLAND:

	Imports	Exports
1697	£ 9,384. — 4d.	£21,659. 10s. 9d.
1698	£ 4,899. 13s. 1d.	£15,620. 9s. 1d.
1699	£18,402. 6s. 1¼d.	£17,661. 8s. 5¼d.

TRADE OF GREAT BRITAIN WITH GREENLAND:

	Imports	Exports
1697	£3,694. 17s. 6d.	——— — —
1698	£ 273. 17s. 6d.	——— — —
1699	£ 469. 6s. 3d.	——— — —[1]

[1] Charles Whitworth, *State of the Trade of Great Britain* (London, 1776), p. 1, *et seq.*

Now, with the great expansion of English commerce clearly in mind, something must be said of its effect upon the commercial policy and the organization of the country's business. A new " politico-economic doctrine " — mercantilism, came into being as a result of the growth of world commerce and the rise of centralized governments in Europe which took an interest in developing the national resources.

In endeavoring to cultivate and preserve the wealth of their subjects, European monarchs proceeded upon the assumption that, if a nation exported costly manufactures to its own colonies and imported cheap raw materials from them, the money paid into the home country for manufactures would more than counterbalance the money paid out for raw materials, and this " favorable balance of trade " would bring gold to the nation. This economic theory and the system based upon it are called mercantilism. In order to establish such a balance of trade, the government might either forbid or heavily tax the importation of manufactures from abroad, might prohibit the exportation of raw materials, might subsidize the export of manufactures, and might attempt by minute regulations to foster industry at home as well as to discourage competition in the colonies.[1]

Moreover, in accordance with the policy just mentioned, as the British colonial trade grew in importance and the competition of the Dutch, the great carrying nation of the time, became more strenuous, the government under Cromwell's leadership, believing itself justified in taking steps to make sure that in future the benefit from this traffic should come to England, passed the first Navigation Act in 1651. This measure, which was later followed by another of similar import in 1660, provided that only English or colonial

[1] Carlton J. H. Hayes, *A Political and Social History of Modern Europe*, vol. i, p. 277.

vessels could bring to England or its territories the commodities of Asia, Africa or America, and on the other hand
any goods of European production had to be imported in
English vessels or those of the producing country. Through
this regulation it was possible to secure to the mother-
country all the business of providing the colonists with
European merchandise, and likewise make it " a staple for
the distribution of the more valuable American products in
other parts of the world." [1]

Another means of taking advantage of and securing for
England the many opportunities which new commercial expansion afforded was the creation of strong monopolistic
chartered companies to promote the national interests and
their own in distant lands. These organizations provided a
greater amount of capital than had previously been accu-
mulated in English business ventures, and thus could push
to a successful conclusion many an undertaking that might
have proved the ruin of individual enterprise. However,
even the large concerns were often unable to succeed; for
out of a total of fifty-eight companies, forty-six failed completely and eight were suppressed or surrendered their charters. The East India Company, indeed, was the only really
successful organization of the sort, but it was not until it
was put on a national basis and a moneyed class created
who invested their savings in it, that its greatest development was attained.[2]

Just as oversea expansion was responsible for the creation of the chartered companies, so their privileges and
activities in turn evoked much hostile criticism of organiza-

---

[1] *Ibid.*, pp. 277, 304; Gardiner, *History of the Commonwealth and
Protectorate*, 1649-1660, vol. ii, p. 80; Cunningham, *op. cit.*, pt. i, pp. 471,
472.

[2] W. A. S. Hewins, *English Trade and Finance, chiefly in the 17th.
Century*, p. 14; E. J. Payne, *History of European Colonies*, pp. 13, 101.

tions that relied too much on their monopoly for success and excluded many capable young merchants from the chief branches of foreign trade, or compelled them to act as " interlopers ".[1]   As early as 1604 bills were passed in the House of Commons, abolishing many of the restrictions upon membership in trading companies.   These salutary bills were brought to naught by the action of the peers who were always anxious to protect vested interests.[2]   As the century advanced, more and more discontent with the business conditions caused by the great companies manifested itself.[3]

[1] *Infra*, p. 243.
[2] Traill, *Social England*, vol. iv, p. 133.
[3] *Infra*, pp. 131, 136, 241.

CHAPTER V

INDUSTRY

DURING the sixteenth century social and material progress in England was greatly impeded by the disorganized condition of the previous system of production, consequent upon the system of enclosures and the dissolution of the monasteries, followed by the entanglement with Spain and religious troubles, which caused for some time serious unrest throughout the country.[1] Although great stores of foreign treasure gained from privateering brought luxury to the upper classes, and added to the comfort of the lower ranks of society, they proved detrimental to industrial progress, for voyages of the sort became so popular that in the craze for making wealth quickly much of the capital which would otherwise have been invested in the cloth trade, or in opening up new enterprises, was withdrawn and devoted to this particular purpose. Since the Hapsburgs controlled in Spain, Portugal, the Netherlands and Germany the very markets which England found most valuable for its trade, the privateering exploits had aroused a feeling of ill will on their part. Commerce with the possessions of Philip II and his royal relative of Austria was made uncertain, thus striking a blow at England and producing a crisis in industrial conditions which on the whole

[1] William R. Scott, *The Constitution and Finance of English, Scottish and Irish Joint Stock Companies to 1720*, vol. i, p. 23.

proved a greater loss to the country than was made up by the bullion seized.[1]

In spite of these retarding circumstances commerce was leaving its old channels and extending in many directions, and naturally the demand thus caused for English goods tended to stimulate domestic production. English woolen goods, the main English manufacture, were being marketed in Russia, the Levant, northern and western Africa and Brazil.[2] Likewise some trace may be found of the disposal of the products of English mines and of hardware in the Levant,[3] of various trinkets such as bracelets, glass beads, hawks bells, etc., in Africa.[4]

With the Stuart period English industry soon began to experience salutary effects from the activities of the chartered companies which furnished new markets and new raw materials for home manufactures, as well as increased the store of available capital. The growth of English industry would have been much more quickly expanded by the enlargement of commerce, had it not been for the retarding effect of the political and religious conditions of the time. Heavy customs and large loans were exacted from the trading and industrial companies by the Stuart sovereigns, which often they were unable to afford, while many of them were prevented from launching out upon industrial enterprises by the system of special privileges and monopolies. The Civil War and the disturbing conditions which preceded and followed it furnished additional obstacles. A period of great industrial and commercial advancement, however, at last arrived with the Restoration, when many economic,

[1] Scott, *op. cit.*, vol. i, pp. 84, 88.

[2] H. de B. Gibbins, *Industry in England*, pp. 231, 241; Froude, *op. cit.*, vol. viii, pp. 440, 442; Macpherson, *Annals of Commerce*, vol. ii, pp. 72, 81.

[3] *Infra*, pp. 138, 139.

[4] Macpherson, *Annals*, vol. ii, p. 183.

social and political abuses were corrected. It was then that the full effect of the vast progress in colonization and oversea commerce began to be felt.

A few actual figures may be to the point at this juncture. Between 1601 and 1620 the East India Company had sent to the Orient as much as £292,286 worth of broadcloths, kerseys, lead, tin and other commodities. By 1674-75 [1] the trade had reached such a height that £110,000 in woolen goods and other merchandise was exported by the Company, while to this amount may be added £40,000 in goods dispatched on private account.[2] The West Indies, likewise, proved a most valuable market for English wares. In 1676 as much as £50,000 worth of the mother country's manufactures was bought by Barbados alone; and by 1697 the annual exports to this colony had reached £146,849, and Jamaica disposed of £120,744 more.[3] It was estimated that about half of the profits from the sale of the planter's sugar was returned to him in merchandise.[4] Virginia and Maryland were enabled through their large sales of tobacco to buy immense quantities of English goods. In 1664 the commodities imported into these colonies were declared to be worth £200,000, a sum equal in purchasing power to perhaps five times that amount at the present time. A single shipment in 1681 was worth £12,000 and cargoes of £20,-000 were not unusual.[5] New England also, through supplying the West Indies with provisions and engaging in the

[1] Thomas Mun, *A Discourse of Trade from England unto the East Indies* (London, 1621), p. 20.

[2] *A Treatise Concerning the East India Trade, wrote at the instance of Thomas Papillon* (London, 1680), p. 7.

[3] *Cal. S. P. Col. Series, Am. and W. I.* (1675-76), p. 500; Beer, *The Old Colonial System*, vol. ii, p. 81.

[4] Oldmixon, *op. cit.*, vol. ii, p. 163.

[5] *Ibid.*, vol. i, pp. 84, 88.

sugar trade, was given means to buy many English manufactures.

The impetus thus created by oversea demands for manufactures was of immense value in this period of the beginnings of modern English industrial progress. For example, the woolen industry had been launched during the latter part of the sixteenth century. At that time immigrants had come from France and Flanders, and not only commenced to manufacture the wool, but also taught the English their secrets. Somewhat later, in 1614, King James I attempted to encourage the infant industry by creating a monopoly in dyeing cloth and by prohibiting the exportation of white or unfinished textiles.[1] This measure, for a while at least, instead of helping the situation, appears to have had very disastrous consequences. The English finished cloth was at first nowhere well received. The people of the Netherlands, who were formerly the great customers of England, refused to buy it. They began to raise wool themselves, as well as to import it from other countries, and the English failed to recover their former trade with them even in this raw commodity.[2] Moreover, cloth of native manufacture was not popular in England itself. Even as late as 1678 it was declared that the wool trade was very much hindered by the people wearing foreign textiles, and that even when they did make use of woolen cloth, they preferred that made from the Spanish rather than the English wool.[3]

[1] Scott, *op. cit.*, vol. i, p. 143.

[2] The exportation to the Low Countries and Germany diminished from 100,000 unfinished cloths to 30,000. Samuel Brothers, *Wool and Woolen Manufactures of Great Britain* (London, 1859), p. 76, *et seq.*

[3] R. L'Estrange, *The Ancient Trades, Decayed, Repaired Again* (London, 1678), pp. 13, 16; William Crook, *A Treatise of Wool and the Manufacture of It* (London, 1685), p. 9.

It may be seen how the English, when confronted by these discouraging results of their first attempt to manufacture their own wool, were encouraged and sustained by the commerce which they had developed with distant lands. In 1641 it was reported that only a third part of the woolen goods were sold in Germany and the Low Countries which used to be sold there, and that there was fear that " our woolen staple, and manufacture especially, will by degrees wheel away from us." However, " to recompense those losses and encourage our further endeavours, Divine providence hath discovered us how to utter a considerable quantity of cloth (though not answerable to the decay in Germania and the Low Countries) for Turkie and Muscovia." To Turkey alone had been sent 20,000 dyed and dressed cloths yearly.[1]

Besides the Turkey or Levant Company, there was the Eastland Company, trading chiefly in English woolens to Russia and to other countries about the Baltic Sea. Its trading route even extended across the northern seas as far as Greenland and Hudson Bay.[2] Before the African Company of 1662 was incorporated, the cloth-makers in Suffolk yearly sold 25,000 cloths to Africa.[3] When this company

[1] Henry Robinson, *England's Safety in Trades Encrease* (London, 1641), p. 141. A contemporary author speaks of the Turkey Company exporting vast quantities of white coarse cloth. This might lead one to think that part of the cloth was not dyed and perhaps only partly finished. *England's Danger by Indian Manufactures* (London, 1690), p. 4.

[2] Joseph Travers, *An Essay to the Restoring of our Decayed Trade* (London, 1678), p. 9.

[3] Roger Coke, *Reflections upon the East Indy and Royal African Companies* (London, 1695), p. 330. Many thousands of the workmen of this county had been employed in manufacturing for this trade. *Journals of the House of Commons*, vol. x, p. 380; vol. xi, p. 96. The East India Company was said to export £70,000 worth of English manufactures, especially woolen goods, annually to Guinea. Davenant, *op. cit.*, vol. v, p. 88.

was established some privileged English textile manufacturers were greatly benefited; while loud complaints at loss of trade came from others.[1]   The East India Company was also a large exporter of English woolen goods.[2]   As early as 1612 it was said that 1,000 broadcloths and 500 Devonshire kerseys could annually be sold at Surat, India, and for the trade in Ispahan, Persia, by the year 1617 as many as 1,000 broadcloths and 1,000 kerseys were in demand.[3]   In fact, so great was the effect of this new commerce that wool was advanced 50% in value.[4]   During the trying years at the latter part of the century when Europe was plunged in war, many of the English woolens which were debarred in consequence from their customary markets were disposed of to the East India Company.[5]

In spite of this evident benefit to the English woolen in-

---

[1] The cloth workers of the town of Shrewsbury depended upon this company for employment; while many hundred families in Worcestershire chiefly relied upon it for support. *Journals of the House of Commons*, vol. xi, p. 639.   Objections to the Company's monopoly may be found in *ibid.*, vol. xi, pp. 618, 639.

[2] *Cal. S. P. Col. Series, E. I.* (1513-1616), pp. 107, 145, 192; (1622-24), p. 376.

[3] *Letters received by the East India Company from its Servants in the East, etc.* (1608-1613), p. 239; (1617), p. 281.

[4] *The British Merchant, containing the sentiments of the most eminent and judicious merchants of London concerning the trade and commerce of these kingdoms, etc., published by Charles King, now republished compleat with improvements* (London, 1748), pp. 162, 163.

[5] In 1693 clothiers and woolen manufacturers in the county of Wilts and that of Gloucester petitioned Parliament in favor of the East India Company, stating that when they were discouraged by the stopping of trade with other European countries during the war, the Company had within three months bought all their supply of manufactures and encouraged them to make more. *Journals of the House of Commons*, vol. xi, pp. 43, 44.   The manufacturers of special grades of cloth were also much benefited by this trade. Thus "rash," a coarse grade of cloth made at Winton and Southampton, had ever since the middle of the century found a ready market with the company. *Ibid.*, vol. xi, p. 656.

dustry, many complaints were heard concerning the harm
done by the importation of India goods. Thus, for example, the clothiers in Wilts and Gloucestershire declared
that they used to sell great quantities of their woolen manufactures to Turkey, but this trade had been destroyed by
the large amounts of manufactured silk imported into
Turkey from the East Indies.[1] Moreover, Indian muslins,
chintzes and cottons came to flood the English market.
Besides transporting the plain and stamped calicos, the
Company brought over thicker kinds which could be used
in place of domestic flannels, and cotton hose to replace the
woolen and silken ones worn by Englishmen.[2] The manufacturers then succeeded in bringing so much influence to
bear upon the government that in 1700 an act of Parliament
was passed restricting the introduction of cotton goods.[3]

To what extent the oversea trade and newly discovered
lands may have assisted the textile manufacturers by furnishing dyes and methods of coloring cloth is an interesting
matter to consider. From the early years of English expansion interest in discoveries of new dyes, and processes
of dyeing was shown. In 1579 Richard Hakluyt drew up
instructions for a certain Morgan Hubblethorne, sent to
Persia by the city of London largely to discover dyes and
learn the Eastern methods of coloring textiles. Hakluyt
remarked that " the price of a cloth for a fifth, sixth and
seventh part riseth by the color and dyeing," and therefore
Hubblethorne was to take " great care to have knowledge
of the materials of all the country's " which he should
" pass thorow " that might be used for this purpose, " be

[1] *Ibid.*, vol. xi, pp. 649, 656, 657, 659.

[2] *Ibid.*, vol. xi, p. 491; *England's Danger by Indian Manufactures*
(London, 1690), pp. 3, 5.

[3] Cunningham, *op. cit.*, pt. i, pp. 465, 517.

they hearbs, weeds, barks, gummes, earths, or what els soever." He instructed him further to find out how the Persian carpets and silks were given their tints and hues. If he could find anil, or procure the herb from which it was made, either in the form of seed or as a plant, he was to bring it to England. He was also to learn " to fixe and make sure the color to be given by logge-wood," so that the English need not buy " wood so deare, to the enriching of their enemies." [1]

The very same year in which these instructions were issued an agreement was made with Sultan Murad III, whereby the English were placed upon the commercial footing enjoyed by other European nations in the Levant. This resulted in the formation of the Turkey Company (1581), and the trade which then arose with the Near East " exercised a very striking influence upon the improvement in weaving and dyeing." The Turkey Company, as well as the Eastland Company, imported Eastern dyes.[2] It seems quite probable that they may have also introduced some of the Eastern methods of manufacture, as the cloth was made especially to suit this market.

Upon the discovery of the Cape route to India larger supplies of indigo were able to reach Europe.[3] · This useful dye had formerly been very costly and therefore had not commonly been used. Unfortunately when it did become available in greater quantities, the government forbade its use by an act passed in Queen Elizabeth's reign and not repealed until 1661.[4] Africa also is known to have furnished the English with dyes. In fact, one of the reasons

---

[1] Hakluyt, *op. cit.*, vol. iii, p. 249, *et seq.*

[2] Brothers, *op. cit.*, p. 63.

[3] *Supra*, pp. 116, 118.

[4] Reinhardt, *op. cit.*, vol. iv, pt. ii, p. 118.

why the trade to this continent was favored, was because it supplied this commodity.[1]

The introduction into Europe of new dyeing materials was a noticeable result of the opening of the West India trade during the sixteenth century. Among the most important were red ones derived from various woods known as logwood, brazil or braziletta wood, and campeachy wood. The best qualities of these grew on the shores of Yucatan, but they were also plentiful in many of the Caribbean islands.[2] Although campeachy wood was first brought to England from Mexico and Central America in 1570, its use was forbidden for over a century, because the English dyers had failed to produce fast colors from it.[3] The English were thus for a long time obliged to send this commodity which they obtained in their West-Indian colonies to other European countries. That some campeachy wood was smuggled into England seems probable. In 1632, for example, the " Little Hopewell " returned to England from Providence Island with a cargo of wood which apparently was not exported. By the end of the century, since the prohibitive acts had then been removed, much dyeing material was sent to England from America and used in English manufactures.[4]

Cochineal employed as a purple dye was first exported from Mexico in 1526. In 1650 Cornelius Drebbel, a Dutchman, established dye-works in England in which it was used. A countryman of his, Adrian Brauer, is also said to have started there in 1667 a wool-dyeing industry.[5] The

---

[1] Cunningham, *op. cit.*, pt. i, p. 274; *supra*, p. 115.

[2] Newton, *The Colonising Activities of the English Puritans*, p. 107; *supra*, pp. 109, 110.

[3] Reinhart, *op. cit.*, vol. iv, pt. ii, p. 127, *et seq.*; Newton, *op. cit.*, p. 108.

[4] Newton, *op. cit.*, p. 108.

[5] Reinhardt, *op. cit.*, vol. iv, pt. ii, p. 119.

English, however, in spite of any assistance they may have received from other countries, seem to have been very slow in developing the processes of dyeing. In 1650 it was stated that the Dutch manufactured their cloths " to that perfection that they will not fail colour or be threadbare in seven years wearing "; while the English dressed and dyed their cloth so " basely " that they were losing trade to foreign countries.[1]

Besides gradually bringing new coloring material into use, oversea trade led to the manufacture of new textiles, and supplied raw materials such as cotton, unfinished calico and raw silk. The Venetians had become familiar with cotton and its manufacture through their trade with Asia, and they first brought cotton cloth to England. The Venetian fabrics won considerable favor there, but the acquaintance with them was comparatively limited until in the sixteenth century the Levant trade was thrown open to English enterprise.[2] As has already been stated,[3] when the English came to trade directly with India, great quantities of Indian calicos, muslins and chintzes were introduced, and became very popular. The popularity of these large importations of cloth, together with its greater cheapness, promoted its manufacture in England.[4]

As early as 1605 it was said that the Levant Company, trading with Turkey and the Near East, had been instrumental in employing more than 40,000 persons making fustian, a coarse cotton cloth, for their trade.[5] Lewis Roberts

---

[1] *A Clear and Evident way for Enriching the Nations of England and Ireland, etc.,* p. 8.

[2] Brothers, *op. cit.,* p. 63, *et seq.*

[3] *Supra,* pp. 38, 40.

[4] They cost only an eighth part of the price of the woolen fabrics they supplanted. Cunningham, pt. 1, p. 517.

[5] M. Epstein, *The English Levant Company: Its Foundation and its History to 1640,* p. 55.

in 1641 mentions that this manufacture had become quite well established at Manchester. Still, not many of the finer kinds of cotton cloth, as "chintz and calico printed in imitation of the fabrics of India," were made in England before the eighteenth century, although there is a reference to their manufacture as early as 1676. For a long time the country relied upon importations from the East for this textile. Much was brought, as has been seen, in its finished state, while considerable amounts of white cloth of Oriental make were printed in England. The supplies of cotton used in this industry were first imported as "cotton wool" from Cyprus and Smyrna by the Levant Company.[1] Later many unfinished calicos, and much cotton "yarn" and "wool"[2] were brought by the East India Company from India, and when the West India colonies were established "cotton wool" came to be exported from there in large quantities. It was claimed in 1690 that 1,000 tons were produced yearly in the Caribbean islands and that as a result the price of raw cotton had fallen from one shilling to five and a half pence a pound.[3] These direct and cheaper supplies of raw material undoubtedly must have promoted the cotton industry.

As a result of the large quantities of raw silk imported from Persia and other Eastern countries, English silk manufactures increased four fold.[4] In 1664 those in London alone employed about 14,000 men, while thirty-five years previous there were only 300 people in the industry.[5] In 1681, Sir Josiah Child stated that there were 40,000

---

[1] Bains, *op. cit.*, pp. 66, 84, 100, 106.

[2] *Supra*, p. 117.

[3] *Harleian Miscellany*, vol. ii, pp. 347, 352, 353; *supra*, pp. 110, 111.

[4] G. Cawston and A. H. Keane, *The Early Chartered Companies*, p. 81.

[5] Thomas Mun, "England's Treasure by Foreign Trade," in McCulloch, *A Select Collection of Early English Tracts, etc.* (1856), p. 132.

families in England engaged in silk manufacturing, and he optimistically exclaims:

Now what should hinder, but that in a few years more, this Nation may treble that number in such Manufactures; since the East India Company have of late years found out a way of bringing Raw Silk of all sorts into this Kingdom, cheaper than it can be offered in Turkey, France, Spain, Italy, or any other place where it is made. Insomuch, as with East India Silks we serve Holland, Flanders, and some other Markets from England.[1]

In 1689 the silk manufacture employed 200,000 artisans living in or near London.[2] This industry by 1695 became important likewise at Canterbury, where 10,000 persons were thus engaged; while 30,000 or 40,000 more prepared the silk for the manufacturers.[3]

In spite of its encouragement of industry by the importation of the raw material, the East India Company came into great disfavor with the silk weavers because it brought home wrought silk. About 1669 the Company sent several skilled English weavers, dyers and " pattern-drawers " to instruct the Indians in their methods, and thus suit the European taste. Before this it was said that manufactured Indian silk was " thought scarce good enough for kitchen maids." [4]

In 1680 the silk-weavers of London petitioned the House of Commons against the trade in wrought silk. Again in 1699 they protested, claiming they were being deprived of

[1] Philopatris, *A treatise wherein is demonstrated, etc.* (London, 1681), p. 8.

[2] *Journals of the House of Commons*, vol. x, p. 285.

[3] *Ibid.*, vol. xi, p. 496.

[4] *England's Advocate—Europe's Monitor, being an Intreaty for Help in Behalf of the English Silk-weavers and Silk-Throsters* (London. 1699), p. 15.

work through the Eastern importations. A mob gathered and attempts were made to storm the East India House. Numerous petitions were sent to Parliament against the importation of manufactured silk [1] and a war of pamphlets arose over the matter.[2] Among the most notable were Davenant's essay on "The East India Trade," and Pollexfen's reply. All opponents agreed that it was a great waste to import merchandise which could be made in England, and to spend large sums in the East to buy such articles.[3] On the other hand, the defenders of the trade held that importation of wrought silk was more than made up by the advantages of a plentiful and cheaper supply of raw silk, and that in any case the finished silk was mostly re-exported to foreign countries, and brought back great profits to England.[4]

The silk-weavers evidently won their case, for by Act ii and xii of William III, chapter 10, it was ordered that from Michaelmas 1701 all wrought silks, Bengals, and other stuffs mixed with silk of the manufacture of Persia, China, or the East Indies, were to be locked up in warehouses till re-exported, so that none of the said goods should be worn or used, in either apparel or furniture, in England. The penalty imposed was forfeiture, and also a fine of £200 on persons having or selling them.[5]

It has just been seen what effect oversea expansion had upon British textile industries. That other manufactures

---

[1] *Journals of the House of Commons*, vol. x, p. 280; vol. xi, pp. 496, 621, 633, 647, 653; vol. xiii, p. 42.

[2] *Ibid.*, vol. xi, p. 667; Cawston and Keane, *op. cit.*, p. 115.

[3] *The British Merchant, etc.*, p. 4.

[4] George C. M. Birdwood, *Report on the Old Records of the India Office, etc.*, p. 46.

[5] *Ibid.*

were promoted is evident. Thousands of dozens of shoes were sent to the plantations. In 1653 as many as 21,600 pairs, and five years later 24,000 pairs were sold to Virginia alone.[1] The leather industry was still further helped by the demand for harnesses, saddles, and bridles.

The hardware, gunsmith, tinsmith, coppersmith and pewter industries were encouraged by the sale of large quantities of ironware, thousands of dozens of hoes, barrels of nails, many sets of carpenter's, smith's and cooper's tools, swords, pistols, muskets, all sorts of tinware, earthenware, woodenware, brass, pewter and lead for the American colonial trade.[2]

The East likewise furnished a market for English hardware, guns and swords, for example; "fair knives" were presented to the Shah of Persia, and it was said that for the trade to this country, copper and ironware were especially in demand. Sword blades, drinking glasses, trenchers, looking-glasses and wrought iron and tinware were among the wares taken to India.[3] In 1616 it was said that 100 sword blades and 20 or 30 dozen knives might annually be sold at good profit in India.[4] When a new factory was started at Berhampur, India, as many as 700 sword-blades were sent for the new business there.[5] The trade to Turkey made many demands for warlike implements; for example, in 1596 a "vast quantity of swords" is said to have been sent to Constantinople.[6] In 1603 there is a further refer-

---

[1] Bruce, *op. cit.*, vol. ii, p. 343.

[2] *The Groans of the Plantations, etc.* (London, 1689), printed by M. Clark, p. 28.

[3] *Cal. S. P. Col. Series, E. I.* (1513-1616), pp. 192, 481; (1625-1629), pp. 28, 29; (1630-1634), p. 201.

[4] *Letters Received by the East India Company, etc.* (1616), p. 297.

[5] *Ibid.*, vol. v, p. 53.

[6] *Cal. Ven. S. P.* (1592-1603), p. 516; (1603-1607), p. 325.

ence to the export of arms, and in 1606, 1000 arquebus barrels, 500 mounted arquebusses, and 2000 sword-blades were sent to that port.[1]

The British mining industry, especially that of tin, lead, iron and quicksilver, was encouraged by oversea commerce. The Italian cities had for long been the distributors of tin to the East, but when the Levant and East India companies were created, they took over this trade. As early as 1585 an English ship arrived at Constantinople freighted with cloth and tin, and others came in quick succession carrying cloth, tin and lead.[2] Tin as well as lead was also taken to Algiers, Tunis and Tripoli.[3] Indeed, these three were the chief articles exported in the Levant trade.[4] By 1682 it was stated that there was £22,000 worth of tin at Smyrna.[5] The effect of the Levant trade upon lead was so great that its value commonly rose at the departure of the " Turkey ships." [6]

Numerous references to the sale of tin, lead, iron, ver- milion and quicksilver by the East India Company may be cited. Its fleet which left England in 1600 carried iron, tin and lead to the value of £2,720.[7] In 1608 the Com- pany's factor at Bantam ordered 200 tons of English iron and 20 tons of lead.[8] In 1623, 200 tons of lead, 20 tons of iron and 20 or 30 " bullions " of quicksilver were to be

[1] *Cal. Ven. S. P.* (1603-1607), p. 325.

[2] *Ibid.* (1581-1591), p. 113; (1592-1603), pp. 44. 183; George Randall Lewis, *The Stannaries: a Study of the English Tin Miner*, p. 63.

[3] *Cal. Ven. S. P.* (1603-1607), p. 92.

[4] Epstein, *op. cit.*, p. 129.

[5] John Collins, *A Discourse about the Several Ways of Making Salt in England* (London, 1682), p. 55.

[6] Samuel Lamb, *Seasonable Observations Humbly Offered to his Highness the Lord Protector* (London, 1657), p. 7.

[7] *Cal. S. P. Col. Series, E. I.* (1513-1616), p. 107.

[8] *Letters Received by the East India Company* (1608-1613), p. 21.

provided for the trade at Surat.[1]   As much as 1,600 hundred-weight of lead, 50 hundred-weight of quicksilver and
15 hundred-weight of vermilion by 1630 might be annually
sold at Masulipatam.[2]   These commodities were also mentioned in connection with the trade to Japan and Persia.[3]
In the latter country it was thought 100 tons of tin, 20
" chests " of quicksilver and 20 barrels of vermilion might
be sold yearly.[4]

The salt industry, which was in its infancy during the
seventeenth century, was encouraged by the demands for
salt to preserve fish and meat, so they could be kept for
months on long sea voyages and for the use of the colonists.[5]   Although the English used the salt they manufactured in their herring fisheries, they do not seem to have
employed it in those of Newfoundland for salting the fish
sent to Spain and France.   Instead, these latter were
usually washed in seawater and then dried.[6]

The English soap industry, established in 1622, was
somewhat benefited by oversea expansion.   Large quantities
of whale-oil and fish-oil were used by the soap-makers of
London.[7]   It was estimated that the value of these ingredients came to £30,000 a year.[8]   When the colonies in
North America were well established they proved to some

[1] *Cal. S. P. Col. Series, E. I.* (1622-1624), p. 161; other references
(1625-29), pp. 6, 7, 18, 579, 580.

[2] *The English Factories in India, etc.* (1630-1633), p. 84.

[3] *Cal. S. P. Col. Series, E. I.* (1513-1616), pp. 209, 343, 433; (1625-1629),
pp. 28, 29, 580; *Letters Received by the East India Company* (1616),
pp. 132, 163, 183, 193.

[4] *Letters Received by the East India Company* (1617), 281.

[5] Collins, *op. cit.,* p. 15.

[6] *Ibid.,* p. 104.

[7] *A Short and True Relation concerning the Soap business* (London,
1641), printed for Nicholas Brown, p. 3, *et seq.*

[8] Scott, *op. cit.,* vol. i, p. 211; *supra,* p. 104.

extent a source of supply for potash and wood-ash.[1]

That there was a noticeable Oriental influence exerted upon the manufacture of English furniture is evidenced by the statement made in 1683 that several new kinds of Eastern varnishes had come into use in that industry. These gave a beautiful " gloss to Musical instruments, Cabinets, Tables and Picture-frames, and the like." As the methods of varnishing employed in China and Japan became somewhat familiar in England, it was said that the English varnished cabinets might vie even with those of the Oriental countries.[2] Supplies of gum-lac were imported from the Orient.[3] Special kinds of varnish were used on coaches. The " Lacka-varnish which imitates the Gold-color hath saved much cost that was formerly bestow'd in the gilding of Coaches," was first brought to England about 1653 by " Mr. Evelin, of Says Court by Deptford." [4]

In 1693 a patent was granted to Thomas Martyn to form a company which was known as " The Patentees for Laquering after the manner of Japan." In 1696 the Company advertised that it had made ready for sale " a considerable and most curious parcel of goods, viz., Cabinets, secretaries, tables, stands, looking glasses, tea-tables, and chimney pieces " which were to be disposed of by lottery.[5]

Woods from America were employed in the manufacture of furniture. Oldmixon tells of " great quantities " of cedar exported from Barbados, and says it was used for " Wainscoting, Stair-Cases, Drawers, Chairs and other Household Furniture," but that the smell of the wood, which

---

[1] *Cal. S. P. Col. Series, America and the W. I.* (1661-68), pp. 73, 99, 291.

[2] *The Present State of England* (London, 1683), printed for William Whitwood, pt. iii, p. 92.

[3] *Cal. S. P. Col. Series, E. I.* (1625-1629), p. 259.

[4] *The Present State of England*, pt. iii, p. 93.

[5] Scott, *op. cit.*, vol. iii, p. 119.

was " so pleasing to some," was offensive to others, and this added to its cost, " hindered its coming as much in Fashion as it otherwise would." The material sold at such a high rate that as much as £400 was made from one tree.[1] Cedar is likewise spoken of as having been found in Bermuda and Virginia. That of the former colony was " a finer tree than any of the sort in other parts of America." [2] As early as 1586 Hariot names cedar as one of the commodities of Virginia and describes it as

a very sweet wood, and fine timber, whereof if nests of chests be there made, or timber thereof fitted for sweet and fine bedsteds, tables, desks, lutes, virginals, and many things etc. (of which there hath bene proofe made already) to make up freight with other principall commodities will yeeld profit.[3]

Quantities of mahogany from Honduras were also used in English furniture. The price of the wood varied from £40 to £16 a ton as the fashion for mahogany furniture increased or declined.[4]

An English industry that was derived from the imitation of Oriental articles was the manufacture of chinaware or porcelain, which, however, did not get much of a start until the eighteenth century. About 1690 the first pottery of importance was established at Bridewell. Here John Philip Elers who came over with the Prince of Orange made imitations of the red wares of Japan. It was much later before the English succeeded in producing a pottery white and translucent like the Chinese ware.[5] Throughout

---

[1] Oldmixon, *op. cit.*, vol. ii, p. 96.

[2] *Ibid.*, vol. ii, p. 374.

[3] Hakluyt, *op. cit.*, vol. viii, p. 355.

[4] Tilby, *Britain in The Tropics 1527-1910*, pp. 9, 10; also *supra*, p. 111.

[5] W. C. Prime, *Pottery and Porcelain of all Times and Nations*, pp. 318, 319.

the first years of the industry the influence of the East was constantly and openly acknowledged, for instance the works at Bow were described as " New Canton," and those at Worcester as the newly established " Tonquin Factory." [1]

An entirely new industry which originated from the introduction of the custom of smoking from the New World was the manufacture of clay pipes. Broseley in Staffordshire, Vauxhall, Derby, and Bath were early centers of pipe-making; while Winchester pipes were considered superior to all others.[2] Fine clay was also brought from Poole to Dorsetshire, and from the Isle of Wight as ballast for ships bound for London. Here it was worth about thirty shillings a ton, and when the clay from these two places was mixed and burnt for fifteen hours it made a hard and handsome pipe.[3] There came to be such a demand for pipes that in 1619 the pipe-makers received a charter of incorporation from James I. Their privileges as a company extended all over England and Wales.[4]

Thomas Gauntlet and John Legge were among the most famous pipe-makers of the seventeenth century. The small, barrel-bowled, short pipes of Elizabethan times were the ones made until the time of the Revolution; then larger bowled ones with long, straight stems after the Dutch style were used.[5]

The great influx of silver and gold into Europe from the Spanish possessions in America and of jewels from the East and precious stones from the New World, as well as

---

[1] W. Burton, *A History and Description of English Porcelain*, p. 26.

[2] Penn, *op. cit.*, p. 148.

[3] Fuller, *The History of the Worthies of England*, vol. iii, pp. 315, 452.

[4] Penn, *op. cit.*, p. 148; Frederick Hackwood, *Inns, Ales, and Drinking Customs of Old England*, p. 377.

[5] Penn, *op. cit.*, p. 149.

the growing wealth of the people, greatly increased the demand in England for the products of silversmiths and jewelers. About one-fifth of the precious metals came to be devoted to the arts. They were not only applied to the making of ordinary plate, but were manufactured into a variety of articles for which they had previously never been employed. Thus silver-plate was used toward the end of the reign of Charles II on tables, bedsteads, bath-tubs, braziers, mirror-frames, etc.[1]

English jewelry not only found a large home market, but was taken to the East and sold, or perhaps more frequently given as bribes, to the native princes and their followers.[2] Jewels were very highly esteemed, especially " diamonds sumptuously set," which could be sold for twice what they would bring in Europe.[3] Many references are made to the disposal in India and Persia of amber beads and coral. In 1625 it was said that the sale of the former article to the value of £500 or £1,000 could be depended upon for the yearly trade to Persia.[4] In 1616 the Company's agent wrote home:

I would advise you to bestow three or four hundred pounds at least in curious toys, rich glasses, figures, French toys, cabinets, embroidered scarfs, swords with fair cut and inlaid hilts, broad blades—whatsoever is curious work and rich. Will in one month yield five, ten, twenty, yea forty for one profit.[5]

Indeed, many trifling articles which might serve as orna-

---

[1] Jackson, *op. cit.*, vol. i, p. 220, *et seq.*; Jacob, *op. cit.*, vol. ii, p. 131.

[2] It required a bribe of 2,000 rupees to sell goods for a year at Surat. *Cal. S. P. Col. Series, E. I.* (1630-34), p. 269.

[3] *Ibid.* (1625-29), p. 371.

[4] *Ibid.*, pp. 29, 580.

[5] *Letters Received by the East India Company* (1616), p. 19.

ments, " such as slight jewels, set with topazes and other
little stones," wrought silk flowers and fruit, hawking
gloves, gold and silver lace, needlework and cloth of gold
and silver were in demand there. In 1624 quicksilver,
amber beads, cloths, green and crimson satins, gold and
silver lace to the value of £300 or £400, and gold and silver
cloth worth £1,000 were shipped to India.[1]

Spectacles also were in demand in the East. Chinese
importers requested an agent of the East India Company
to procure some of the best of these articles for them.
Since they had taken all he could spare, he suggested to the
Company that 1,000 or 2,000 more pairs in the best gilt
cases be sent him for sale.[2] These were given as presents
and sold in both Persia and India as well. In 1616 four
boxes of spectacles and ten telescopes comprised part of the
cargo to Persia.[3] Small looking-glasses, "burning-glasses"
and the larger pier-glasses were also greatly in favor.[4]

Among the fanciful kinds of merchandise made to please
the Oriental taste were pictures. In 1615 the Company's
agent reported that he believed five or six dozen of the
finer kinds would sell. He advised them to supply those of
" feigned gods, histories, gardens, banquets and the like,
with some two or three hundred pictures, which are
cheaper." Presents were made to the Great Mogul of pic-

---

[1] *Cal. S. P. Col. Series, E. I.* (1630-34), p. 467.

[2] *Cal. S. P. Col. Series, E. I.* (1625-1629), p. 377.

[3] *Letters Received by the East India Company* (1616), p. 194.

[4] *Ibid.* (1613-15), p. 214; (1615), pp. 64, 85; vol. iv, p. 198. These commodities had not sold well after the first importations; for in 1616
it was stated that looking-glasses, pictures, comb-cases and spectacles
were not merchantable wares, but were very useful for presents. Elsewhere it was stated that hot waters, drinking-glasses, looking-glasses,
spectacles, burning-glasses, swords, cony-skins, baize and pots were
"mere idleness and commodities not fit to deal in" in India. *Ibid.*
(1616), pp. 232, 243, 298.

tures of the king, queen, Lady Elizabeth and Sir Thomas Smith.[1]

There must likewise have been some sale for gaudy trifles for the African and American trade, as these could be disposed of at a great profit to the negroes for their gold, ivory and slaves, and to the Indians for their furs. Towards the close of the seventeenth century, for example, glass beads, boxes of red lead, combs, laced coats and looking-glasses were among the articles sent to Hudson Bay for the trade at that place.[2]

The influence of the Orient was clearly felt by the English gunpowder industry through the large stores of saltpetre brought from India,[3] and through the sale of gunpowder to Eastern princes. This industry must have been well established in England by the beginning of the seventeenth century, for large amounts of powder were then sent to Turkey. In 1606 as many as 700 barrels of powder were shipped to Constantinople, and it was said at that time that gunpowder was a commodity in which England abounded, and that 500 barrels were exported every year to Turkey.[4] Later in the century the East India Company sold the product in the East. In 1629 they petitioned to be allowed to export 1,000 barrels of powder, and this request was granted.[5]

This industry was under the control of the government which contracted with some favored individual to deliver large quantities to the government arsenal. John Evelyn, who was the royal powder-maker, received £1,700 a month to furnish the commodity. In 1626 the East India Com-

---

[1] *Ibid.* (1615), pp. 19, 63, 67, 91.

[2] Bryce, *op. cit.*, p. 20, 22.

[3] *Supra*, p. 117.

[4] *Cal. Ven. S. P.* (1606), pp. 312, 318.

[5] *Cal. S. P. Col. Series, East Indies* (1625-29), p. 685.

pany also secured the right to make powder. Mills were set up at Windsor Forest; but the king soon ordered their removal on the ground that they disturbed the deer. Later Evelyn was so successful in his protest to the crown that the Company's privilege was suspended, and in 1637 definitely taken away.[1]

The sugar-refining industry was organized in England about 1544, at which date two sugar houses were in operation in London. These were not very profitable, as the large number of refineries at Antwerp were able to supply England with better and cheaper sugar than could be made at home. However, when commerce with Antwerp was stopped for awhile in 1585, all England was supplied for twenty years by these two factories, which became so prosperous that many other persons embarked in the business. After 1585 London was the important refining center for the European trade. With the great importations of sugar in the latter part of the century,[2] the industry became very extensive.[3]

It is quite apparent that agriculture, the greatest of English industries, must have been promoted by oversea expansion. Apart from the introduction of new products from America susceptible of cultivation in England, farming profited from the rise in prices, due to the greater abundance of gold and silver and to the increased demands of a population, which as a consequence of the prosperity of English trade was growing both in numbers and in wealth. Produce soon came to be paid for in money, and the farmer having capital at his disposal was enabled to improve his methods of cultivation. He soon felt the need

[1] *Ibid.*, pp. 235, 432, 559; *The Court Minutes of the East India Company* (1635-1639), p. xxxiii.

[2] *Supra*, p. 109.

[3] Reed, *op. cit.*, p. 9; Surface, *op. cit.*, p. 24.

of an increased output, not merely because of the greater demand from a larger population, but also because there was less competition in agriculture, as many of those formerly engaged in it had become artisans, sailors, traders and colonists.

Although the continental colonies in America were agriculturally quite independent after they were once well established, the supplying of the early settlers in America sometimes nearly exhausted the stock of provisions in the sections of England where these stores were bought. In 1638, for example, a letter to " the High Sheriffs and Justices of Dorsetshire and Hampshire " speaks of large exportations of foodstuffs from this part of England to America:

Whereas wee are informed of the great and secrett abuses committed in that countrie and other the westerne partes, by the Company of New England and such as send commodities thither, who underhand provide and secrettly transport extraordinary quantities of Wheate, Beanes, Butter, Beere, Cheese, Bacon and like provisions to the great prejudice of the poore thereaboutes, and the enhanceing of the prices of those commodities, whereof wee having taken consideration have thought good to recommend it to your especiall care.[1]

The colonies in the West Indies depended almost entirely upon England, and later upon the continental colonies, for their provisions. Considerable quantities of grain, meal, peas, oatmeal, butter, cheese and beef were exported thither during the seventeenth century. One ship, the " St. Peter of Plymouth," carried in 1666 as much as 2,000 barrels of beef to Barbados.[2] Upon another occasion it was said that if 4,000 hogsheads of bread, beans and peas had not been

[1] *A. P. C. Col. Series*, vol. i, p. 230.
[2] *Ibid.*, vol. i, pp. 268, 440.

sent from England the inhabitants of Barbados would have
starved.[1] During one period of twenty years, more than
150 ships were laden in England with bread, butter, cheese,
beer, meat and other foodstuffs, besides all sorts of merchandise, and sent to the West Indies.[2]

The East India Company, moreover, required large amounts of provisions. The supplying of four ships and a
pinnace carrying 500 men upon the East India voyage in
1600, cost 6,679 pounds, 9 shillings and 10 pence. Of
this amount 1,028 pounds, were for bread, 267 pounds, 17
shillings, 4 pence for meal, 2,150 pounds for beer, cider and
wine, 1,721 pounds, 8 shillings for meat, and 1,511 pounds,
16 shillings for cheese, butter and other provisions.[3] In
1625 the victualling of two ships which were to be gone
for twenty months upon the Persian trade came to 7,000
pounds.[4] In 1628 the East India Company contracted for
200 oxen and a proportionable quantity of pork.[5]

By the end of the seventeenth century large herb gardens
to supply the apothecaries with their drugs had been started.[6]
Undoubtedly the great numbers of new medicinal plants
imported from beyond the seas tended to establish the raising and compounding of drugs as a regular industry. The
new flora from America and the Orient led to the building

---

[1] *Some Considerations Humbly offered to Both Houses of Parliament
Concerning the Sugar Colonies, and Chiefly the Island of Barbados*
(London, 1701), printed and sold by A Baldwin, p. 8.

[2] *Some General Considerations offered relating to our present Trade*
(London, 1698), p. 13.

[3] *Cal. S. P. Col. Series, E. I.* (1513-1616), p. 107. For further particulars regarding the commodities and the localities from which they were
purchased see Henry Stevens, *The Dawn of British Trade to the East
Indies, etc.* (1599-1603), pp. 66, 67, 75, 114.

[4] *Cal. S. P. Col. Series, E. I.* (1625-29), p. 18.

[5] *Ibid.,* p. 560.

[6] *Infra,* p. 223.

of greenhouses and must have induced some to go into the business of cultivating flowers for sale. At any rate care of delicate plants began to be studied, and led to works like Evelyn's *Sylvia* giving directions regarding transplanting and protection of plants.

The shipbuilding industry naturally was given a great impetus by the voyages to distant parts of the globe. Until the defeat of the Armada, the English merchants bought many of their ships in the " East Country," but after 1588 a great English shipbuilding industry was started.[1]   In 1605 as many as 250 ships were employed in the New-foundland fishing trade, in 1670, 35 to 40 sail were engaged in commerce with the East Indies, 28 ships a year were used by the African Company, and by the close of the century as many as 400 in the plantation trade. The tonnage of merchant ships had increased from about 7,600 tons in 1560 to about 500,000 in 1691 ; while that of the Royal Navy had grown from 23,600 in 1607 to 112,400 in 1695.[2]

With the transfer of the center of trade from the Mediterranean to the Atlantic ocean, long voyages had to be undertaken in the open sea, and great changes in marine architecture were the necessary result. Heretofore the ships were mostly galleys depending largely upon oars for propulsion. Now the vessels had to be larger and more strongly built in order to withstand storms of the Atlantic, and the chief propulsion was the sails. As late as the be-

[1] Sir William Monson, " Naval Tracts," in *A Collection of Voyages and Travels* compiled by John Churchill (London, 1704), vol. iii, p. 382.

[2] M. Oppenheim, *A History of the Administration of the Royal Navy and Merchant Shipping, etc.*, p. 172, *et seq.*; Anderson, *op. cit.*, vol. i, p. 226; vol. iii, pp. 17, 149, 266; Traill, *op. cit.*, vol. iii, p. 454; Wood, *op. cit.*, p. 34, 185; Davenant, *op. cit.*, vol. i, p. 363; Child, *op. cit.*, p. 205; William Petty, *Several Essays in Political Arithmetic* (London, 1755), p. 205; George Chalmers, *An Estimate of the Comparative Strength of Great Britain*, p. 66.

ginning of the seventeenth century a ship of 1,000 tons was considered a very large and unusual one. In 1609 the East India Company, mindful of the long voyage to be undertaken, and the need of more space to carry valuable cargoes, built the " goodliest and greatest ship that was ever framed in the kingdom." This was a vessel of 1200 tons burden.[1] The English "Indiamen" continued, during this century of expansion, to be the largest ships constructed. In the actual construction and equipment of the vessels some improvements had been made during the second half of the sixteenth century by the invention of jointed topmasts, the chain-pump, studding sails, the method of weighing anchor by a capstan, and by raising the ports.[2]

After the accession of James I the galley-shaped prow, so characteristic of the shipping of earlier times, was largely dispensed with. The " enormously high towering poops " and the " no less extravagantly formed forecastles " were no longer used. The immense square stern copied from the Dutch likewise changed to a more tapering one and a sharper bow. Ships, moreover, were much better built and the material used in them was more carefully selected.[3] However, as late as 1697 a learned Jesuit, Paul Hoste, in a work on the theory of naval architecture, remarked that it could not be denied that the art of constructing ships was the least perfect of all arts. " The best constructors built the two principal parts of the ship, the bow and the stern almost entirely by the eye, consequently it happened that the same constructor who built two ships at the same time, after the same model, most frequently made them so unequal that they were quite different." The author further remarks

---

[1] Churchill, *op. cit.*, vol. iii, p. 382.

[2] John Charnock, *A History of Marine Architecture of all Nations*, vol. ii, pp. 31, 66, 68.

[3] *Ibid.*

that more good ships were seen among the merchantmen than in the royal navy.[1]

In addition to the improvements wrought in marine architecture by the requirements for longer and longer voyages, unsuccessful efforts were made to devise means of propelling ships otherwise than by sails and oars,[2] and to safeguard them in various ways. Evelyn mentions a boat with a double-bottomed keel which was lost in the Bay of Biscay.[3] In 1691 a pamphlet was written by Thomas Hale describing a new invention of "milled lead" for the sheathing of ships. Its purpose was to protect the vessel from water and worms. It appears to have been used in some cases, though it did not turn out to be very serviceable.[4]

At a time when shipwrecks were frequent and when the destruction of a ship often involved the loss of immense sums of bullion, it was natural that much attention should be given to devices for recovering the cargoes from the depths of the sea. This was notably the case toward the close of the seventeenth century. Captain William Phipps of New England was the first to make the industry of salvaging popular. As a result of a voyage in 1686-7 he was successful in recovering a large amount of silver and many jewels from a Spanish ship that had been wrecked many years before near Hispaniola. In the next year another voyage was made and between £200,000 and £250,000 was recovered.[5]

[1] John Fincham, *A History of Naval Architecture*, p. xv.

[2] W. S. Lindsay, *A History of Merchant Shipping and Ancient Commerce*, vol. iv, p. 17, *et seq.*

[3] "Evelyn's Correspondence," in *Memoirs*, vol. vi, p. 408.

[4] Thomas Hale, *The New Invention of Mill'd Lead for the Sheathing of Ships* (London, 1691), *passim.*

[5] *Cal. S. P. Col. Series, America and the W. I.* (1685-1688), p. 392; Narcissus Luttrell, *A Brief Historical Relation of State Affairs from September 1678 to April 1714*, vol. i, p. 407; Anderson, *op. cit.*, vol. iii, p. 73; Scott, *op. cit.*, vol. ii, p. 485.

The securing of so large an amount of treasure could not fail to arouse much interest in this sort of enterprise. Many curious and interesting patents were granted to inventors of diving apparatus. A few may be worth mentioning. In 1689 Francis Smartfoot obtained a patent for a " sea crab " to raise ships, guns and goods. The same patent also granted the exclusive right for fourteen years, " of enabling a man to breathe under water by attaching a pair of lungs to his back as he swims." Other patents awarded to companies in 1691, were for " a new engine for carrying four men fifteen fathoms and more under water, whereby they may work for twelve hours at a time " invented by John Williams; a similar contrivance which would " enable the person using it to walk up and down by himself and work or view any wreck in the sea and have fresh air to breathe," discovered by John Tyzack; and a diving dress, " which gives liberty for a man to see, walk and work for a considerable time many fathoms under water."[1]

Another group of companies sought to locate wrecks, and to recover valuables from them. They were to get as salvage either a cash payment or one-tenth part of the treasure secured. A number of companies were formed, but none of them was successful. The most notable were the ones organized by Thomas Neale in 1691 to recover silver from a ship off Broadhaven, Ireland, and in 1692 for the Bermudas, and the district from Carthagena to Jamaica.[2]

[1] Scott, *op. cit.*, vol. ii, p. 487.

[2] *Ibid.*, vol. ii, p. 488; *Notes and Queries, Sixth Series*, vol. x, p. 404.

CHAPTER VI

FINANCE

HAVING seen in the preceding chapters what effect English colonization and oversea trade were commencing to have upon the development of the commercial and industrial interests of the nation, it is now desirable to consider the relation of the process to its financial prosperity. As to the enhancement of material welfare in general produced by English endeavor overseas, Daniel Defoe, in "A Plan of the English Commerce," printed in 1730, says:

Now, whence is all this poverty of a country? 'tis evident 'tis want of trade, and nothing else: And we go back for an example of it to our own country, when the product of the land, and the labour of the people were as low here, when good wheat was worth about 4d. per bushel, a fat sheep about 3s. 4d. and a fat ox about 18 to 24s. and when was this? But when we had no trade, and because we had no trade; neither is the present difference owing to anything else, but to the increase of commerce, as well here as in other parts of the world; and 'tis evident the rate of provisions, and the value of lands in all parts of the world are high or low, great or small, as the people have or have not trade to support it.

Trade encourages manufacture, prompts invention, employs people, increases labour, and pays wages: As the people are employ'd, they are paid, and by that pay are fed, cloathed, kept in heart, and kept together; that is, kept at home, kept from wandering into foreign countries to seek business, for where the employment is, the people will be.

This keeping of the people together, is indeed the sum of the whole matter, for as they are kept together, they multiply together ; and the numbers, which by the way is the wealth and strength of the nation, increase.

As the numbers of the people increase, the consumption of provisions increases ; as the consumption increases, the rate or value will rise at market ; and as the rate of provisions rises, the rents of land rise : So the gentlemen are with the first to feel the benefit of trade, by the addition to their estates. . . .

As the consumption of provisions increase, more lands are cultivated ; waste grounds are inclosed, woods are grubb'd up, forrests and common lands are tile'd, and improv'd ; by this more farmers are brought together, more farm-houses and cottages are built, and more trades are called upon to supply the necessary demands of husbandry : In a word, as land is employ'd, the people increase of course, and thus trade sets all the wheels of improvement in motion ; for from the original of business to this day it appears, that the prosperity of a nation rises and falls, just as trade is supported or decay'd.

As trade prospers, manufactures increase ; as the demand is greater or smaller, so also is the quantity made ; and so the wages of the poor, the rate of provisions, and the rents and value of the lands rise and fall, as I said before.

And here the very power and strength of the nation is concern'd also, for as the value of the lands rises or falls, the taxes rise or fall in proportion ; all our taxes upon land are a kind of pound rate ; and bring in more or less, as the stated rents of land are more or less in value ; and let any one calculate, by the rate of the lands in England, as they went in the times of Edward iv, or even in Henry vii's time, when trade began, as it were, just to live in England ; and tell us how much they think a land tax would then have brought in : For example,

If a tax of four shillings in the pound now brings in above two millions, I suppose it would have been thought very well then, if it had brought in three hundred thousand pound, all the rest is an increase occasion'd by trade and nothing else ;

trade has increas'd the people, and people have increas'd trade; for multitudes of people, if they can be put in condition to maintain themselves, must increase trade; they must have food, that employs land; they must have clothes, that employs the manufacture; they must have houses, that employs handicrafts; they must have household stuff, that employs a long variety of trades: so that in a word trade employs people, and people employ trade.[1]

Stating the case in figures, Sir John Hawkins, treasurer of the navy, estimated in 1584 that since 1558, the wealth of England had trebled.[2] Another author states that the total national wealth was about £17,000,000 in 1600, but by 1630 it had nearly doubled and could be calculated at £28,000,000. By 1660 it had reached about £56,000,000, and by 1688 had become £88,000,000.[3]

As evidence of the growing wealth of the country may be cited the increased value of real estate and the low rate of interest on money. Before England became a commercial nation, the general price of land was twelve years' purchase, and the legal interest on money was 10%. About 1666 the value of the land in the best counties was from eighteen to twenty years, and in the worst from fourteen to sixteen years, while the legal rate of interest was 6%; and money was more plentiful than securities in which to invest it. After 1666 the price of land in the best countries, was from twenty-six to twenty-seven years, while in the counties where it had formerly been at fourteen, it had now become seventeen and eighteen. Money upon landed security was at that time lent much more at the rate of 4% and 4½%

[1] Daniel Defoe, "A Plan of the English Commerce," in McCulloch, *Collection* (1859), pp. 112-114.

[2] Scott, *op. cit.*, vol. i, p. 84.

[3] Davenant, *op. cit.*, vol. i, p. 375; Wood, *op. cit.*, p. 37. See *infra*, p. 161.

than at 5% or 6%. Estimating the value of the land of England in 1600 at a rental of £6,000,000, at twelve years purchase it was worth £72,000,000, whereas in 1688 it could be rented for £14,000,000, and this at eighteen years purchase would bring its value at that date to £252,000,000.[1] Not only country real estate, but the houses in London and other cities of England had greatly increased in value. According to Sir Josiah Child, newly built houses in London were yielding " twice the rent they did before the Fire," and houses just before that event yielded about one fourth more rent than they did twenty years earlier.[2] As already observed, this increase in the value of real estate was largely due to the expanding commerce of England.

The growth of material welfare of the nation as well as in the sovereign's resources is further evidenced by the ease with which it bore the large taxes of the years 1652-53, when an assessment was made of £120,000 per month, in addition to the other fixed taxes. Child, in fact, asserted that England could pay a greater tax in his time in one year, than his forefathers could in twenty.[3] During the twenty-two years of the reign of Richard II there was so little wealth in London that the town hazarded its charter rather than loan the king £1,000. The government was able for the first time in 1559 to obtain a loan of money in England. Even as late as 1587, when the queen sent to the citizens of London to borrow £60,000, they were uncertain whether they could pay it. With the next century the case was much different, for in December 1607, certain private citizens lent the king £120,000 for a year without

---

[1] Wood, *op. cit.,* p. 29, *et seq.,* Davenant, *op. cit.,* vol. i, p. 359, *et seq.*

[2] Child, *op. cit.,* pp. 10, 34, *et seq.*

[3] Anderson, *op. cit.,* vol. ii, p. 557.

going to much trouble in raising it. Again the next year they lent him £63,000.[1]

The royal revenues were not merely indirectly benefited through the effects of expansion upon national prosperity, but they soon derived a large direct income from the customs laid upon the rapidly growing oversea trade.[2] At Elizabeth's death in 1603 the customs dues amounted to £36,000, and at the restoration of Charles II in 1660 they had reached £400,000.[3] Twenty-eight years later they had risen to almost double this sum.[4] Of this increase in the national customs revenue a large part was due to the oversea trade. In 1635 the East India Company paid the crown £50,000 in customes and imposts, besides £400 special duties on spices,[5] and by 1681 the customs upon the East India trade amounted

[1] "Stow's Annals," edited by Howe, 1615, p. 896, col. 2 quoted in Harrison, *op. cit.*, vol. ii, p. 22; Traill, *op. cit.*, vol. vii, p. 371.

[2] In spite of the fact that the customs duties in themselves added little to the national resources, it seems evident that they were an indication of the increased wealth created for the most part by commerce and in this manner placed at the disposal of the government as its share of the general prosperity. See Beer, *The Old Colonial System*, vol. i, p. 36, *et seq.* for a complete discussion of the idea that the customs in themselves added to national wealth.

[3] Anderson, *op. cit.*, vol. i, p. xxx; Child in 1681 says that "since Queen Elizabeth's time, our customs are increased from £14,000 per annum to about £700,000 per annum." Philopatris, *A treatise wherein is demonstrated, etc.*, p. 27.

[4] July 24, 1660—

September 29, 1661	£421,582	7s.	11d.
1665	519,072	4s.	2d.
1670	516,229	19s.	7½d.
1675	674,133	16s.	0¼d.
1680	633,562	8s.	4¾d.
1688	781,987	2s.	9½d.

George Chalmers, *An Estimate of the Comparative Strength of Great Britain, etc.*, p. 49.

[5] *A Calendar of the Court Minutes ... of the East India Company, 1635-1639*, edited by Ethel B. Sainsbury, p. 50.

to £60,000 per annum.[1]   The duty upon tobacco and sugar
at the commencement of the Revolution of 1688 was £148,
861; while that upon tobacco alone for the year ending
September 1693 was £75,611.   The revenue derived from
silk for the same year was £148,430.[2]

Another point to notice in estimating the profit to the
English government resulting from the founding of colonies
and the establishment of a colonial trade, is that, in contrast to its neighbors France, Spain and Portugal, it went
to little expense of its own in establishing colonies in
America, and in promoting trade with the East.   As a
rule, whatever expenses and losses there might be were
borne by the individuals or companies who promoted the
enterprises.   Queen Elizabeth sometimes invested in the
profitable buccaneering voyages of her reign, and always
received her share for connivance at them.[3]   In the same
way when trading voyages had become the investment of
the day, the East India Company, whose ventures were the
most lucrative, not only made large loans to the government, but also paid an annual tribute of £400,000 to the
treasury.[4]

It was only when possessions were acquired through
force of arms as in the case of Jamaica, which was not at first
self-sustaining, and when the colonial governments were
taken over by the crown and royal colonies created, that
large governmental expenses were incurred.   Even the early
defense of the trading posts, as for instance in the case of

---

[1] Philopatris, op. cit., p. 8.

[2] Davenant, op. cit., vol. i, p. 20, et seq.; Journals of the House of
Commons, vol. x, p. 37.   In 1677 Governor Berkeley stated that
Virginia yielded nearly £100,000 per annum in revenue to the crown.
Cal. S. P. Col. Series, Am. and W. I. (1677-80), p. 106.

[3] Infra, p. 166.

[4] Earl of Cromer, Ancient and Modern Imperialism, p. 43.

the East India Company, was maintained at the expense of the company.

Due in part to the decrease in the value of money and to the more or less corresponding rise in the prices of commodities caused by the great influx of the precious metals from the New World, the royal funds, as the larger share of them were fixed revenues, were at first diminished rather than increased. Later, with a constantly increasing customs' revenue and other means of taxation, as well as the actual enlargement of the civil list, the situation of the English sovereigns and their government became the reverse. How rapidly the royal revenue increased during the later years of the seventeenth century is shown by the fact that, while the annual income of James II was £2,061,856, that of William III was more than double that amount, or £4,415,360.[1]

It is evident that under the prosperous conditions just described, an ever growing class of capitalists would be created. In the fifteenth century, when the " Merchant Adventurers " were organized, it was recorded " as a most memorable fact," that one citizen had invested as much as £50 in the enterprise. In the early part of the seventeenth century, on the other hand, many merchants advanced £5,000 and a few as large a sum as £20,000 in similar undertakings. So, too, the farmer, although his rent was raised to £40, was not only able to have plate and feather-beds, but he could also purchase a renewal of his lease six years before the expiration of the old one, or else he might buy the land outright. If he chose to rent rather than purchase his land,

---

[1] The net income paid into the exchequer in 1691 was £4,249,757. Chalmers, *An Estimate of the Comparative Strength of Great Britain*, p. 80.

[2] " Stow's Chronical," edited by Howe, p. 903, col. 2, 1, 21 in Harrison, *op. cit.*, vol. ii, p. 45.

he might then have money saved for his stock of cattle and implements, and to pay his laborers until he secured further resources at harvest time. This great prosperity among the farmers was due largely to the cheapening of money, and the higher prices for produce.[1]

With the increase of English capital, London was rapidly becoming, not merely a great commercial emporium, but also an important financial center. Foreign as well as English capitalists made that city their home. There was a trace of this inflow of foreign capital during the time of Elizabeth, and it steadily increased under James I and Charles I[2]

This accumulation of money for investment purposes was greatly aided by the larger quantities of precious metals from America, which were brought to England through trade and piracy and made available for coinage. The following table shows the amounts of gold and silver actually coined between 1599 and 1697:

From October, 1599 to March, 1619	£4,779,314 13s. 4d.
From March, 1619 to March, 1638	6,900,042 11s. 1d.
From March, 1638 to May, 1657	7,733,521 13s. 4½d.
From May, 1657 to November, 1675	2,238,997 16s. ¾d.
Under Charles II and James II	6,500,000 in gold and 4,200,000 in silver.
From December 31, 1619 to August 14, 1697	7,157,116
"　　　"　　　"　　　"　　　"　　　"　　　"　　　"	312,000 coined in plate.
Total money in the country in 1697	8,136,000.[4]

[1] Jacob, *Historical Inquiry, etc.*, vol. ii, p. 107. See also *infra*, p. 162.

[2] Cunningham, *op. cit.*, pt. i, p. 324, *et seq.*

[3] " Britannia Languens " in McCulloch, *Collection* (1859), p. 387, *et seq.*

[4] Davenant further states that the amount of coin in England in 1600 was £4,000,000; while at the beginning of the reign of Charles I it was £5,500,000; in 1660 about £16,000,000 or £14,000,000 after deduction for wear, loss, etc.; in 1688 about £18,500,000 after proper deductions. Davenant, vol. i, pp. 364, 437.

The impetus given to financial activities by the abundance of precious metals and the rapidly expanding commerce with new lands did not stop here. As soon as specie no longer sufficed, bills of exchange, notes of banks of deposit and of circulation, and all the institutions of public and private credit were utilized to increase the number and means of exchanges.[1]

Another phase of the financial influence of oversea expansion to be considered, is the effect of these large supplies of gold and silver as such from the New World upon English social and economic conditions. England, like other European countries, had her portion of the precious metals. Spain made futile efforts to retain the inflowing stream of wealth, but through its buccaneering expeditions, and its expanding trade, England began to divert part of the Spanish treasures to its shores. The increase in the supply of gold and silver is shown, as has already been seen, by the amount of coinage.[2] The average annual coinage of Elizabeth's reign was £125,311, while in James the First's reign it was £241,216.[3]

While it is generally conceded that plentiful supplies of money have a most beneficial effect upon business conditions, and indeed in this instance they had much to do with the increasing prosperity of the kingdom, the sudden transition from a limited supply of money to a bountiful one could not help but cause suffering among certain classes of the population. The value of money depreciated, while there was a rapid rise in the prices of all the principal kinds of grain used in the sixteenth and seventeenth centuries as food.[4]

---

[1] J. A. Blanqui, *History of Political Economy*, p. 253.

[2] *Supra*, p. 161.

[3] Cunningham, *op. cit.*, pt. i, p. 165, *et seq.*

[4] J. E. Thorold Rogers, *History of Agriculture and Prices in England*, vol. v, p. 787.

The principal rise in prices appears to have taken place
between the years 1583 and 1642, when they more than
doubled.   The cheapening of silver by the large supplies of
this precious metal brought into the country had its con-
tributory part in the rise of prices; but other factors, like
the greater demand for grain products, due to a population increased by trade, in a country like England where
the supply was limited, like governmental interference
in keeping rents high and depressing wages, like the engros-
sing of supplies of grain, and the actual scarcity during
many years of the seventeenth century, likewise had considerable influence upon the prices of grain.[1]

The landed proprietors whose rent was still partly paid
in produce gained, if there was a surplus of commodities
which they could sell above what they themselves used, provided this surplus was more than the goods purchased.
When their estates, as was generally the case, were leased
to tenants for life, or for long terms of years, the fines on
renewals as well as the rents would be fixed at the commencement of the leases, at the value of the money of the
period when they were granted.   During the term of such
leases the landlord, by receiving payment in money which
had depreciated, would get less than the value the land
should have brought him.   Wherever for example an estate
was heavily mortgaged or settlements were to be paid to
other branches of the family, the annual depreciation of
money would tend to relieve it of the burden.

The real cultivators, the husbandmen, would be greatly
benefited, as their leases were for a considerable period of
time and the rate of rent was fixed according to the prices
of produce at the commencement of the term of leasing.
The tenants would thus be saved more in the course of the

[1] Rogers, *op. cit.*, vol. v, p. 788; Cunningham, *cp. cit.*, pt. i, p. 166, *et seq.*

century, during which prices had advanced to five times their former rate, than would be sufficient to purchase their own farms.[1]

On the other hand, the condition of the agricultural laborers was at first not benefited. The rates of wages do not seem to have advanced as rapidly as prices. Eden thinks that though the rise in wages was comparatively small, there is no reason to believe that they failed to share somewhat in the general improvement of the country. Industrial laborers, however, who depended upon wages for their sustenance, would suffer severely from the effects of the large importations of precious metals.[2]

Not only the people but the sovereign, as has already been seen,[3] suffered from the sudden financial changes. The income of the crown was unelastic. Although the increasing trade brought in a large revenue, the land was still the principal source from which taxation was obtained, and the tenths and fifteenths and general subsidies had become fixed payments. On the other hand all the expenses of living had been raised four or five times as much as they had been a hundred years before the Stuart period.[4]

Two classes who especially profited from the new financial conditions were the manufacturers and the merchants. Although the prices of raw materials which the manufacturer had to buy were rising, the demand for manufactured articles was constantly growing, and their prices were much higher. The merchants, whether wholesale or retail, benefited in proportion to the stock of goods which they had

[1] Jacob, *op. cit.*, vol. ii, p. 103, *et seq.*

[2] *Ibid.*, vol. ii, p. 110; Blanqui, *op. cit.*, p. 257; Eden, *State of the Poor*, vol. i, p. 119; Cunningham, *op. cit.*, pt. i, p. 170.

[3] *Supra*, p. 160.

[4] Jacob, *op. cit.*, vol. ii, p. 103; Cunningham, pt. i, p. 170.

kept in their warehouses and shops. In the case, of the
commodities which they had to buy, even if they did have
to pay more than usual for them, they were able to make
up for this greater expense by selling these goods which
they bought dear at a still high rate.[1]

One important means of spending the largely increased
stores of bullion was in the trade with the East Indies.
Many in England, led by false economic ideas regarding the
hoarding of bullion, believed that certain kinds of con-
merce, especially that with the East Indies, brought an
actual loss to the mother country. Sir Thomas Mun expresses the objection in the following:

It were a happie thing for Christendome (say many men)
that the navigation to the East Indies, by way of the Cape of
Good Hope, had never bene found out. For in the fleetes of
shippes, which are sent thither Yearly out of England,
Portingall, and the Low countries the gold, silver, and Coyne
of Christendome, and particularly of this Kingdome, is exhausted to buy unnecessarie wares.[2]

Advocates of trade with the East Indies, among whom was
Mun, on the other hand, agreed that England gained in
wealth through this commerce.[3] Some were of the opinion

---

[1] Jacob, *op. cit.*, vol. ii, p. 111.

[2] Mun, "A Discourse of Trade, etc.," in McCulloch, *Collection* (1856),
p. 7. Jacob estimates that during one hundred and twelve years after
the discovery of America the amount of precious metals which passed
from Europe to Asia amounted to one-tenth of the whole quantity
produced. Jacob, vol. ii, p. 69, *et seq.*

[3] Mun argues that much expense was saved England by direct Eastern
trade. Formerly it had to send more than double the amount of
bullion to Turkey to get commodities. About £953,543 might thus be
saved on a year's trade. £100,000 spent for Eastern wares would procure goods worth £494,223. Thus about £394,233 might be added to the
nation's wealth by the transaction. McCulloch, *Collection* (1856),
pp. 12,202.

that the bullion was finally returned to England at the expense of other European countries, through the sale of the surplus spices and other Eastern commodities.[1] However this may be, it is certain that the demand for bullion to be used in the Eastern trade had a salutary effect in helping to counteract the influence of the large importation of precious metals from the New World.

Turning now to the topic of the creation of individual fortunes by those directly engaged in the new ventures resulting from the discoveries and the attendant growth of commerce, it may be said that during Elizabeth's reign the English privateering expeditions proved to be the most thriving business and profitable investment that could be made. The first generation of Englishmen to invest capital put it into these enterprises, as money is put today into railways or manufacturing industries.[2] A bold venture in a privateering expedition might easily make a very wealthy man out of one with little means, and often such newly enriched gentlemen created the fortune of their native town. A few examples will suffice to show how profitable these ventures were. The value of the treasure from Drake's expedition of 1577-80 was £600,000 or over. Of this amount the queen's share was from £250,000 to £300,000. Drake's voyage in 1585, however, resulted in a loss, but that undertaken in 1587 made a gross profit of 138%. Of this Elizabeth's profit was 87%. The returns of voyages made from about 1590 to 1596 brought the queen about

---

[1] It was estimated that £470,000 in bullion was brought in every year by the India trade, and added to the wealth of the kingdom. *A Treatise Concerning the East India Trade, wrote at the instance of Thomas Papillon* (London, 1680), p. 12.

[2] J. R. Seeley, *The Expansion of England*, p. 3.

£200,000.[1] John Oxenham is said to have taken £60,000 in "massie gold" and £200,000 in silver from the Spaniards.[2] In 1592 the Portuguese ship, "Mother of God," of 1,600 tons burden and a cargo worth £150,000, was towed into Dartmouth.[3] The privateering industry became so profitable that it led to preying not only on the Spanish and their dependencies, but also on French and Dutch commerce.[4]

Not all the actual gain in wealth at the time was due to privateering, as England for some years during the latter part of Elizabeth's reign made considerable profit from the carrying trade between European countries.[5] As has already been said, in the end privateering brought about a loss rather than a gain to the English, for it resulted in a most serious restriction of commerce with European ports.[6] Besides, as time went on, less spoil was taken, for the Spaniards, when once aroused to the danger from privateers, kept their bullion in the interior of their colonies

---

[1] Scott, *op. cit.*, vol. i, pp. 82, *et seq.*, 501, 507.

[2] J. Evelyn, "Navigation and Commerce, their Original and Progress," in *Literary Remains of John Evelyn*, edited by William Upcott, p. 664.

[3] E. J. Payne, *History of European Colonies*, p. 56.

[4] Throughout the entire reign of Elizabeth, English buccaneers were preying on the commerce of their Dutch allies. Henry IV of France in 1603 declined an invitation to visit England for fear that the English privateers would capture him while crossing the Channel. D. Campbell, *The Puritan in Holland, England and America, etc.*, vol. i, pp. 382, 389.

[5] There had been quite a large carrying trade in Eastern wares brought through Russia and taken direct to Spain and Portugal. The Spanish in retaliation for their losses to the English sea-rovers stopped this traffic. The English likewise had a carrying trade with Germany which they afterwards lost. *Calendar of Letters and State Papers relating to English Affairs . . . in the Archives of Simancas* (1580-86), p. 651, *et seq.*; Scott, vol. i, p. 170.

[6] *Supra*, p. 125.

instead of at the ports, and transported it to Europe in heavily armed fleets.[1]

It was commonly thought at the time that the shareholders of the great trading companies, which grew up as a result of English expansion, made immense profits. Doubtless there were very large gains, but there were also many losses, even of entire fortunes. The mania for speculation once aroused would carry men of fortune far; while others who were prominent investors in such successful ventures as the East India Company would, as in the case of the Virginia Company,[2] support losing enterprises for patriotic as well as commercial reasons.

Much was said of the fabulous dividends from investments in the East India Company. The average profit of twelve voyages made to the East Indies during the early part of the seventeenth century was 138%; but none of these voyages were made in less than twenty months, and often they extended over three or four years. After the arrival of goods from India, they sold at long credits of eighteen months or of two years, and owing to the irregularity of the factors in keeping and transmitting their accounts, the returns from a voyage could not be finally adjusted sooner than six or eight years. Taking the duration of the business of a voyage at a medium of seven years, the profit would be somewhat under 20% per annum, which, when the current rate of interest was 8%, scarcely proved an adequate premium for the risk the adventurers ran in establishing a new trade in unknown countries, and would

[1] Scott, *op. cit.*, vol. i, p. 85.

[2] In 1618 after twelve years of effort and an expense of more than £80,000 of public stock, besides other sums of private planters and adventurers, the Virginia Company was left in debt nearly £5,000. Stith, *op. cit.*, pp. 159, 281.

perhaps be reduced to a level with the common interest of the time, if the expense of insurance were deducted.[1]

Although the average returns were not excessively large, taking into consideration the risks, expenses, delays etc., investment in the East India Company and in a number of other oversea trading companies was on the whole very profitable. From 1683 to 1692 inclusive, the East India Company paid 200% on their stock. Besides this they had as early as 1676 given a bonus to every stockholder in the form of an amount of stock equal to that he already held. Thus the 200% paid to such people would really amount to 400% on their original investment. During the same period, besides giving a bonus in stock, the African Company paid at least 49¼% and the Hudson's Bay Company 275%. The East India Company, therefore, distributed an average annual dividend of 40%, the African Company, of about 5%, and the Hudson's Bay Company, of 27½%. Most of the quotations of the East India stock during the years mentioned stood at about 300, although at one time it rose as high as 500, and at another sank to 122½. Taking 300 as the average rate for these years, the payment of 200% during ten years on 100 nominal capital stock would yield an annual average return of about 8⅓%.[2]

It is evident that the holders of the original stock and those who bought when the stock was comparatively low, were the ones who had the chief opportunity for profit. At one time the stock was as low as 60. In 1664 it was 70,

---

[1] Macpherson, *The History of European Commerce with India*, p. 92. Stockholders who had subscribed for stock in 1630 had by June 20, 1634 received no dividend. The Governor then told them they must look for no returns for a year or two longer. Investors in the first voyage received 40% profit, those in the second, 50% and in the third, 35%. *Cal. of the Court Minutes of the E. I. Co.* (1635-39), p. vii, *note*.

[2] Scott, *op. cit.*, vol. i, p. 318, *et seq.*; Macaulay, *op. cit.*, vol. iv, p. 236.

while in 1677 it had reached 245. As has been seen, the average from 1683 to 1692 was 300, with some sales made as high as 500. A holder of the original stock who sold it in 1685 at 500, would have made a net profit on his capital of 1,190½%, after allowance for interest was deducted.[1]

John Evelyn tells how in 1688 he had just sold his East India venture for £750. This he had originally bought for £250 and then held for twenty-five years.[2] It is said that the annual income of some of the fortunate speculators was £10,000. Sir Josiah Child was so judicious and lucky in his purchase of stock that he made a fortune of £200,000, from which he received an annual income of £20,000. He obtained a baronetcy and purchased an estate at Winstead, where he spent vast sums in excavating fish ponds, and planting whole square miles with walnut trees. He married his daughter to the eldest son of the Duke of Beaufort, giving a dowry of fifty thousand pounds with her.[3]

Besides the chance to sell stock bought at a low figure for a high one, there was likewise, as has already been seen, the chance of a bonus being granted, which might double or even further increase the investor's stock. In the period from the Restoration to the Revolution the nominal capital of the East India Company was doubled, the Hudson's Bay Company trebled, and the African Company quadrupled, by giving bonuses out of reserved profits.[4]

Another opportunity to make large sums of money was offered the factors in the East India Company's service.

---

[1] Macaulay, *op. cit.*, vol. iv, p. 236.

[2] "Diary," December 18, 1682, in *Memoirs*, vol. iii, p. 73.

[3] Evelyn, "Diary," March 16, 1683, in *Memoirs*, vol. iii, p. 77. Child is said to have bought his stock in 1665 when it was at a low figure. *Dictionary of National Biography*, vol. x, Sir Josiah Child.

[4] Scott, *op. cit.*, vol. i, p. 447.

These brought home what they could save of their salaries, and also in many cases large profits made through private trade, which proved a genuine addition to the country's wealth.[1] The salaries of the factors in the East varied. Thirty-six factors were engaged in 1600 to go with the first expedition sent by the Company to establish posts. Of this number there were three factors of the first class who were to be allowed £100 for equipment and £200 as an investment; four factors of the second class were to be paid £50 for equipment and £100 for investment; four factors of the third class were to have £30 for equipment and £50 for an investment; and four factors of the fourth class were secured at the rate of £20 each for equipment and £40 for investment. These factors had to pledge themselves not to engage in private trade.[2] A few other typical examples of factors' salaries are as follows; in 1608, Richard Reave and in 1609, Thomas Keinsworth £4 per month with £10 for provision, and in the case of the latter £25 allowed for private trade; in 1614, Edmund Blithman £30 a year and Nicholas Hawkins £75 a year; in 1626, Henry Glasscock £20 per year for the first two years and £30 thereafter, and Robert Fotherby, clerk of the stores and yard, £80 per year. In 1623 a merchant was given £150 yearly, and four general auditors were to each have £100 annually.[3]

Immense sums were frequently made by these factors through legitimate and often illegitimate private traffic with the natives. Thus it was stated that the private trade in

[1] Macpherson, *The History of European Commerce with India,* p. 133, note.

[2] John Bruce, *Annals of the Honourable East India Company from their Establishment by the Charter of Queen Elizabeth 1600 to the Union of the London and English East India Companies, 1707-1708,* vol. i. p. 131.

[3] *Cal. of S. P. Col. Ser. E. I.* (1513-1616), p. 286.

Persia for one year, 1630, amounted to as much as £30,000.[1] Boothby, in his " Five Declarations," stated that two of the Company's servants made through private trade in less than six years £30,000 and £20,000 respectively.[2] George Page in that same year boasted that he made £1,000 a year through private trade, although he only had £60 with him when he came. Another factor was said to be worth £15,000 or £20,000 gained during his short stay in India.[3] Three other factors were reported to be worth, respectively, 80,000 rials, 20,000 rials, besides goods to the value of 10,000 and 12,000 rials.[4]

Ship-captains and other officers of the East Indiamen had many chances to save a comfortable fortune. They secured on the whole very good salaries and often had chances for private trade. Captain Davis, who was in charge of one of the ships of the first expedition in 1600, was to have £100 as wages and £200 on credit for an investment. On his return, if the profits of the voyage " should yield two for one, he was to be allowed £500, if three for one £1,000, if four for one, £1,500 and if five for one, £2000." [5] The well known Captain Middleton was secured in 1609 to head the expedition to the East at a salary of £13, 6s, 8d. per month, and £60, 13s., 4d. for equipment. The equally renowned Captain Newport was paid in 1615 a salary of £15 per month, provided he renounced private trade.[6]

Besides his salary the officer of the East Indiaman had the

[1] *The English Factories in India* (1630-1633), p. 17.

[2] *Cal. of the Court Minutes of the E. I. Co.* (1635-39), p. v.

[3] *The English Factories in India* (1630-1633), pp. 151, 153.

[4] *Ibid.* (1642-1643), p. 76. A rial was equal to 15 shillings.

[5] Bruce, *Annals, etc.*, vol. i, p. 129.

[6] *Cal. S. P. Col. Ser. E. I.* (1513-1616), pp. 180, 372.

right to take fifty tons of goods from England free of any freight charge.   On his homeward voyage he was allowed twenty tons of free freight, to consist of certain scheduled goods, upon which duties had to be paid to the Company. As the rate was twenty-five pounds a ton this privilege was a very valuable one, and much could be made from the profits of the sale of the goods which could thus be carried. The other officers were also allowed a certain amount of freight.   Thus the chief mate could take eight tons, the second mate six tons, the purser three tons, the surgeon six. the midshipman and the quartermasters each one ton on the voyage from England.

On the China ships as goods were not convenient, the captain might take three thousand pounds of bullion, the chief mate three hundred and so on down.   On the homeward voyage the commanders of the China ships were allowed thirty-eight tons, the chief mate eight tons, second mate six tons and so on down to the carpenter who might take one ton.   On the other homeward bound ships from the Orient the commander was allowed thirty tons or thirty-two feet, the chief mate six tons or sixteen feet, and so on to the carpenter who might have the use of thirty-two feet.   Upon their importations these officials had to pay the customs dues, and three percent to the Company for warehouse room on the gross amount of the sale in the case of Indian products, and a larger percentage in the case of China goods.[1]

A further source of private as well as public wealth was furnished by the West India plantations.   Many men of small or moderate means were made very wealthy through the cultivation of sugar.   Others who had formerly been gentlemen of means but who had lost nearly all they possessed in the Civil War came to retrieve their fortunes in

[1] Edward Keble Chatterton, *The Old East Indiamen*, pp. 133, 227-230.

the West Indies.[1]   A few typical examples of the fortunes
made in the sugar plantations will serve to show the importance of these possessions for creating new wealth for
Englishmen.   Col. James Drax who invested £300 in a
Barbados plantation made so much money that he refused
to return to England until he was able to purchase an estate
there which would yield £10,000 in annual income.   In
1677 he shipped sugar from Barbados to the value of £5,000.
He appears to have about secured the fortune he desired,
for Oldmixon states that he acquired an estate which would
yield from £8,000 to £9,000 a year income, and married the
Earl of Carlisle's daughter.[2]   Colonel Thomas Modiford
who resolved not to return to England " until he made his
voyage, and employment there worth him a hundred
thousand pounds sterling " may be cited as another example
of an Englishman who became a wealthy planter.[3]

These planters were in every way of great financial benefit to England.   The mortgages on their estates, because of
the high rate of interest which they paid for the loan of
capital, were a most desirable investment for English capitalists.   Money invested in the plantations, moreover, was of
much more value to the mother country than if it had been
put out at interest at home, for it became a means of re-
taining settlers in the colonies who in every way increased
the consumption of English manufactures.   One thousand
pounds spent by a planter in Jamaica produced in the end
better results and greater advantages to England than twice
that sum expended by the same family in London.[4]

[1] Oldmixon, *op. cit.*, vol. ii, p. 13.

[2] Lignon, *op. cit.*, p. 96; *Cal. S. P. Col. Ser. Amer. and the W. I.*
(1677-1680), p. 110.   Oldmixon, *op. cit.*, vol. ii, p. 11.

[3] Lignon, *op. cit.*, p. 96.

[4] E. Long, *History of Jamaica*, p. 387.   William Wood calculates that
if a man brought to the public 6 shillings, 8 pence above his mainten-

When planters made large profits, their savings were deposited in England. Besides this, they sent their children home to be educated, which proved a still further benefit to the mother country. Finally, when there was enough wealth saved to support their family in luxury, they came to England to live. If their fortune was large enough, an estate might be purchased and the former planter would become a rich country gentleman.[1] Oldmixon speaks of the removal of " several of the most eminent Planters to England, where they purchas'd Estates and live in great Affluence and Splendour." [2] It was estimated that as much as £50,000 a year was spent in England by those who had returned from the West Indies and by the children of others, sent there for their education.[3]

A further evidence of English expansion having helped to build up a class of well-to-do English country gentlemen is the case of the West Country squires who made their money through buccaneering and the Newfoundland fisheries. No country in England contained so many small proprietors as Devonshire; and it is said that during the Tudor and Stuart periods, it produced more courtiers than any other shire in England.[4]

ance he would very much enrich the country. The planters brought as much as £7, 4 shillings, besides the employment they gave to 100.000 tons of shipping. Wood, *op. cit.*, p. 156.

[1] Joshua Gee, *The Trade and Navigation of Great Britain* (London, 1731), p. 101, *et seq.* Long, *op. cit.*, p. 387. Davenant gives 300 as the number of wealthy planters' children who yearly returned to England; but whether he meant that they came for education or to stay permanently and enter English social life is uncertain. Davenant, *op. cit.*, vol. ii, p. 7.

[2] Oldmixon, *op. cit.*, vol. ii, p. 112.

[3] *Some Considerations Humbly Offered to Both Houses of Parliament concerning the Sugar Colonies, etc.* (London, 1701), p. 8.

[4] Prowse, *A History of Newfoundland*, p. 144.

CHAPTER VII

Morals and Religion

It is probably due to the discovery of the New World and the subsequent growth of commerce that we owe in part the beginnings of religious toleration. Trade drew the attention of mankind more and more from the visionary realms of the hereafter to the more real wonders of the world about. Human nature at high tension in striving to realize the spiritual world and live in it suddenly was diverted to lands that could be seen and explored. Man began to think more of earthly things and of his own gain.[1] One can readily imagine that his nerves would have been eased,

[1] This tendency is well described by Edward Dowden in his *Shakespeare—A Critical Study of his Mind and Art*, p. 10, as follows: " But in the Renaissance and Reformation period, instead of substituting supernatural powers and persons and events for the natural facts of the world, men recurred to those facts, and found in them inspiration and sustenance for heart and intellect and conscience. Of Paradise men knew somewhat less than Angelico had known, or Dante; but they saw that this earth is good. Physical nature was not damnable; the outlying regions of the earth were not tenanted by vampires and devils. Sir John Mandeville brought back stories of obscure valleys communicating with Hell and haunted by homicidal demons; Raleigh brought back the tobacco plant and the potato. In the college of his New Atlantis, Bacon erects a statue to the inventor of sugar. Dreams of unexplored regions excited the imagination of Spaniard and Englishman in the later Renaissance; but it was of El Dorado they dreamed, with its gold-roofed city and auriferous sands. . . . Men found that the earth is in heaven, that God is not above nature, touching it only through rare preternatural points of contact—rather that he is not far from everyone of us; that human life is sacred, and time a fragment of eternity."

and his mind rested and refreshed by the new fancies and facts. Bigotry and religious intolerance when analyzed are often found to arise in large measure from an overwrought and oversensitive nature, which has become tired and morbid with dwelling on the one theme. Now America and the East offered to curiosity, imagination, zeal for adventure and self-realization, a ready outlet. Besides this, the long voyages had insensibly detached a great number of people from absurd ideas which superstition inspired.[1]

But all this was slow in coming. There were the struggles of the Reformation first to be passed through. Spain wasted her new-found treasures in the Netherlands to oppress the Dutch; while England continued to hate the Spaniard for his religion and his cruelty, and persisted in making this an excuse to despoil him of his treasures. It is noticeable, however, that after the Thirty Years War the great religious conflicts cease, and those of trade commence. Very gradually through the centuries a feeling of tolerance for strange customs and ideas developed. Narrow minds were somewhat broadened by the scenes of a New World, and their sympathies were aroused by the spiritual needs of more unfortunate races; while the variety of religious worships and the differences of nations which were encountered accustomed the more vulgar minds to a kind of indifference for their particular faith. Religious prejudices began to appear of less account, as worldly and material things grew in importance. The Englishman began to be a cosmopolitan, not only in his dress but in his thoughts. It is quite interesting to notice how similar had been the case centuries before, when Rome became an empire most tolerant of the customs and religions of the world, and

[1] Raynal, *op. cit.*, vol. vi, bk. xix, p. 137; l'Abbé Genty, *L'Influence de la Découverte de l'Amérique sur le Bonheur du Genre Humain, passim.*

largely indifferent and even skeptical in the matter of her own religion.

Again we must notice a second important influence in the direction of tolerance. New lands had been found whither those who were dissatisfied or were not tolerated in the Old World could go. The medieval law of intolerance had been based on the Scriptures, which led men to believe the Omnipotent was a jealous God, visiting the sins of men, not only upon their descendants to the third and fourth generations, but also upon the nation to which they belonged.

To believe or conceive of Him, or to worship Him, otherwise than in accordance with the revelation made by Him for the guidance of man, was something more than an offense against Himself. It was an intolerable wrong to society, for it exposed the pious many to the penalty incurred by an impious minority. Plague and pestilence, famine and destruction in war, were brought on a nation by religious apostasy; and it was therefore, not merely lawful, but a national duty, to stamp out apostasy in its beginnings.[1]

It was different in the New World, for there was virgin soil. Here in this vacant continent colonies could be planted at considerable distances from each other, and could settle their religious principles for themselves at their own risk. Here, the most diverse sects, the Puritan, the Catholic, the Quaker, which were not tolerated in their native land, could seek and find refuge.[2]

Not only must there have been a reflex influence upon the nations of the Old World, of the toleration, liberty and independence of thought and action in the New World; but likewise religious tension in England doubtless was much

[1] E. J. Payne, "The New World," in *Cambridge Modern History*, vol. i, p. 47.

[2] *Ibid.*

lessened by having the most energetic and earnest of the Dissenters and Catholics remove to America. These were the ones who would have kept the struggle active at home. In fact, as will be shown later, many of the important leaders in the Puritan Party during the Civil War were those who had returned from New England.[1]

America afforded the Puritans a refuge, where they could develop unimpeded their concepts of theology. The opportunity to expand their ideas of government proved of value to the English race;[2] similarly much theological philosophy and thought must have been preserved free from the suppression of the home government, and the influence of the foreigner.

It is interesting to notice the idea quite prevalent at the time, of the purity of life in a primitive land close to nature, where a new and wholesome religion and system of morality could be started. In the words of George Herbert:

> Religion stands tip-toe in our land,
> Ready to pass to the American strand,
> When height of malice and prodigies, lusts,
> Impudent sinning, witchcraft, and distrusts,
> The marks of future bane shall fill our cup:
> When Seine shall swallow Tiber, and the Thames:
> By letting in them both, pollutes her streams;
> When Italy of us shall have her will,
> And all her calender of sins fulfil;
> Whereby one may foretell what sins next year
> Shall both in France and England domineer:
> Then shall religion to America flee,
> They have their time of Gospell, e'en as we.[3]

Another evidence of this sentiment is found in a letter of Dr. Twisse to the learned churchman, Mede:

[1] *Infra*, p. 343.

[2] *Infra*, p. 343.

[3] Neill, *The English Colonization of America during the Seventeenth Century*, p. 178.

Now, I beseech you, let me know what your opinion is of this English plantation in the New World. Heretofore I have wondered in my thoughts at the providence of God concerning that world, not discovered till this Old World of ours is almost at an end, and there no footsteps found of the true God, much less of Christ. And then, considering our English Plantations of late, and the opinion of many grave divines concerning the Gospel's fleeing westward, sometimes I have such thoughts—why may not that be the place of the New Jerusalem? [1]

It is evident that the discoveries had some tendency toward causing a sceptical, and in many cases an indifferent, attitude in regard to the old form of religion. The many new revelations, coming suddenly as they did, shook the system of belief upheld by the church. From such questioning the newly aroused minds came to the conclusion that the accepted religious doctrine and practice could not possibly represent the true construction of God's will revealed in Scripture. A sense of general intellectual insecurity, best named scepticism, resulted.[2]

Toward the end of the seventeenth century men prominent in public life who were also known as sceptics, or as having sceptical tendencies, were met with. So threatening did the inclination appear, that Evelyn wrote to the Bishop of Oxford in 1681-82, urging that he have some of the scholars there do something to defend Christianity against the rising atheism. He spoke of the necessity of confuting the modern atheists as " these start new and later notions," and " the men of this curious and nicer age do not consider what has been said or written formerly, but expect something fresh, that may tempt and invite them to consider." [3]

[1] Neill, *op. cit.*, p. 78.

[2] *Cambridge Modern History*, vol. i, p. 156.

[3] " Correspondence " in *Memoirs*, vol. iv, p. 263.

In another place Evelyn speaks of the profane temper of the age. A good illustration of this characteristic is a story told regarding the great scholar Sir William Petty, who entertained his friends one day

by holding forth in tone and action, passing from the court pulpit to the Presbyterian, and then the Independent, Anabaptist, Quaker, Fanatique, Frier, and Jesuit, as entertained the company to admiration, putting on the persons of those secretarys with such variety and imitation, that in coming to be told the King, they prevail'd with him to show his faculty one day at court.[1]

Pepys relates that the clergy received affront in all places of England from the gentry and ordinary persons of the parish.[2]

It appears quite evident that the awakened commercialism and spirit of gain resultant from expansion tended to materialize men's natures and therefore make them less religious. This is shown by the fact that a new commercial morality had become common among moneyed men who no longer felt the moral obligation as formerly of employing the poor during hard times. The paternal spirit of the preceding ages more or less changed to the modern one, each looking out for his own personal gain without consideration for his neighbor.[3]

Men's natures were not merely materialized, but in many cases their morals were seriously impaired as a result of the inpouring wealth and the customs it engendered. A growing class composed of newly enriched merchants, courtiers, and nobles became great lovers of extravagant display. Youths from the country were ruined by the fast city life.

[1] " Correspondence " in *Memoirs*, vol. iv, p. 409.
[2] *Pepys' Diary*, vol. ii, p. 315.
[3] Cunningham, *op. cit.*, pt. i, pp. 205, 206.

Men of otherwise innocent characters were led astray, through pressing need of money to continue their expensive entertainments and other aristocratic excesses. While courtiers stole, the monarch became deeply indebted.[1]   Thus in the matter of dress and adornment, childishly fond of what was then called " bravery," the courtiers of Elizabeth, James I and Charles I, to please their sovereign's vanity and their own, were extravagant in the jewels worn on court dresses. A court suit of the Duke of Buckingham, the favorite of James I, cost £8,000; while Lord Fanshaw, the English ambassador to Spain, wore a black beaver decorated with a jewel worth £1,200, and around his neck a curious wrought chain made in the Indies.[2]

Ladies of the higher class made each new fête a pretext for greater extravagance, and efforts to outshine their neighbors. During the reign of James I the love of personal adornment among men as well as women was even more widespread than before. John Chamberlain, an interesting contemporary, wrote in 1608 to a friend unable to attend a masque:

Whatsoever the devise may be, and what success they may have in their dancing, yet you should be sure to have seen great riches in jewels, when one lady, and under a baroness, is said to be furnished far better than a hundred thousand pounds; and the Lady Arabella goes beyond her, and the Queen must not come behind.[3]

---

[1] Traill, *op. cit.*, vol. iv, p. 162.

[2] De Barrera, *op. cit.*, p. 77. Great luxury in jewelry was also associated with the court of Charles II. Smith, p. 305. The fact that a great courtier about the year 1620, spent as much as £18 a year for shoe strings may be cited as an example of the extravagance of the time. *Journals of the House of Commons*, vol. i, p. 523.

[3] Smith, *op. cit.*, p. 235.

A further example of the excessive extravagance of
the time is afforded by the large popular demand for
tobacco.   One of the strongest objections to the herb was
its ruinous cost.   When it was first introduced into England
it cost about three shillings an ounce.   In modern money
this would be equivalent probably to eighteen shillings.
Threepence was the usual charge in taverns for a pipeful
of tobacco.   In the reign of James I the best tobacco cost
eighteen shillings a pound, and an inferior article, ten shillings.[1]   A single bill for tobacco amounted to £36, 7s. 8d.,
or reduced to modern money, about £145, 10s., 8d.[2]   Edmund Gardiner, author of *The Trial of Tobacco,* com-
plained in 1610 that " the patrimony of many noble young
gentlemen, have been quite exhausted, and have vanished
clean away with this smoky vapour, and hath most shame-
fully and beastly flyen out at the master's nose; " and that,
" othersome there be that spend whole daies, moneths times,
and years (for the most part) in tabacco taking, not sparing
to take it even in their bed.[3] . . . . John Deacon, whose
opinions have already been mentioned, throws much light
on the situation as follows:

Concerning therefore that former superfluous and riotous
waste, which those Tobacconists do so wilfully make about
their beastly Tobacco fumes, do tell me in good sadness,
whether it be not a superfluous waste, for any man of great
place, to paddle forth yearly one hundred pounds at the least
for a hundred gallons of filthy fumes? for a Gentleman of
meaner condition, to be at fortie pounds annuall expenses, about
bare fortie pottles of stinking flames? for a Yeoman, an Hus-
bandman, an Artificer, a Trades-man, a Tinker, a Shooemaker,

[1] Penn, *op. cit.,* p. 68.

[2] Fairholt, *op. cit.,* p. 70.

[3] *Ibid.,* p. 75.

or a Cobbler, to bestow weekely some three shillings four pence at the least for but one onely ounce of fantastical fooleries?[1]

King James himself continues in this vein: "Now how you are by this custome disabled in your goods, let the Gentry of this land become witnesse, some of them bestowing three, some four hundred pounds a year upon this precious stinke, which I am sure might be bestowed upon many farre better uses."[2]

Sir William Vaughan, also, in his pamphlet, *The Golden Fleece etc.*, published in 1626, takes into consideration the evil effects of tobacco:

> Three hundred thousand pounds yee yearly spend
> In hastning griefes unto a deadly end.
> Yee need not Hellebore. Tobaccoes fume
> From Court and Cottage will expell the rheume.
> Alas fond Fooles! which spend your meanes and health,
> With Sathans joy, and hurt to Commonwealth.[3]

He even ascribes a decline in trade to " Prodigality, Excesse of Aparrell, Tobacco, and other enormities in this iland."[4]   In fact, one of the objections raised against the importation of tobacco was because it was thought that there was no real return of bullion to England from the traffic.[5]

In addition to the evils resulting from the great expense of smoking, it was regarded as a vice akin to immoderate drinking, and was associated with other forms of intemperate life.   Charles I, in 1639, asserted that. " through the

---

[1] Deacon, *op. cit.*, p. 61.

[2] *English Reprints*, no. 19, p. 110.

[3] Sir William Vaughan, *The Golden Fleece Divided into three parts, etc.* (London, 1626), pt. ii, p. 82.

[4] *Ibid.*, p. 29.

[5] Beer, *The Origins of the British Colonial System, 1578-1660*, p. 79.

immoderate taking of tobacco, provoking the takers to excessive drinking and other inconveniences, the health of many of our subjects has been impaired." [1] In 1621, it was stated in the House of Commons that: " Tobacco and Ale (are) now made inseparable in the base vulgar Sort: These (are) accompanied with Idleness, Drunkenness, Sickness, Decay of their Estates etc." [2]

A spirit of rather coarse hilarity and love for extravaganza,—echoes from the dare-devil buccaneers who seized the Spaniard's glittering gold, and spent as freely as they seized — stole into the society of the times. Life was so aroused and shaken from its old restraints, imagination was so unloosed and the spirit of reckless freedom and power was so invigorated, that greater coarseness as well as immorality among the people of the new age was bound to follow. [3]

On the other hand, England's increasing commerce and wealth had a far different effect upon an ever growing class of hardheaded merchants, artisans and traders. Among these form and ceremony, at the expense of time and money, were most distasteful. This feeling was more clearly shown in religion perhaps than in any other phase of life. The business man with his practical outlook was less addicted to religious formalism than the old-fashioned country gentleman; while the new industrial laborer frequently exchanging thought with his fellows needed a more vitalized religion than the conservative peasant. Peter Pett, writing at the time, remarks:

Finding the genious of trading people averse from cere-

---

[1] Beer, *op. cit.*, p. 82.

[2] *Journals of the House of Commons*, vol. i, p. 605.

[3] Campbell, *The Puritan in Holland, England and America, etc.*, vol. i, p. 353.

monies, Puritan preachers by their disesteem of ceremonies and external pomp in the worship of God, were the more endeared to corporations, and the greater part of persons engaged in trade and traffic, who hate ceremonies in general, and what does unnecessarily take up time, which is natural to men, who live by trade and whose being rich or beggars depends much on that preaching passionate and loud against what looks like luxury and is apt to occasion unnecessary expense to them.[1]

This utterly practical bent of mind may have been a reason why so many disputes between the Dissenters and the Church of England took the form of a wrangle over vestments and the elaborateness of church services.

True religion has always gained new impetus when Chrisians have become interested in the uplifting of weaker peoples; so it is with a sense of relief that we turn from our study of the influence of the new conditions upon religious thought, and the conduct of everyday life to the newly awakened zeal for foreign missions. It may rightly be said that, when the settlements made in America and the voyages to India aroused interest in missionary activities, a new era dawned for the Church of the old world. From a zealous, but rather selfish regard for the individual soul's salvation, and from endeavor that the tenets of orthodox faith, whatever they might be, should prevail to the care for the redemption and civilization of unheard-of multitudes who had never learned of God's grace, was surely an important step toward the realization of the Christian ideal.

The settlements made in America and the voyages to India aroused interest in missionary activities. As early as 1519 English sentiment regarding the conversion of the natives is clearly voiced:

[1] P. Pett, *The Happy Future State of England, etc.* (London, 1688), p. 239.

O what a great meritorious deed,
To have the people instructed
To live more virtuously,
And to learn to know of men the manner,
And also God their maker,
Which as yet live all beastly!
For they nother know God nor the devil,
Nor ever heard tell of heaven or hell,
Writing, or other scripture.[1]

The settlement of America was represented by the preachers of the day as a crusade to win the heathen. William Crashaw, preacher at the Temple, delivered a stirring sermon on February 1, 1610, upon the conversion of the savage and the founding of the English church and commonwealth in America. Addressing those about to start, he said:

And you right honourable and beloved, who engage your lives and are therefore deepliest interested in this business, who make the greatest ventures, and bear the greatest burdens,—who leave your ease and honour at home, and commend yourselves to the seas and winds for the good of the enterprise,—you who desire to advance the gospel of Jesus Christ, though it be with the hazard of your lives, go forward in the name of the God of Heaven and earth, the God that keepeth counsel and mercy to thousands.

After exhorting them to allow no Papist, Atheist or Brownist to go, thus strangely mingling philanthropy and intolerance, he continued:

Then shall Heaven and earth bless you, and for the heroical adventure of thy person and state in such a godly course the God of Heaven will make thy name to be mentioned throughout all generations, and thousands of people shall honour thy memory, and give thanks for thee while the world endureth.[2]

[1] John Rastell, "A New Interlude and a Mery of the Nature of the IIII Elements," quoted in E. J. Payne, *History of the New World called America*, vol. i, p. 239.

[2] Neill, *The English Colonization, etc.*, p. 35, *et seq.*

John Donne, Dean of St. Paul's, in closing his sermon before the Virginia Company, remarked:

Those among you that are old now shall pass out of the world with this great comfort, that you contributed to the beginning of the Commonwealth and Church, although not to see the growth thereof to perfection. . . . You shall have made this island, which is but as the suburbs of the Old World a bridge, a gallery to the New, to join all to that world that shall never grow old, the kingdom of Heaven.

The Rev. Daniel Price, in 1609, portrays the "angel of Virginia, crying to this land, as the angel of Macedonia to Paul, " Come over and help us.",[1] Sir William Alexander, Secretary of State for Scotland and proprietor of Nova Scotia, in his poem called " Doomsday," written about 1614, has a verse with the ring of a modern missionary hymn:

> In this last age, Time doth new worlds display,
> That Christ, a Church, o'er all the earth may have,
> His righteousness shall barbarous realms sway,
> If their first love more civil lands will leave,
> America to Europe may succeed,
> God may of stones raise up Abram's seed.[2]

Even in the charters of the trading companies and the instructions issued to their governors interest was expressed in the moral condition of the Indians. In the Letters Patent of the Virginia Company, granted in 1606, it was hoped that the colonization of Virginia would tend to the propagation of the Christian religion among the tribes; while the accompanying instructions directed that the inhabitants should use " all good means to draw the savages and heathen people of those territories to the true knowledge of God."[3] Like

[1] *Ibid.*, pp. 177, 178.

[2] Alexander Brown, *The Genesis of the United States, etc.*, vol. ii, p. 758.

[3] Bruce, *Economic History of Virginia in the Seventeenth Century*, vol. i, p. 67.

wise in the first charter of Massachusetts it is stated: " To win and invite the natives of the country to the knowledge and obedience of the only true God and Savior of Mankind and the Christian faith, in our royal intention, is the principal end of this plantation." [1]

As evidence of some degree of active interest in the missionary movement, it may be said that the East India Company early in its career sent ministers along with its merchandise, although it never allowed religion to interfere with its trade.   Patrick Copeland, who may be considered the first English missionary, entered the service of the Company as soon as it had established a trading post at Surat. In 1614 he returned to England with a native youth whom he had taught to speak, read and write English.   It was his intention to educate him as a religious helper.   A feeling of curiosity more than anything else appears to have been aroused by the sight of the native; for when he walked the streets large crowds of children followed, and the housewives also peeped at him.   When the ceremony of baptism was administered to him, so many people were attracted that the Privy Council, Lord Mayor, Aldermen and members of the East India Company had difficulty in pushing through the crowd.   King James, ever ready with his ideas, gave the native the name of Peter Pope. [2]

Another reference to missionary work in the East, and the interest shown in the new movement is given by Evelyn, who in 1661 mentions going to the Abbey to hear a Dr. Basire, " that great travailler, or rather French Apostle, who had been planting ye Church of England in divers parts of ye Levant and Asia." [3]   Many learned Englishmen, also,

---

[1] Young, *Chronicles of the First Planters*, pp. 142-143.

[2] *Cal. of S. P. Col. Ser. East Indies* (1513-16), p. 316.

[3] *Diary*, November 10, 1661, in *Memoirs*, vol. i, p. 181.

went to the Near East as the chaplains of the Levant Company. Upon a number of occasions this organization gave evidences of a philanthropic spirit. It contributed liberally, as a body or individually, whenever there was distress in the East. It redeemed Christian captives and helped the Greeks when persecuted by the Turks.[1]

The spirit of missionary endeavor was strong enough in 1618 to warrant collections being made by royal order four times in the next two years throughout all the parishes of England for the education of native as well as white children in Virginia. In this manner as much as £1500 was secured for the first church offering for missions.[2] Private contributions further added to the amount raised. One of £500 was sent by an unknown gentleman " for the converting and educating of three score Infidel's children." In 1620 Nicolas Ferrar bequeathed £300 for the purpose. As its share in the undertaking, the Virginia Company gave 5,000 acres of land, 1000 of which were to be especially devoted to the Indians. Unfortunately the school never materialized during the Company's existence, although its founding was constantly agitated.

The case was different in Massachusetts. Here the General Court in 1646 passed an order, "that the county courts in this jurisdiction should take care that the Indians residing in their several shires should be civilized, and that they should have power to take order from time to time to have them instructed in the knowledge and worship of God." This order provided that two ministers should be chosen by the elders of the churches each year at the Court of Election,

[1] Robert Walsh, *Account of the Levant Company*, p. 14.

[2] *Records of the Virginia Company*, vol. i, p. 220; Neill gives £2,043, 2s., 12½d. as the amount of the collections taken up in England in 1619. Edward Duffield Neill, *Memoir of Patrick Copeland, Rector Elect of the First Projected College in the United States*, pp. 17, 88.

and sent with the consent of their churches, together with whoever else should freely offer themselves for that service, " to make known the Heavenly counsel of God among the Indians." The General Court of Massachusetts might thus be called the first missionary society in the history of Protestant Christendom.[1]

News of this missionary work in New England soon reached the motherland, where it was received with great delight. A pamphlet called " The Day-Breaking " soon drew public attention to the new undertaking. This perhaps was the first missionary tract in England. Shepherd, the minister at Cambridge, then sent further information. So important was this considered that twelve of the most eminent Presbyterian and Independent ministers in England provided for its publication. In this work there was an address under their names to the " Lords and Commons assembled in High Court of Parliament," and another " to the godly and well affected of the Kingdom of England." Evangelizing the natives of New England was commended to the patronage of the State and of private Christians. Winslow promoted the matter with such diligence that he finally succeeded in getting Parliament to take action in furtherance of the cause. It instructed the Commissioners for Foreign Plantations to prepare and bring in an " Ordinance for the encouragement and advancement of learning and piety in New England." It is said that four or five years before an attempt to accomplish the same thing had been made by William Castell, who had addressed Parliament on the subject in a memorial approved by a large number of English divines. For some time nothing was done, but finally in 1649 an ordinance was passed constituting a society called " The Corporation for Propagating the Gospel

[1] John G. Palfrey, *History of New England*, vol. ii, pp. 188-189; John Fiske, *The Beginnings of New England*, p. 229.

in New England." This may be considered as the first society definitely organized in England for promoting missions.[1]

A general collection was ordered throughout all the parishes, counties and cities of England to obtain funds for the undertaking. By it enough money was raised to enable the society to purchase property which would yield a yearly income of between 500 and 600 pounds.[2] By the second charter granted the Corporation, in 1661, it had power to purchase £2,000 worth of goods per annum, and liberty to transport yearly £1,000 in bullion or foreign money from the kingdom.

From its origin, the " Corporation for Propagating the Gospel in New England " had in its membership some of the most eminent personages in England, such as the Earl of Clarendon, Lord Chancellor, Earl of Southampton, Lord Treasurer, Lord Robers, Privy Seal, Duke of Ormond, Earl of Manchester, Lord Chamberlain, Earl of Anglesey, Viscount Say and Seal etc. When the work was at its height, as many as twelve or fifteen missionaries both English and Indian were maintained.[3]

However strong the interest in missions may have been for a time, there were soon evidences of lack of interest in the subject. In the *Calendar of State Papers* for 1699 the complaint is made from New York, that no minister could be found " who will go and live with the Indians and teach them Christianity." As much as £100 a year was

[1] Palfrey, *op. cit.*, vol. ii, pp. 197, 198.

[2] Neal, *History of New England*, vol. i, p. 260, Fiske gives the much larger figure of £2000 as the annual income which shortly after 1649 was at the disposal of the Society. He further states that this came from voluntary contributions and that with these resources schools were set up in which agriculture was taught to the Indians as well as religion. Fiske, *op. cit.*, p. 229.

[3] Neal, *History of New England*, vol. i, pp. 260-263.

offered for preaching to the Five Nations, but no one was willing to go.[1]   It is quite possible, however, that the young divine who would make the venture was at last discovered, as Evelyn in 1702 says that the " Society for the Propagation of the Gospel," had just sent a young minister to New York.[2]

Although certain examples of interest in the problem of converting the people of the East have been cited, not much real concern for promoting the good work seems to have been shown until a later date. ` The Dutch as well as the Portuguese and French appear to have felt more responsibility in the matter than the English did.   Dr. Prideaux, Dean of Norwich, drew up a paper in 1694 entitled, " An Account of the English Settlements in the East Indies, together with some Proposals for the Propagation of Christianity in those parts of the World."   In this he complains that, while the Dutch settlements were provided with missionaries and in their factories and ships were able ministers, the English crews were left " wholly without prayer, instruction or sacraments," the chaplains at their factories were discouraged by the inadequacy of their salaries and the promotion of Christianity among the natives was altogether neglected.[3]

[1] *Cal. S. P., Col. Series, America and West Indies* (1699), p. 555.

[2] " Diary," May 3, 1702, in *Memoirs*, vol. iii, p. 395.   It may, however, have been that this divine only ministered to Europeans.

[3] James Hough, *History of Christianity in India*, vol. ii, p. 414.

CHAPTER VIII

Thought

THROUGHOUT history periods of national expansion and contact with new lands and people have provided great intellectual stimulus and have been accompanied by advancement in the arts and sciences of civilization. Western Europe was privileged to receive impulsion from two such periods, that of the Classical Age, which was revived in the Renaissance, and that of modern discovery and colonization. The former gave the medieval world a cool and reviving draught from the distant past when men had conceived large thoughts; had conquered lands on the outskirts of civilization; had sought with the all-aspiring Alexander to forge their way to far-distant India; had dipped with the Roman legions into the deep reaches of the German forests and viewed their semi-barbarous tribes described by Tacitus, the Hakluyt of old; had seen Albion on the very western edge of the then known world; had ventured into Armenia, and met many a barbarian from the heart of Asia and heard his weird Oriental tales. In other words, they had realized the vastness of an existence which filled their souls with the passion for achievement, and their minds with the craving for the knowledge which gives the fuller earthly life. Herodotus, traveling throughout little known lands and writing of distant peoples, Aristotle, staying at home and receiving large collections of natural objects brought by Alexander's expedition from the heart of Asia, Plato,

194   [194

speculating upon the ideal republic which lay far off over the visionary seas, the elder Pliny, with his compendious knowledge gathered about the whole known world, Strabo [1] and many others were predecessors of Hakluyt, of Bacon and More, of Gerard and those scholars of the Royal Society, who in another cycle of great thoughts and great men, likewise inspired by a vast mysterious nature, led forward human progress. So, too, the writings of a Homer, a Vergil, a Shakespeare and a Spenser were inspired and filled with the surging spirit of new life which flowed from distant lands.

A medieval world that had lived more or less unto itself, except perhaps for the Crusades; Europeans, whose more adventurous spirits had been for long satisfied with the excitements of European wars, whose supreme vision had been that of regions which rose in mysterious grandeur beyond the grave, whose finer spirits despised the worldly and the human and sought the abstract and the visionary, yet for lack of the broader concrete experience had often become narrow, superstitious and pedantic, whose coarser minds were rough, crude and self-centered, were suddenly confronted with a glorious active past and an unfathomable future in vast lands never before viewed by them. Thus men of the fifteenth and sixteenth centuries were furnished a tremendous impulse to activity, a desire to search out and to know all things. A nature which had hitherto seemed so unimportant and uninteresting now was full of new surprises which might stir the imagination and delight the fancy of the most ordinary person.

It is with such an individual for a companion as the freshly awakened man of the new era to whom the super-

---

[1] Hakluyt speaks of Herodotus, Strabo, Plutarch, Pliny and Solinus as well as a "great many of our new principall writers" as having reported strange things. Hakluyt, *op. cit.*, vol. i, p. liii.

stitions, the credulity and also the spiritual strivings of the Middle Ages continued to cling, but whose face was set toward the future, that we are to embark for many a long sea voyage. We must see the new sights with his eyes, feel his enthusiasms, hopes and disappointments, and realize what it all meant to the intellectual history of the age.

Reading the accounts of voyages and other works of the time which evince an interest in the New World seems to show that the impressions made upon the minds of contemporaries were substantially the following: some conception of the vastness of the new revelations, accompanied by an uncertainty as to what they might lead, and a very real sense of the dangers which confronted the discoverer; a feeling of wonder; a stimulus to courageous enterprise; enthusiasm, credulity, curiosity, scientific interest, philosophic speculation and deliberate calculation for future advantages.

No better example of the first impression mentioned can be cited than a poem,—probably the first written in English about America—entitled " A new interlude and a mery of the nature of the iiii elements," which was printed by John Rastell about 1519. In part it makes a navigator say:

> " Right farr, Syr, I have ridden and gone,
> And seen straunge thynges many one
>   In Affrick, Europe and Ynde;
> Both est and west I have ben farr,
> North also, and seen the sowth sterr
>   Bothe by see and lande.

>   .   .   .   .

> There lyeth Iselonde where men do fyshe,
> But beyonde that so colde it is
>   No man may there abyde.
> This see is called the Great Occyan;
> So great it is that never man

Coulde tell it sith the worlde began
Tyll nowe within this XX yere,
Westewarde be founde new landes
That we never harde tell of before this
By wrytynge nor other meanys.
Yet many nowe have ben there;
And that contrey is so large of rome,
Muche lenger then all Crestendome,
Without fable or gyle;
For dyvers maryners had it tryed,
And sayled streyght by the coste syde
Above V thousande myle!
But what commodytes be wythin,
No man can tell nor well imagin." [1]

Writing in a like spirit, Ralph Lane in a letter of 1585 to Richard Hakluyt says: " It is the goodliest and most pleasing Territorie of the world, for the continent is of a huge and unknown greatnesse.[2] . . . .

George Best, who had undertaken a voyage to the New World, expresses in a most vivid manner a realization of the perils of the ventures then being made:

How dangerous it is to attempt new Discoveries, either for length of the voyage, or the ignorance of the language, the want of Interpreters, new and unaccustomed Elements and ayres, strange and unsavoury meates, hugenesse of woods, dangerousnesse of Seas, dread of tempests, feare of hidden rockes, steepnesse of mountaines, darknesse of sudden falling fogges, continuall paines taking without any rest, and infinite others.[3]

In direct contrast he pictured the intellectual pleasure and profit derived from these enterprises:

[1] Justin Winsor, *Narrative and Critical History of America*, vol. iii, p. 16.

[2] Hakluyt, *op. cit.*, vol. viii, p. 319.

[3] *Ibid.*, vol. vii, p. 251. For another vivid account of the dangers of a voyage to Virginia, see Copeland's sermon, delivered April 18, 1622, in Neill, *Memoir of Rev. Patrick Copeland*, pp. iv, v.

How pleasant and profitable it is to attempt new Discoveries, either for the sundry sights and shapes of strange beastes and fishes, the wonderfull workes of nature, the different manners and fashions of divers nations, the sundry sorts of government, the sight of strange trees, fruite, foules, and beasts, the infinite treasure of Pearle, Golde and Silver, the newe founde landes, the sundry positions of the Sphere, and many others.[1]

Thus, after the first shock of the new revelation, had come a great enthusiasm and a devouring curiosity:

And although we everywhere feele his present Deitie yet the difference of heavenly climate and influence, causing such discording concord of dayes, nights, seasons; such varietie of meteors, elements, ailments; such noveltie in Beasts, Fishes, Fowles; such luxuriant plantie and admirable raritie of Trees, Shrubs, Hearbs; such fertilitie of soyle, insinuation of Seas, multiplicitie of Rivers, safetie of Ports, healthfulnesse of ayre, opportunities of habitation, materialls for action, objects for contemplation, haps in present, hopes of future, worlds of varietie in that diversified world; doe quicken our mindes to apprehend, whet our tongues to declare, and fill both with arguments of divine praise.[2]

" Both the imagination and the interest of men were stimulated.   Pictures of far away oceans, novel landscapes, strange races of astounding habits and features and faiths, boundless riches lying in some distant clime, flashed before the excited brains of the dwellers in the ' stout ' little isle." Mysteries which had long troubled humanity might perhaps now be solved.   Limitless hopes leading to infinite daring, cravings after power and mastery, intellectual as well as political. aspirations for the ideal, were aroused by the magnificent possibilities opened on every side.[3]

[1] Hakluyt, *op. cit.*, vol. vii, p. 251.
[2] " Virginia's Verger " (1625), in Purchas, *op. cit.*, vol. xix, p. 231.
[3] F. S. Boas, *Shakespeare and His Predecessors*, p. 41.

Such was the spirit breathed in the lines from " Tamburlaine " :

> " Nature that framed us of four elements,
> Warring within our breasts for regiment,
> Doth teach us all to have aspiring minds :
> Our Souls whose faculties can comprehend
> The wondrous architecture of the world,
> And measure every wandering planet's course
> Still climbing after knowledge infinite,
> And always moving as the restless spheres,
> Will us to wear ourselves, and never rest,
> Until we reach the ripest fruit of all,
> The perfect bliss and sole felicity,
> The sweet fruition of an earthly crown." [1]

" It is this same spirit which instills itself into Sir Thomas More's visions of a perfect society, Spenser's pattern of the highest manhood, Bacon's call to the conquest of all knowledge, and into the heroic deeds and speeches of Sidney, Gilbert and Granville." [2]

The imagination once aroused by new and unlooked-for splendors was unwilling for many a day to accept the ordinary and usual. All thought and interest, even in such commonplaces of daily life as dress, had to be of the most extravagant and varied sort. Versatility of interest and experience was the accepted token of human excellence. As a result, the Elizabethan age was not over critical of its information, so long as it was new and attractive. In fact, things that seemed unreal might, according to the reasoning of the time, well be believed. Spenser expresses this feeling when he justifies his " Land of Faerie " in the following lines :—

---

[1] Christopher Marlowe, " Tamburlaine the Great," pt. i, act ii, sc. vii, in *Marlowe's plays*, Mermaid Series (London, 1887).

[2] Boas, *op. cit.*, p. 141.

" But let that man with better sence advize,
That of the world least part to us is red:
And daily how through hardy enterprize
Many great regions are discovered,
Which to late age were never mentioned.
Who ever heard of th' Indian Peru?
Or who in venturous vessel measured
The Amazons huge river, now found trew?
Or fruitfullest Virginia who did ever view?

Yet all these were, when no man did ever them know,
Yet have from wisest ages hidden beene;
And later times thinges more unknowne shall show,
Why then should witlesse man so much misweene,
That nothing is, but that which he has seene?
What if within the moones fayre shining sphere,
What if in every other starre unseene
Of other worldes he happily should heare?
He wonder would much more; yet such to some appeare." [1]

With the knowledge thus suddenly forced upon them unorganized, with credulity often appearing wiser than experience, there was danger that Englishmen's minds, filled with the splendors of new revelations, should accept all as true. In reading the accounts of voyages and discoveries we meet with strange and interesting evidences of credulity scattered among many quite careful observations. One of the most interesting cases of this credulity was Sir Walter Raleigh's belief in the fabled city of Manoa. This scholar and valiant adventurer was completely bedazzled by tales of the golden city and the Emperor's palace, where

all the vessels of his house, table and kitchin were of gold and silver, and the meanest of silver and copper for strength and hardnesse of metall. He had in his wardrobe hollow statues of

---

[1] *The Complete Works of Edmund Spenser* (Cambridge edition), p. 23. Spenser was one of Raleigh's greatest friends, and lived near him in southern Ireland. He joined with Raleigh in his colonization schemes. Prowse, *op. cit.*, p. 54; Sidney Lee, *Great Englishmen of the XVIth Century*, p. 177.

gold which seemed giants, and the figures in proportion and bignesse of all the beasts, birds, trees, and hearbes, that the earth bringeth foorth: and of all the fishes that the sea or waters of his kingdome breedeth. He also had ropes, budgets, chestes and troughs of golde and silver, heapes of billets of gold, that seemed wood marked out to burne. Finally, there was nothing in his countrey, whereof he had not the counterfait in gold: Yea and they say, The Ingas had a garden of pleasure in an yland neere Puna, where they went to recreat themselves, and when they would take the aire of the Sea, which had all kinde of garden hearbs, flowers and trees of golde and silver, an invention, and magnificence till then never seene.[1]

Raleigh upon recounting and commenting upon this story says it may seem strange, yet when the many millions which were daily brought to Spain from Peru were considered, the account might well be believed.

Robert Thore, who proposed to Henry VII the organization of an expedition for the discovery of the northwest passage, furnishes an interesting evidence of the misconceptions of his time. He thought the expedition should proceed in a northwesterly direction until it reached the shores visited by John Cabot, and then sail northwards until it had passed out of the icy region into the warmer climate which he believed to be in the neighborhood of the North Pole.[2]

An account given of Sir Richard Hawkins' voyage to the "South Sea" in 1593 states that the heat of Africa caused sickness, which is most likely the truth, and shows correct observation in other respects; but immediately following says that the moon in hot countries was most prejudicial to one's health, for shining on a man's shoulder it caused sharp pains.[3] Thus a strange mingling of fact

[1] Hakluyt, *op. cit.*, vol. x, p. 357, *et seq.*
[2] Henry R. Fox-Bourne, *English Seamen under the Tudors*, vol. i, p. 84.
[3] Purchas, *op. cit.*, vol. xix, p. 231.

and superstition may be discovered, and that superstition was often accepted as truth. The rest of the account speaks of the various fruits to be found in the "South Sea" and shows a great deal of painstaking examination.

Another interesting narrative to study for the mingling of evidences of rather careful observation, credulity and preposterous rumor is that of a second voyage to Guinea made about 1554 by Captain John Lok. After speaking of people without heads who had their eyes and mouth in their breasts, and of satyrs "which have nothing of men but onely shape," he tells of a beast which they called "rhinocerotes." Later he dwells upon the climatic conditions in Africa and narrates how, instead of winter, "they have a cloudy and tempestuous season, yet it is not cold, but rather smoothering hote, with hote showers of raine also, and somewhere such scorching windes, that what by one meanes and other, they seeme at certaine times to live as it were in fornaces, and in maner already halfeway in Purgatorie or hell." He then mentions an account of Gemma Phrisius which asserts that, "in certaine parts of Africa, as in Atlas the greater, the aire in the night season is seene shining, with many strange fires and flames rising in manner as high as the Moone; and that in the element are sometimes heard, as it were, the sound of pipes, trumphets and drums." This shows that Lok had been reading what he could find on that part of the world, and was quite ready to consider and accept all sorts of strange tales. It is most likely that he received his ideas of satyrs, etc., from similar sources.

Mention is next made of sailors' tales, that they had felt a heat come from the beams of the moon. Lok thinks this may be reasonable, as Pliny wrote that the stars and the planets consisted of fire. He thinks that David, when he says in Psalm 121, "In the day the Sunne shall not burne thee, nor the Moon by night," affirms the fact that the moon gives out heat. The sailors told of seeing "certaine streames of water, which they call spouts, falling out of the aire into the sea," and some of these were "as bigge as the great pillars of Churches: insomuch that sometimes they fall into shippes." Some thought these were "Cataracts of heaven which were all opened at Noes floud." Lok, however, judges that they may be the same "fluxions and eruptions" as those which Aristotle wrote about.

The writer repeats a weird tale told him by Richard Chancellor concerning some adventures of Sebastian Cabot. When Cabot was near the coast of Brazil or Rio de la Plata, his ship was suddenly lifted from the sea and cast upon the land. Lok, to justify this strange story, remarks of this as well as other equally strange natural phenomena, when he takes into consideration "the narrownesse of man's understanding and knowledge, in comparison of her [i. e. nature's] mightier power," that he has to "confesse with Plinie, that nothing is to her [i. e. nature] impossible, the least part of whose power is not yet knowne to men." He further states there were many more things seen by his men which he had "thought good to put some in memory, that the reader may as well take pleasure in the variety of things, as knowledge of the historie." [1]

The account just given illustrates the manner in which the awakened and excited intellects of Englishmen went about the discovery of new facts. They observed, accepted tales and superstitions, although with wonder, were willing to believe nothing impossible, because all was so strange and marvelous, and yet sometimes they criticised. Their interest in the unusual and sensational is clearly shown, and there is apparent an intense craving for variety even at the expense of accuracy.

[1] Hakluyt, op. cit., vol. vi, p. 169, et seq.

The effect upon the imagination of the people of the time, amounting to nearly a mania for hearing tales of strange and unnatural creatures, and for viewing them with their own eyes, was a most marked influence of the discoveries. This popular craving naturally tended to encourage voyagers in their marvelous tales and in their production of new ' rarities ' for the popular gaze. Moreover the willingness of the people to believe could not help but be contagious, keeping credulity alive until the human mind, becoming satiated ever more and more with what at first appeared to be wonderful and unnatural, came to seek something still more marvelous. Thus many objects lost their first charm and were accepted as being, after all, merely a part of the real and the natural in the world about.

" Long before the Elizabethan period the inhabitants of strange lands were looked upon as beings, monstrous and brutal in every physical characteristic, and yet in some not clearly defined sense, human." [1] The Hungarians, for instance, who ravaged Germany, Italy and France in the ninth and tenth centuries were described by medieval chroniclers as " hideous boar-tusked child-devouring ogres." According to Marco Polo, the Andaman Islanders were " a most brutish, savage race, having heads, eyes and teeth resembling those of the canine species, cruel cannibals who ate human flesh raw, and devoured everyone on whom they could lay their hands." [2] Raleigh, in his account of Guiana, tells of Indians who " had the points of the shoulders higher than the crownes of their heads." [3] Such monstrous beings were afterwards referred to by Shakespeare

[1] Daniel Wilson, *Caliban the Missing Link*, p. 14.

[2] *Ibid.*

[3] Hakluyt, *op. cit.*, vol. x, pp. 437, 438.

in " The Tempest " and in " Othello." [1]   As late as 1625
the anonymous author of *Virginia's Verger,* calls the American Indians a

bad people, having little of Humanitie but shape, ignorant of
Civilitie, of Arts, of Religion; more brutish than the beasts they
hunt, more wild and unmanly than the unmanned wild Countrey, which they range rather than inhabite; captivated also to
Sathan's tyranny in foolish pieties, and bloody wickednesse . . .[2]

" For voyagers to return from the New World with
stories of its being peopled with human beings like themselves was actually at first a kind of blasphemy intolerable
to all honest Christians, because to assert that there were
inhabited lands on the opposite side of the globe would be
to maintain that there were nations not descended from
Adam, it being impossible for them to have passed the in-
tervening ocean, therefore they were inclined to refuse the
belief that human beings had been discovered in the Antipodes; while they welcomed at first the most monstrous
exaggerations about these little understood creatures." [3]

Let us now notice some of the creatures and objects
which at first appeared so wonderful to Englishmen.   By
the seventeenth century Indians and curious fishes and
crocodiles seem to have been singularly numerous in London, and crowds were attracted from all parts of the country to see them.[4]   Many marvels were related of them.

---

[1] *The Tempest,* Act iii, sc. 3; *Othello,* Act i, sc. 3.

[2] Purchas, *op. cit.,* vol. xix, p. 231.

[3] Wilson, *op. cit.,* pp. 70, 71.

[4] Frobisher on his first voyage carried home three or four savages.
Indians were also brought to England in the expeditions which went
to various parts of America, in the years 1605, 1611, 1614; and when
settlements in Virginia became established, they came to be still better
known in England.   Nathan Drake, " *Shakespeare and His Times,*" vol.
i, p. 387; Karl Elze, " *Essays on Shakespeare,*" (translated by L. Dora
Schmitz), p. 17; Rye, *op. cit.,* p. 205.

Curious fishes seemed to have aroused their share of popular interest. In 1578 Frobisher's crew found " a strange fish dead, that had been caste from the sea on the shore, who had a boane in his head like a unicorn, which they brought away and presented to the prince, when they came home." In 1586 on a voyage to the South Sea there was encountered " a great foule monster, whose head and back were so hard that no sword could enter it: but being thrust in under the belly in divers places, and much wounded, hee bowed a sword in his mouth, as a man would do a girdle of leather about his hande, and likewise the yron of a boare speare. He was in length about nine foot, and had nothing in his belly, but a certain quantitie of small stones." In the Stationer's Books of the year 1604 an account was printed of a monstrous fish, that appeared in the form of a woman from the waist upward, while in the office book of the Master of the Revels is the entry on September 3, 1632 of a license to James Leale to show a strange fish for half a year. The records of London exhibitions and the chronicles of Bartholomew and of other fairs give evidence that a succession of these favorite shows was held.[1]

The popular craving for exhibitions of unusual creatures furnished a chance for ridicule to the dramatists of the time. Shakespeare pictures Trinculo, upon discovering Caliban extended on the ground, and supposing him to be a species of fish, as remarking: " Were I in England now, as once I was, and had but this fish painted, not a holiday fool there but would give a piece of silver: there would this monster make a man; any strange beast there makes a man; when

---

[1] Drake, *op. cit.*, vol. i, p. 388; Chambers, *The Book of Days*, vol. ii, p. 311; Hakluyt, vol. xi, p. 206. That the highest society was interested in the new " rarieties " is shown by the fact that Captain Weddell brought from the Indies a leopard for Charles I, and a cage of birds for the queen. *Cal. of S. P. Col. Series, E. I.* (1630-34), p. 153.

they will not give a doit to relieve a lame beggar, they will lay out ten to see a dead Indian." [1]

In the " City Match " of Jasper Mayne, a set of knaves are described as hanging out the picture of a strange fish which they affirm is the fifth they have shown, and the following dialogue takes place regarding the sign which advertised the monster's presence:

> " Holland—Pray, can you read that Sir? I warrant
> That tells where it was caught, and what fish 'tis.
>
> " Potwell—Within this place is to be seen,
> A wondrous fish, God save—the Queen.
>
> " Holland—Amen! She is my customer, and I
> Have sold her bone-lace often.
>
> " Bright—Why the Queen? 'Tis writ the King.
>
> " Potwell—That was to make the rhyme.
>
> " Bright—'Slid thou didst read it as 'twere some picture of
> An Elizabeth fish." [2]

The larger part of the curiosity of the earlier period was quite unscientific, but it was at any rate an advance when interest was shown and when an attempt was made to discover all the facts possible about the new lands. The very voyages of discovery could not help but force men to regard as ridiculous many of their preconceived notions and beliefs concerning ccsmography, history and natural phenomena.

Thus from the first the appearance of a new continent proved of great value in promoting a search for the natural causes of things. As Humboldt remarks: " Never before since the establishment of society had the sphere of ideas relative to the exterior world been increased in a manner so

[1] *The Tempest*, Act. ii, sc. 2.

[2] *Ancient British Drama*, vol. ii, p. 377, *et seq.*

prodigious; never had man felt a·more pressing need to observe Nature, and to multiply the means of successfully questioning it." [1]

A vast coast line was offered to sailors by the new lands, and the boundless seas presented many problems which had to be solved regarding the tides and the winds. The new families of vegetables and quadrupeds hitherto unknown proved of great interest to naturalists, while immense chains of mountains, rich in precious metals, drew the attention of geographers. The philosopher on his part might contemplate a race of men of different temperaments, manners and languages from those of Europe.

One is impressed with the fact that Sir Francis Bacon must have been greatly inspired and encouraged in his search after knowledge which lay all around him in the universe, by the contrasts and comparisons, the phenomena and the natural problems afforded by the New World. Moreover, the general attitude of curiosity, of interest in the world about, rather than in the spiritual realities, or in the far distant past, lent him the sympathy of the people of his time, which his predecessors had not possessed.

It is apparent on glancing over Bacon's inquiries about the New World, that he had read extensively the accounts of the voyages of his time and was filled with their wonder as well as his own scientific interest concerning the puzzling natural problems presented by the New World. He particularly comments upon Acosta's statements concerning the trade winds constantly blowing from the East to the West; the manner in which the breezes carry the perfumed air from the Florida coasts, and the inhabitants of Canada perceive the cold from the icebergs which break loose and float about the northern ocean and are finally

---

[1] Alexander von Humboldt, "Histoire de la Géographie du Nouveau Continent," *Oeuvres*, vol. i, p. 3.

borne toward their shores; the conflicting or according
phenomena of the tides on the coasts of Florida, Africa and
Spain.   Mankind, not less than nature, draws his attention.
Was it the heat of the sun which made the African negro
black?   If so, why were not glass blowers who work where
the heat is intense made dark-complexioned?   Was the
practice of painting the skin practiced by the American Indians connected at all with their extraordinary longevity? [1]

Here and there through the narratives of the voyages
one feels the desire of the author to know more of the why
and the wherefore.   Still more these queries must have
presented themselves to the thoughtful reader of these
accounts as they had done to Bacon, but to him was given
the task of speaking the words and forming the ideal of
scientific research which bore fruit later in the seventeenth
century.

Richard Hakluyt was another who certainly displayed
the scientific spirit that had been aroused by interest in the
New World.   He tells how as a youth, he resolved that,
if he ever went to a university, he would make a careful
study of geography and the accounts of voyagers.   True
to his resolution, he gradually read " whatsoever printed
or written discoveries and voyages " he could find, " either
in the Greeke, Latine, Italian, Spanish, Portugall, French
or English languages."   He " produced and showed both
the olde imperfectly composed, and the new lately reformed
Mappes, Globes, Spheares and other instruments of this
art of demonstration in the common schooles."   He grew
acquainted with " the chiefest captaines at sea, the greatest

---

[1] *The Works of Francis Bacon*, vol. ii, pp. 472, 473; vol. iv, pp. 181,
207; vol. v, 147, 151, 152.   *Cambridge Modern History*, vol. i, p. 63.
Bacon was a shareholder in Guy's plantation in Newfoundland, thus
having material as well as intellectual interests in America.   Prowse,
op. cit., p. 54.

Merchants, and the best Mariners," and in this way obtained
" more than common knowledge." He later went to France
in connection with the British embassy and there continued
his studies.

Hakluyt was stirred by the exploits of foreign navigators,
and was so aroused by the taunts he heard concerning the
" sluggish security " of the English and their " continuall
neglect of the like attempts," that he resolved to undertake
the collecting and publishing of the accounts of the exploits
of his own nation on the seas. This was a great task, as
the records of the voyages " lay so dispersed, scattered and
hidden in severall hucksters' hands." He tells of the " restlesse nights," "painefull dayes," " the many long and
chargeable journeys " undertaken, and the large numbers of
famous libraries he had searched, where he had perused a
great variety of ancient and modern writers. His whole
life was spent in this, to him, entrancing work.[1]

Hakluyt's attitude furnishes an excellent example of men
who were aroused by the newly awakened knowledge of the
great world which was day by day being revealed. According to his own words, the objects which drew his particular interest were " beastes, birds, fishes, serpants, plants,
fruit, hearbes, rootes, apparell, armour, boates " and other
" rare and strange curiosities." [2] Although his main interest may have been to promote natural history, geography
and navigation, he likewise strove to arouse his countrymen
to the opportunities afforded by the new lands for the advancement of the commerce and industry of England and
the relief of social conditions. According to his opinion,
it is the story of man's travels which gives us complete
knowledge of the world.[3]

[1] Hakluyt, *op. cit.*, vol. i, pp. xvii, xxxix.

[2] Hakluyt, *op. cit.*, vol. i, p. xxx.

[3] *The Cambridge History of English Literature*, vol. iv, p. 96.

Bacon and Hakluyt had led the way, and by 1645 a number of persons residing in London were so interested in the natural and new experimental philosophy which the former had promoted, and in the problems presented by an unknown continent, that they agreed to meet weekly to discuss such things. In this way the idea of " Salomon's House " of " The New Atlantis " [1] was realized, for this gathering developed into the famous Royal Society of London.[2]

One of the earliest undertakings of the Society was the drawing up of a list of things upon which it desired to be informed. A committee to consider suitable questions was appointed as early as 1661. From published accounts of the new lands queries were compiled and were given to ship captains or to travelers who were to obtain accurate information. Seamen bound for the West Indies and on other far voyages received special directions as to geographical, meteorological, astronomical and other observations. These were prepared and printed as early as 1666. The Master of Trinity House had the duty of supplying the masters of ships and others who kept diaries with these helpful suggestions. One copy of the voyager's observations was to be sent to the Lord High Admiral and another to Trinity House, where it might be examined by the Royal Society. Such inquiries as those just mentioned were prepared in 1663 for John Winthrop upon his return to New England, another in 1667 for Virginia and the Bermudas, again for Virginia in 1669, queries for Greenland in 1662, 1663, and in 1668 for Hudson Bay and the Antilles.[3]

---

[1] *Infra*, p. 260.

[2] Thomas Birch, *The History of the Royal Society of London*, p. 10; Martha Ornstein, *The Rôle of Scientific Societies in the Seventeenth Century*, pp. 55, 56 (Columbia University Studies in History, Economics and Public Law).

[3] C. M. Andrews and F. G. Davenport, *Guide to the Manuscript Ma-*

That " Plinylike " gentleman and prominent member of the Royal Society, John Evelyn, writing to a Mr. London, who was travelling in Barbados, in September 27, 1681, ends his letter in this manner:

Sr, the Royal Society have lately put their Repositorie into an excellent method, and it every day encreases, thro' the favour and benevolence of sundry benefactors, whose names are gratefully recorded. If any thing incurr to you of curious (as certainly there daily do, innumerable) you will greatly oblige that assembly of virtuosi in communicating any productions of the places you travelled thro' upon the occasion of the returne of vessells from these parts. The particulars they collect are animals, and insects of all sorts, their skins, and sceletons, fruits, stones, shells, swords, gunnes, minerals, and whatever nature produces in her vast and comprehensive bosome.[1]

These collections appear not merely to have been made by the Royal Society, but wealthy and fashionable people. were quite eager to procure all sorts of " rarities " somewhat, perhaps, in the manner that the modern millionaire makes his art collections. In 1686 Evelyn mentions going to see the " rarities " of one Mr. Charleton:

Who shewed us such a collection as I had never seene in all my travels abroad, either of private gentlemen or princes. It consisted of minatures, drawings, shells, insects, medailes, natural things, animals (of which divers, I think 100, were kept in glasses of spirits of wine), minerals, precious stones, vessells, curiosities in amber, christal, achat, etc., all being very perfect and rare of their kind, especially his bookes of birds, fish, flowers, and shells, drawn and miniatured to the life.

terial for the History of the United States to 1783, in the British Museum, in Minor London Archives, and in the Libraries of Oxford and Cambridge, p. 356.

[1] " Private Correspondence," in *Memoirs*, vol. iv, p. 253.

This collection was afterward purchased by Sir Hans Sloane, and now forms part of the British Museum.[1]

James Petiver, living in the latter part of the seventeenth century, although a man of little means, was also an ardent collector and writer. His chief interest was botany. He not only gathered English plants but also through the help of others, secured a vast number of specimens from foreign countries. He carried on an extensive correspondence with people abroad, exchanging " rarities " with them from time to time. Besides, he employed captains and doctors of ships to bring home the seeds of plants, birds, stuffed animals, insects, as well as botanical specimens, " giving them careful printed directions and such information as enabled them to choose and select the most desirable objects for collections." Sir Hans Sloane sometime before Petiver's death is said to have offered him £1,000 for his museum. He afterward secured the collection. Petiver between 1697 and 1717 wrote more than twenty papers which may be found in the *Philosophical Transactions* of the Royal Society. These dealt with such diverse matters as Guinea, Madras and Maryland plants, minerals and shells, insects and corals from various parts of the world.[2]

Sir Hans Sloane, whose collections constituted the origin of the British Museum, in 1687 sailed for Jamaica and remained there sixteen months, when he returned with eight hundred species of plants and commenced publishing his *Catalogus Plantarum quae in Insula Jamaica sponte proveniunt aut valga culuntur.* Twenty years after that date his natural history collection comprised 8,226 specimens in botany alone, besides 200 volumes of dried samples of plants.[3] The influence which such collections must have had in promoting natural science may readily be seen.

[1] Evelyn, Private Correspondence, in *Memoirs*, vol. iii, p. 219.
[2] G. L. Apperson, *Bygone London Life, etc.*, p. 98, *et seq.*
[3] Chambers, vol. i, p. 92.

The botanical or "physic" gardens were another means of preserving rare and hitherto unknown plants. Beginning with the sixteenth century, many public as well as private gardens of this sort were formed. The first botanical garden in England is said to have been that near John Gerard's house in Holborn. This soon became a center of scientific investigation. Gerard, like Hakluyt and Bacon, had early become interested in the new commodities which were constantly being brought to England by the voyages. He had been particularly impressed by Raleigh's collection of plants, which had caused so much interest at the time that the noted scholar, Clusius, had come from Europe to see it. Lord Hunsdon, who had procured many "rare and strange things from the fartherest parts of the earth," and Lord Zouch, who brought seeds and plants from Constantinople, still further excited his emulation. He became anxious to study for himself the growth and qualities of the many plants first made known to Englishmen by the translations of Monardes' *History of Drugs Brought from America* and the similar book written by Garcia ab Horto on those of the Orient.[1] Consequently, he began to form a garden which should contain all the new species of plants he possibly could secure. Descriptions of them were incorporated in his famous herbal, which was so instrumental in arousing popular interest in the cultivation and study of plants that he has been called "the Father of English gardening."[2] So successful was he in his collection that he is said to have secured 1100 species of plants both native and exotic. Dr. Baker, Queen Elizabeth's physician, writes of Gerard and his garden that

[1] Richard Pulteney, *Historical and Biographical Sketches on the Progress of Botany in England, etc.*, pp. 114, 116, 125; J. R. Green, *A History of Botany in the United Kingdom, etc.*, p. 38.

[2] Green, *op. cit.*, p. 40.

Upon his proper cost and charges he hath had out of all parts
of the world all the rare simples which by any means he could
attain to, not only to have them brought, but hath procured by
his excellent knowledge to have them growing in his garden,
which as the time of yeere doth serve may be seen; for there
you shall see all manner of strange trees, herbs, roots, plants,
flowers, and other rare things that it would make a man wonder
how one of his degree could ever accomplish the same.

Plants and seeds came to Gerard in London from nearly all
the known world.   These he obtained from ship-captains
and travelers and on one occasion, even sent his servant,
William Marshall, as surgeon on one of the ships going to
the Levant in order that he might secure some species of
rare Eastern plants for his collection.[1]   Other herbalists
soon followed Gerard's example.   Among these Parkinson
constructed his " garden of pleasant flowers," containing a
splendid collection of flora from all parts of the world,
particularly from America and the Levant, upon which he
based his *Paradisus,* or flower book, that had much to do
with familiarizing gardeners with exotic varieties.[2]   The
earliest public botanical garden was opened at Oxford in
1621, following a gift of £5250 by the Earl of Danby, and
proved of considerable influence on the development of
science.   The gardens served as centers of study and research, much as botanical laboratories of the present time
do.   Robert Morrison, who was one of the first Englishmen to write a systematic botany, was given charge of this
garden in 1669, and was instructed to give a course in
botany there.[3]   Evelyn speaks of going to visit it and of

---

[1] Green, *op. cit.,* pp. 35, 36.

[2] *Ibid.,* p. 49. Parkinson was also the author of an extensive herbal.

[3] *Ibid.,* pp. 54, 55; J. C. F. Hoefer, *Histoire de la Botanique, de la Minéralogie et de la Géologie,* p. 152.

seeing two large locust trees, plantain trees and some rare plants there. He also mentions visiting similar gardens at Westminster and Chelsea.[1] These were founded by the Apothecaries' Company for medical purposes, but the Company went far beyond this and sought to encourage botany in its widest sense, and particularly the cultivation and study of exotic plants brought from beyond the seas.[2] It was this same Chelsea Garden to which Sir Joseph Banks presented more than five hundred different kinds of seeds he had collected on his voyage around the world.[3]

Collections of living animals also appear to have been made as the beginning of zoological gardens; for Evelyn, in 1684, tells of going with Sir William Godolphin to see a rhinoceros or " unicorn," being the first that he supposed was ever brought to England. He further relates that it belonged to some East India merchants and was sold for above £2,000. He likewise mentions seeing a crocodile which was brought from some of the West India Islands.[4]

Many of the prominent men of the Restoration period were greatly absorbed in the study of these new " rarities " and everything pertaining to natural and physical science. Even those who were busiest and held important positions found time for experimentation. It was the age of Newton. Halley and Boyle. King Charles II had his own private laboratory at Whitehall and he even expected the East India Company to supply him with Arabic and Persian manuscripts.[5] Evelyn was so zealous in these studies that he

[1] Evelyn's Diary, June 10, 1658, August 7, 1685, in *Memoirs*, vol. ii, p. 135; vol. iii, p. 219.

[2] Green, *op. cit.*, p. 149.

[3] Phillips, *History of Cultivated Vegetables*, vol. i, pp. 11, 13, 16.

[4] " Diary," Oct. 22, 1684, in *Memoirs*, vol. iii, p. 119.

[5] *Cal. S. P. Col. Series, E. I.* (1630-34), pp. 523, 623; Macaulay, *op. cit.*, vol. i, p. 376.

injured his eyes by " too intently poring upon a famous eclipse of the sun.[1]

Sir Thomas Browne's *Pseudodoxia Epidemica or Enquiries into very many received tenets and commonly presumed truths, which Examined prove but Vulgar and Common Errors,"* first published in 1646, is one evidence at least of how the critical and scientific spirit aroused by the oversea discoveries was beginning to assert itself during this century. Lord Bacon, years before, had expressed his belief in the value of doubts, falsehood and popular errors. He had said that from their love of truth, men became so anxious to possess it, that they were altogether too ready to imagine themselves " enriched by the possession of counterfeit, instead of real coin." It would, therefore, be of advantage to search out the common errors and make them known.[2]

Browne realized that his task would be difficult and largely original, for he remarked: " We hope that it will not be unconsidered that we find no open tract or constant manuduction in this labyrinth, but are ofttimes fain to wander in the America and untraveled parts of truth." [3] To Browne the New World evidently presented a vast fund of unknown facts, of which many erroneous notions might be held. He conceived as causes of error the infirmity of human nature, the erroneous disposition of the people, false deduction, credulity and obstinate adherence to antiquity:

Men impose a thraldom on their times. . . . Men that adore times past consider not that those times were once present, that

[1] *Memoirs*, vol. iv, p. 200.

[2] *Sir Thomas Browne's Works*, edited by Simon Wilkin (London, 1852), editor's preface, p. lxxxii.

[3] *Ibid.*, vol. i, p. 3.

is, as our own at this instant; and we ourselves unto those to come, as they at present; as we rely on them, even so will those on us, and magnify us hereafter, who at present condemn ourselves.[1]

Browne points out that the works of the ancients often contained fabulous statements:

For they, indeed, have not only been imperfect in the conceit of some things, but either ignorant or erroneous in many more. They understood not the motion of the eighth sphere from west to east, and so conceived the longitude of the stars invariable. They conceived the Torrid Zone unhabitable, and so made frustrate the goodliest part of the earth. But we now know 'tis very well empeopled, and the habitation thereof esteemed so happy, that some have made it the proper seat of Paradise; and been so far from judging it unhabitable, that they have made it the first habitation of all. Many of the ancients denied the Antipodes, and some unto the penalty of contrary affirmations; but the experience of our enlarged navigations can not assert them beyond all dubitation. Having thus totally relinquished them in some things, it may not be presumptuous to examine them in others; but surely most unreasonable to adhere to them in all, as though they were infallible or could not err in any.[2]

With this glance into the spirit of the times, it is evident that it was an age of beginnings of things scientific. The foundations were being laid upon which the real science was to rest. The genius which with time was to become truly scientific, and was then commencing to have some of its attributes, had been aroused largely through that spirit of curiosity and eager searching, or in other words, as Payne phrases it, " that dead lift " which the discoveries in the new

[1] *Memoirs*, vol. i, p. 40.
[2] *Works*, vol. i, pp. 40, 50.

lands gave to the human intellect. As was noticed above, numerous inquiries and questionings about the new " rari-ties " and curiosities were being made. The very words " rarities " and " curiosities " imply that there was still lack of scientific knowledge about them, that they were still to be regarded as something which was not completely un-derstood, that new facts about them might later be dis-covered. Ideas were not suddenly changed by the great reve-lations of what lay overseas. The collections, which many, not only in England but throughout Europe, were busy gathering, were not yet well classified and arranged for study. Indeed, one difficulty to be met then, as now, in going through accounts of the earlier of these collections was the great disorder in the nomenclature of the subject. It was so impossible to determine with certainty the plants spoken of by preceding writers, that thirty or fifty different botanists had given to the same plant almost as many differ-ent names. However, by the period after the Restoration, much improvement apparently had been made, and some-what systematic classifications of plants and other objects of scientific interest appeared in great numbers.[1] So, too, illustrations and sketches of such objects in books on botany, zoology, geography, etc. were often poor. Evelyn writing to a prospective author, advises him to make care-ful illustrations, and says that he mentions it because

most of those authors [especially English] who have given us their relations, fill them with such lame and imperfect draughts and pictures, as are rather a disgrace than ornament to their books, they having no talent that way themselves, and taking no course to procure such as can designe.[2]

[1] William Whewell, *History of the Inductive Sciences from the Earliest to the Present Time*, vol. ii, p. 381, *et seq.*

[2] Correspondence, in *Memoirs*, vol. iv, p. 254.

During part of the seventeenth century progress in almost all the sciences became necessarily languid for a while. The wars and other political troubles that disturbed almost the whole of Europe, and in England the quarrels of Charles I and his Parliament, the Civil Wars and the Commonwealth, left men neither leisure nor disposition to direct their best thoughts to the promotion of science. The baser spirits were brutalized; the better were occupied with high practical aims and struggles of a moral nature.

Soon after the Restoration of the Stuarts, however, came a period of greater tranquility when attention could once more be occupied by the quest of knowledge. Thus in the Elizabethan Age appeared much of the inspiration, the new outlook on the world and a highly aroused curiosity, which promoted the first rudiments of modern scientific knowledge. Then came the period of relapse, when although facts were constantly being collected from the New World, scientific advance was at more of a standstill. This was followed by a bound of the minds of Englishmen to the facts which were collected. This was accompanied by the development of an eager spirit to know further details, this time more systematic and scientific, as the information had gradually widened and new problems suggested by the discoveries were investigated. The craving for the novel still remained, but now it took more the form of seeking the novel in the actual, ascertained facts.[1] Experimentation had advanced and had become the fad of the age. Criticism

[1] " It was almost necessary to the character of a fine gentleman to have something to say about air pumps and telescopes; and even fine ladies, now and then, thought it becoming to affect a taste for science, went in coaches and six to visit the Gresham curiosities and broke into cries of delight at finding that a magnet really attracted a needle, and that a microscope really made a fly look as large as a sparrow." Macaulay, *op. cit.*, vol. i, p. 376.

as has been seen was alive; and when with the closing years
of the century, there began to be a study of statistics by
such able scholars as Petty, Child, King and Davenant, the
era of accurate information opened, and science built upon
collection, experimentation, criticism, accurate mathematical
measurement and statistics, began to be known.

CHAPTER IX

Thought (continued).

Special branches of science affected by activities over-seas were medicine, navigation, geography, history and political economy. The new herbs and drugs found in America and the Far East as well as the enlarged store of old ones,[1] and the contact of Europeans with Eastern physicians, undoubtedly promoted the use of medicine in some cases in the place of blood-letting so generally employed at this time as a remedy. In the words of an eighteenth century writer: "Every new discovery, every new plantation, every new branch of trade furnisheth some new thing, some rarity in nature, some specific in physic for the relief of a distempered world, which lay hid till navigation carried us to America."[2]

The usual method of introducing the new drug was to bring its seeds, roots. or even in some cases the plant or shrub itself, and plant them in a botanical garden, hot-bed or green-house where, under careful attention, they might develop. Here they could be watched and studied, and experiments made of their virtues. William Harrison, in his

[1] Those from China, Persia, India and the Levant which had formerly reached Europe in small quantities were now made available for common use; others became known for the first time. Nearly all that came from America belonged to this latter class.

[2] *Collection of Voyages and Travels from the Library of the Earl of Oxford, printed for Thomas Osborne* (London. 1745-47), Introductory discourse, p. 1.

Description of England, tells how nearly every nobleman or
merchant in England in his day was interested in growing
medical herbs from other lands. He claims to have seen
as many as three or four hundred in one garden, "halfe of
whose names within forty years passed we had no maner
knowledge." He himself had a garden in which there were
about three hundred kinds.[1]

Some idea as to the quantity of new drugs brought to
England from the Orient in the sixteenth century may be
gained from the book of the Portuguese doctor to the
viceroy of India, Garcia ab Horto, or Garcie du Jardin, as
he is known to French authors. In his *History of Certain
Plants from the Indies,* written during the sixteenth century,
and made available in Latin to English scholars about 1567,
he mentions and describes about forty species of drugs
that had been introduced from the East.[2] Nicholas Monardes, a Spanish physician, whose work was translated into
English in 1576, and eagerly read and referred to as an
authority, mentions about seventy-four new kinds of drugs
from America.[3] About the middle of the next century, Jacob
Bobart's *Catalogus Plantarum Horti Medici Oxoniensis,*
published in 1648, stated that a thousand exotic simples were
cultivated in the Oxford physic-garden, and only six
hundred English species.[4]

Among the more important medical plants from America
or the East cultivated in England before the eighteenth

[1] Harrison, *op. cit.,* pt. i, bk. 2, vol. i, p. 326.

[2] Garcia ab Horto, "Histoire de quelques plantes des Indes," *passim,*
in Antoine Colin, *Histoire des Drogues, Epiceries, et de Certaines
Medicamens Simples qui Naissent des Indes en Amérique* (Lyons,
1619), pp. 305, *et seq.*

[3] Nicholas Monardes, "Histoire des Simples Medicamens apportés
de l'Amérique," *passim,* in Colin, *op. cit.,* pp. 1-305.

[4] Green, *op. cit.,* p. 56.

century, the *Hortus Kewensis* mentions as grown in English gardens at the following dates: the castor-oil plant and capsicum (1548); the tamarind (1633); sarsaparilla (1664); sassafras (1633); guaiacum or lignum vitae [1] (1691); Virginia and two-leaved night-shade (1662 and 1699); dwarf cassia [2] (1699); myrobalan plum (before 1629); wild senna (1693); round-podded cassia (1658); horehound (1596); the aloe (1596); and colchicum or broad-leaved meadow saffron (1629). [3] Fistinuts from Persia, Arabia, Syria and India, balsam from both Indies and balm from America, mentioned by Gerard, were also imported as drugs. [4]

Of all the medicines discovered during this period probably the most famous was the quina, cinchona, Peruvian or Jesuits' bark from which quinine is made. Although found in Peru possibly as early as 1535, [5] its virtues did not become conspicuously known until 1638, when the Countess of Chinchon, wife of the Spanish viceroy, was cured of fever through its efficiency. When she returned to Spain in 1640, she took a large amount of the precious bark with her. Dr. Juan de la Vega, the physician of the Countess, followed soon after bringing a further supply. The drug used came

---

[1] Sassafras root as a commodity was imported much earlier. *Supra,* p. 71. Thomas Harriot says that it possessed "most rare vertues in physicke for the cure of many diseases," and that it was found "by experience to be far better and of more uses then the wood which is called Guaiacum, or Lignum vitae." Hakluyt, vol. viii. p. 355.

[2] Parkinson says that, although cassia grew in Egypt and was first procured in Syria and Armenia, most of the drug used in Europe was brought from the West Indies. *Theatrum Botanicum,* p. 235.

[3] Aiton, *op. cit.,* vol. i, pp. 397, 402, 404, 405; vol. ii, pp. 292, 329, 430; vol. iii, pp. 29, 33, 199, 296; vol. iv, p. 123; vol. v, pp. 331, 388.

[4] Gerard, *op. cit.,* pp. 1436, 1527-1529.

[5] Phillips, *History of Cultivated Vegetables,* vol. ii, p. 114.

to be known as the Countess of Chinchon's powders.[1]
Knowledge of it appears to have been disseminated through
Europe by Jesuits. It was sent by their numerous repre-
sentatives in South America to the general of the order at
Rome, and by him dispatched to the Jesuits in Europe at
large.[2] In England possibly the earliest reference to the
use of Peruvian bark was contained in a prescription of
1694.[3]

In no respect was European credulity and the desire to
find all the possible uses a new article might have more in
evidence than in the case of drugs. Herbalists, following
the example of antiquity, attempted above everything else to
discover what medicinal virtues a new plant might possess,
and these were valued more or less proportionately. Hence
the qualities of an unfamiliar herb were very frequently
exaggerated, and where some of its species had been known
by the ancient writers the mythological and astrological
conceptions concerning it which had been handed down were
currently accepted.[4] In the same way the eager student
was all too free to take for granted the tales of voyagers
about the virtues of exotics. Harrison, speaking of the great
credit which was given to compound medicines made with
foreign drugs, exclaims in disgust:

How doo men extoll the use of tobacco in my time, whereas

---

[1] Clements R. Markham, *A Memoir of the Lady Ana de Osorio,
Countess of Chinchon and Vice-Quéen of Peru*, pp. 40, 44, 45, 73.

[2] J. Dronke, "Die Verpflanzung des Fieberrindenbaumes aus seiner
süd amerikanischen Heimat nach Asien und anderen Ländern," in
Abhandlungen der K. K. Geographischen Gesellschaft in Wien, vol.
iv, p. 8.

[3] *The Philosophical Transactions of the Royal Society of London* . . .
to 1800, etc., abridged by Charles Hutton, G. Shaw and R. Peason
(London, 1809), vol. iii, p. 602.

[4] Green, p. 58; Julius von Sachs. *History of Botany, 1530-60*, translated by H. E. F. Garnsey, p. 3.

in truth (whether the cause be in the repugnancie of our constitution or to the operation thereof, or that the ground dooth alter hir force, I cannot tell) it is not found of so great efficacie as they write. . . . I could exemplifie after the like manner in sundrie other, as the salsaparilla, mochoocan, etc.[1]

The large number of new plants and herbs not only stimulated curiosity and credulity, but awakened interest in the study of medicine and led to the employment of many new drugs, and in the end to careful observation. Even during the earlier period of the discoveries, the very criticisms made by contemporary authors showed the beginning at least of a modern science. Thus, Burton for example says: " We are careless of that which is near us, and follow that which is afar off, to know which we will travel and sail beyond the seas, wholly neglecting that which is under our eyes." [2] Le Compte, the traveler, likewise mentions the tendency of Europeans to exaggerate the virtues of new substances. Speaking of tea, he says there were divers opinions concerning it; while some ascribe marvelous qualities to it, " others hold these virtues to be mere fancy and whim of Europeans who always love novelties, and admire what they do not understand." [3] Moreover, during the century under consideration herbals of distinctive merit were written, in which special attention was paid to the medicinal virtues of plants, and the gardens where exotic plants were grown were maintained to a large extent so that students might be better informed about new drugs.[4]

[1] Harrison, pt. i, bk. 2, p. 326.

[2] Robert Burton, *The Anatomy of Melancholy* (New York, 1889), vol. ii, p. 353.

[3] Harris, *op. cit.*, vol. ii, p. 508.

[4] Burton, *op. cit.*, vol. ii, p. 354. It is stated that the Oxford garden was founded " for a nursery of simples, and that a Professor of Botanicey should read there, and show the use and virtue of them to his auditors." Green, *op. cit.*, p. 55.

In the accounts of the voyages of the sixteenth and seventeenth centuries there are some careful observations regarding the use of drugs and the causes of sickness; for instance as early as 1572 certain diseases were attributed to the mosquito. It was said that Vera Cruz was "inclined to many kind of diseases by reason of the great heat, and a certaine gnat or flie which they call a mosquito, which biteth both man and woman in their sleep." [1] Moreover, the new voyages led to the study of tropical diseases and remedies to be employed for them. Hakluyt, in the dedication of the third volume of his voyages in 1600 to Sir Robert Cecil, speaks of a short treatise which he had in his library touching " The curing of hot diseases incident to travellers in long and Southern voyages," written by a George Watson. This, however, was defective, and a certain Dr. Gilbert had promised that the whole College of Physicians would cooperate and produce something authoritative "on the diseases of hot and cold regions." [2] Again, under the influence of the Levant Company, whose " great men not only contributed to England's commercial success, but embellished English literature with admirable studies, both of the past and the present," [3] special study was made of the plague, and *Russel on the Plague* was quite a standard work of its time. It was through the efforts of these men that the gradual diminution and eventual eradication of the malady were due. [4]

[1] Hakluyt, *op. cit.*, vol. ix, p. 379.

[2] *Ibid.*, vol. xii, p. 81.

[3] Montague, Covel and Pococke gave some of the earliest accounts in the English language of the people of the East. Under the Company's influence considerable attention was paid to archaeology. Sir Paul Ricaut and Sir James Porter wrote admirable works on the policy and government of the Turkish people. *Ibid.*

[4] *Ibid.*

With the discovery of America much attention, as a result of expanding commerce, was necessarily paid to the study of meteorology, ocean currents and trade winds, in their bearing upon navigation. In England attention was focused upon the possibility of getting to Asia by another and shorter route than that used by the Spanish and Portuguese.[1] This led to constant search and a careful study of the northern oceans, and the conditions which existed there. England's first great discoverers, the Cabots, had their theories regarding the "north west passage;" while other English navigators like Chancellor and Willoughby, had their ideas about the "north east passage." John Cabot, because of his knowledge that Eastern spices passed through many hands, thought that Cathay must be near the west. Upon making his voyage along the American coast he noticed that the ocean current moved westward, though more gently than those of the Spanish seas to the southward. From this he inferred that there must be an opening from the east to the west through which the waters passed.[2]

Sir Humphrey Gilbert appears to have made a most careful study of the ancient writers and accounts of the Elizabethan voyagers. This led him to the conclusion that America was an island with a great sea lying between it and Cathay. An examination of this belief proves how logical his proofs for this opinion must have appeared to the men of his time, and also illustrates the arguments on the sub-

[1] The respect which Englishmen for some time felt for these nations' rights, the chance of a shorter passage to India and therefore cheaper freights, the opportunity of settling England's needy in new lands of temperate climate, and the disposal of English manufactures to the colonists and aborigines, thus lessening the effect of such large exportations of bullion to the East, were all reasons for the discovery of this passage, which forcefully appealed to the Englishman's practical mind. G. E. Weare, *Cabot's Discovery of America*, p. 172.

[2] H. R. Fox-Bourne, *English Seamen under the Tudors*, vol. i. p. 115.

ject which were in favor during Elizabeth's reign. His
theory is in substance as follows:

First, all seas are maintained by the abundance of water,
so the nearer the end any River, Bay or Haven is, the shallower
it waxeth, although by some accidentall barre, it is sometimes
found otherwise. But the farther you sayle West from Island
towards the place, where this fret is thought to be, the more
deepe are the seas; which giveth us good hope of continuence
of the same Sea with Mar del Sur, by some fret that lyeth
between America, Groneland, and Cathaia.

As a further reason why the New World appeared an island,
he said that otherwise Asiatic animals and tribes such as the
" Scythians " and " Tartarians " would have gone thither.
Moreover, travelers who had been to Asia would in that
case also have seen it. A still further proof made to support his contention was the fact that the current which
runs northward along the eastern coast of America [1] must
of necessity find a passage to the northwest, or else it would
strike the coast of Iceland, Norway, Finland and Lapland.

Furthermore, the current in the great Ocean could not have
beene maintained to runne continually one way, from the
beginning of the world unto this day, had there not been some
thorow passage by the fret afore sayd, and so by circular
motion bee brought again to maintaine itselfe: For the Tides
and courses of the sea are maintayned by their interchange-
able motions: as fresh rivers are by springs, by ebbing and
flowing, by rarefaction and condensation. [2]

These illustrations will suffice to give a notion of the care
with which problems of navigation and geography were

---

[1] Probably Gilbert refers to the Gulf Stream, although he evidently
had not secured accurate information concerning it.

[2] Sir Humphrey Gilbert, "A Discourse to Prove a Passage to the
North-west," in *The Prince Society Publications*, 1903, p. 59, *et seq.*

studied at the time, and to summarize the views of Englishmen about a portion of the world with which they were
somewhat familiar.

Turning to another part of the world, the following instructions, which illustrate the methods of observation employed by navigators of the period, were issued to Arthur
Pet and Charles Jackman in 1580, upon the occasion of a
voyage for the discovery of the northeast passage:

But when you come upon any coast, or doe finde any sholde
banke in the sea, you are then to use your leade oftener, as
you shal thinke it requisite, noting diligently the order of
your depth, and the deeping and sholding. And so likewise
doe you note the depths into harboroughs, rivers etc. . . .
Doe you diligently observe the latitude as often and in as many
places as you may possible, and also the variation of the
Compasse (especially when you may bee at shoare upon any
land) noting the same observations truely, and the place and
places where, and the time and times when you do the same.
When you come to have sight of any coast or land whatsoever, doe you presently set the same with your sailing Compasse, howe it beares off you, noting your judgement how farre
you thinke it from you, drawing also the forme of it in your
booke, howe it appeares unto you, noting diligently how the
highest or notablest part thereof beareth off you, and the
extreames also in sight of the same land at both ends, dis-
tinguishing them by letters, A. B. C. . . .
And also in passing alongst by any and every coast, doe you
drawe the manner of biting in of any and every Bay, and
entrance of every harborow or rivers mouth, with the lying
out of every point, or headland, (unto the which you may
give apt names at your pleasure) and make some marke in
drawing the forme and border of the same, where the high
cliffs are, and where lowe lande is, whether sande, hils, or
woods, or whatsoever, not omitting to note any thing that
may be sensible and apparent to you, which may serve you to
any good purpose.[1]

[1] Hakluyt, *op. cit.*, vol. iii, pp. 259, 266.

The old navigators such as Frobisher often attempted to solve problems of spherical trigonometry, and took globes on their voyages with this end in view.[1] That knowledge of navigation was early considered as most important is evident. The Muscovy Company, in order to instruct their mariners, maintained for some years " one learned man in the science of cosmographie " paying him the liberal salary of £200 a year.[2] Later Sir Francis Drake, realizing the importance of the study, offered £20 a year, with £20 at the start to buy instruments, toward a chair of navigation in one of the universities. It is said that the man to whom the position was offered would not accept it unless he were given £40 a year.[3] Still later, Hakluyt tried to get Charles Howard, then Lord Admiral, in the dedication of the second edition of the *Principall Navigations,* to realize how important the establishment of such a lectureship might prove.[4] Finally the Royal Observatory at Greenwich was started, and Flamsteed became on March 4, 1675 the first "Astronomer Royal," whose duty it was, according to the warrant of Charles II,

forthwith to apply himself with the most exact care and diligence to rectifying the tables of the motions of the heavens and the places of the fixed stars, so as to find out the much desired longitude of the places for the perfecting of the art of navigation.

[1] Sir Clements R. Markham, " The History of the Gradual Development of the Groundwork of Geographical Science," in *The Geographical Journal,* vol. xlvi, p. 184.

[2] Edward Cheyney, *A History of England from the Defeat of the Armada to the Death of Queen Elizabeth,* vol. i, p. 315.

[3] *Hakluyt Society Publications,* 1st. series, no. 7, p. 16.

[4] Hakluyt said that Sir Thomas Gresham had founded " many chargeable Lectures," some of them " mathmeticall tending to the advancement of Marine causes." Hakluyt, *op. cit.,* vol. i, p. xxxiv, *et seq.*

The government, however, was not over liberal, as Flamsteed's salary was only £90 a year and although an observatory building was erected, no instruments were furnished. He had to construct instruments at his own expense, and for thirty years he maintained the observatory out of his private income.   Although Greenwich was founded " for the perfecting of the art of navigation," it was nearly one hundred years after Flamsteed's appointment before the work of the observatory proved of immediate value to the navigator.[1]

Interest in the study of navigation as a practical science is further shown by a large number of tracts and books written from the close of the sixteenth century, giving instructions to seamen, explaining the use of instruments, etc. Among these were William Cuningham's *The Cosmographical Glass*, 1559, Leonard and Thomas Digges' *Pantometrix*, 1571, William Bourne's *A Regiment of the Sea*, 1596, John Davis' *The Seaman's Secret*, 1607, M. *Blundevile His Exercises*, 1613, Robert Hues' *Tractatus de Globis extended by Pontamis*, 1617, Edward Wright's *Certain Errors in Navigation*, 1657, etc.[2]   Among English authors during the Elizabethan Age, Hues gained experience in the Straits of Magellan and in the southern Atlantic, and Wright served under the Earl of Cumberland; while Davis and Baffin were indefatigable observers and inventors, as well as great explorers.   Hulley made voyages for magnetic observations, as also did Harrison, the inventor of chronometers.[3]

It is evident that there was considerable advance in the knowledge of navigation during the seventeenth century.

[1] Charles L. Poor, *Nautical Science*, p. 97, *et seq.*; *The Cambridge History of English Literature*, vol. iv, p. 95.

[2] *The Geographical Journal*, vol. xlvi, p. 181.

[3] *Ibid.*, p. 182.

Dr. Gilbert in 1600 first propounded the theory that the earth itself is a magnet, and Edward Wright by his scientific discoveries associated with the principles of Mercator's projection made himself the father of modern marine cartography.   In 1620 logarithmic tables were applied to navigation by Gunter; while Norwood in 1631 made the application of the mensuration of a degree.[1]

As time went on the English with each successive voyage of their own, and through the accounts of foreign voyagers, gradually corrected old errors and discovered new facts. The voyages of the European nations made in the fifteenth and sixteenth centuries had raised the veil under which for thousands of years half of the terrestrial globe had remained concealed.   Within thirty years of the date of the first voyage of Columbus, the whole coast of America from Greenland to Cape Horn had been explored; the Pacific Ocean had been navigated, and the world circumnavigated by Magellan, the coasts of eastern Africa, Arabia, Persia and India had been visited by the Portuguese and numerous islands in the Indian Ocean discovered.   Through the ardor and rivalry of the Spanish, Portuguese, English, French and Dutch merchants and explorers, the succeeding centuries continued constantly to reveal new geographic facts.

Since foreigners were the pioneers in exploration, the literary impulse for recording voyages reached England from the continent.   In 1522 Peter Martyr was instructed by the Spanish government to examine all navigators who returned, and from their accounts write the history of Spanish exploration.   He therefore had the honor of being the first historian of the discovery of America.   His work was fol-

---

[1] *Dictionary of National Biography*, vol. xxi, p. 338, vol. xxiii, pp. 100, 350.

lowed in 1526 by the *Sumario de la natural y general historia de las Indias* of Gonzalo Fernández de Oviedo y Valdés.[1] After several inferior works had been produced by English authors,[2] Richard Eden undertook the great task of first translating and publishing from the Latin Sebastian Münster's *Universal Cosmography, A Treatyse of the newe India with other new founde landes and Islands, as well eastwarde as westwarde, as they are knowen and founde in these our dayes,* following this in 1555, with a translation from Peter Martyr: *The Decades of the New Worlde or West India, conteyning the Navigations and Conquests of the Spanyards, with particular description of the most ryche and large Landes and Islandes lately found in the West Ocean.* This work was composed of accounts of the voyages of Columbus and his companions, and to it Eden added translations from Oviedo.[3] Thus, for the time being, Englishmen's craving for knowledge of the recently discovered portions of the world was appeased and their desire for more geographical knowledge, for the study of new lands and peoples, whetted. Without doubt, as Eden had intended, his work also had the result of exciting a desire among English navigators and traders to emulate the exploits of foreign voyagers. At any rate voyages soon began to be made, to the western coast of Africa for slaves and gold dust, thence to the Spanish strongholds in the West Indies, and in the opposite direction in the vain quest of northeast and

---

[1] *The Cambridge History of English Literature,* vol. iv, pp. 80, 81.

[2] John Doesborch printed in 1511 the first English book relating to America, entitled " Of the newelandes and of ye people founde by the messengers of the kynge of Portyngale named Emanuel." John Rastell also wrote concerning America in a "A new interlude and a merry of the nature of the iiii elements," printed between 1510 and 1520. *Ibid.,* vol. iv, p. 81.

[3] *Ibid.,* pp. 81, 82.

northwest passages, to the treasures of the Orient. This
resulted in a number of individual accounts of voyages and
treatises to prove the benefits and practicability of these exploits. The most notable were John Hawkins's own personal account of his voyages entitled, *A True Declaration
of the Troublesome voyage of Mr. John Hawkins to the
parts of Guinea and the West Indies in the years of our
Lord 1567 and 1568;* also the notable work already cited,
written by Sir Humphrey Gilbert, entitled *Discourse of a
Discoverie for a new passage to Cataia,* published in 1576,
and Captain George Best's lively and vigorous account of
his friend Frobisher's voyages in search of the northwest
passage, entitled, *A true discourse of the late voyages for
the finding of a passage to Cathaya by the north-west, under
the conduct of Martin Frobisher, Generall,* published in
1578.[1]

Besides these original narratives, English geographical
knowledge was further increased and zeal given to those
studies by a new edition, 1577, of Eden's *Decades of the
New World,* which was edited and augmented by additional
accounts of voyages, by Richard Willes and published under
the title of *The History of Travayle in the West and East
Indies, and other countreys lying either way towards the
fruitfull and ryche Moluccaes . . . . with a discourse of
the North west Passage.*[2] Englishmen's desire for information concerning the geography of the world was not
rewarded as it deserved, however, until the matchless collections and compilations made by that painstaking and zealous scholar and patriot, Richard Hakluyt, appeared. He
had long been gathering material and his first published
work, *Divers Voyages touching the Discoverie of America*

---

[1] *The Cambridge History of English Literature,* vol. iv, pp. 84, 85, 86.
[2] *Ibid.,* vol. iv, p. 87.

and the Islands adjacent unto the same, came into print in
1582, while the first edition of the *Principall Navigations*
was issued in 1589.[1] Probably no other Englishman did
so much to promote the study of the geography and natural
history of the oversea lands. Indeed Hakluyt's whole life
was devoted to the literature of navigation and discovery.
His efforts bore rich fruit, not only in the increased study
of geography and navigation, but in literature notably as
exemplified by Shakespeare and Milton,[2] who show how
thoroughly English minds were filled with the great
thoughts and the striking facts he suggested. More still,
the national spirit was aroused to undertake exploits which
led to later geographical discoveries. Through his diligent
searching of chroniclers and the papers of merchant companies Hakluyt brought to light many facts which later
formed the basis of scientific geographical study and
writing.

Samuel Purchas was Hakluyt's successor as a great editor
of narratives of travel. *Hakluytus Posthumus,* or *Purchas
His Pilgrimes contayning a History of the World, in Sea
Voyages and Lande Travells by Englishmen and others,* was
published in 1625. Purchas never traveled more than two
hundred miles from his birthplace, but made up for this
by indefatigable industry. His work, which in its most recent edition contains twenty volumes, is made up of travels
in ancient times including those of Biblical characters, personal narratives of seamen and travelers which Purchas had
himself written down, and some öf Hakluyt's papers which
remained unpublished at his death and of the narratives
given in Hakluyt's collections.[3]

Thus geographical theory had been overcome by the

---

[1] *The Cambridge History of English Literature,* vol. iv, p. 92.

[2] *Infra,* pp. 289, 292, 295-303.

[3] *The Cambridge History of English Literature,* vol. iv, pp. 106, 107.

great mass of material which had been collected concerning the new discoveries. The work of Ptolemy, who for many centuries had enjoyed the distinction of being the source of nearly all geography, was now made practically obsolete through the large number of new facts that had been found out. Moreover, before the end of the seventeenth century a new turn was given to the study of geography by bringing other sciences as biology, astronomy, physical and natural science to bear upon it. Perhaps the chief characteristic of the study of this science during the period under consideration was the interest shown by so many scholars in the newly discovered facts without reference to classical tradition. This was undoubtedly due to the spirit of inquiry and interest in the universe aroused by the new discoveries and the fact that they revealed so many errors in the writing of the old authorities as to cause the new generation to distrust them.

The new geographical discoveries exercised a most marked influence on the perfecting of maps. Throughout the sixteenth and seventeenth centuries the rapidly accumulating fund of geographic facts was organised by a generation of cartographers, among whom Mercator was the most important; and since the exploits of the navigators had caused Elizabethan Englishmen to have imperial ambitions and their minds were fired by the many wonderful oversea tales, they wished to let their eyes roam at will over the charts of the world, while dreams of empire floated through their minds. Therefore map engraving became for both native and foreign engravers in England the chief and most lucrative employment. Maps were still inaccurate, but vivid in their interesting portrayal of strange savages, animals, sea-monsters and exotic vegetation.[1] The appeal, therefore, was rather to curiosity than to rational thought. Among

[1] *Infra*, p. 319.

the well known map-makers of the time were Humphrey Cole, Benjamin Wright, William Hale, Ralph Aggas, the Flemish brothers, Francis and Remigius Hogenberg, and the accomplished Theodore de Bry who contributed maps to Hakluyt's "Voyages;"[1] while Edward Wright, a mathematician of Cambridge, produced the first English map on Mercator's projection.[2]

Since Englishmen, led by the new spirit, were so earnestly seeking a wider knowledge of the world, desire for the acquaintance with the history of hitherto unknown peoples and their institutions was aroused. Tiring of histories of local and rather limited scope a demand was soon felt for universal histories and special historical and descriptive accounts of familiar peoples. Among histories of the former type was Sir Walter Raleigh's *The History of the World*, written in 1611.[3] The second class was represented by Richard Knolles, *General Historie of the Turkes from the first beginning of that Nation to the rising of the Othoman Familie,* published in 1603, and Captain John Smith's *The Generall Historie of Virginia, New England, and the Summer Isles.*[4] These histories were written in clear, vigorous style, often in a rather popular vein, and especially in the case of Smith's work were full of descriptions of the land and its resources, the people, their life, characteristics and institutions. Instead of a mere account of the reigns of sovereigns and their military campaigns, these histories laid emphasis upon institutional, social and economic phases. This may have been due, not only to the growing curiosity concerning all manner of

[1] Malcolm C. Salamon, *The Old Engravers of England in their Relation to Contemporary Life and Art, 1540-1800*, pp. 3, 4.

[2] J. Scott Keltie, and O. J. R. Howarth. *History of Geography*, p. 120.

[3] *The Cambridge History of English Literature*, vol. iv, pp. 67, 68.

[4] *Ibid.*, vol. iv, p. 111.

things which made up the sum of life, but also to the fact
that Raleigh, Knolles and Smith were writing for the benefit
of the people rather than a select group of scholars.   This
is still further emphasized by the fact that they were about
the first histories to be published in the English language
instead of Latin, in order that every one might read them.[1]

Much of the thought of the seventeenth century was directed into the channels of trade, and the chief impetus to
the study and publication of discourses upon economic subjects was afforded by the problems of colonial trade, which
followed the enterprise of the navigators and adventurers.
Child and Davenant, Petty and Mun, and a host of others
were actively interested in these questions, of which the following may be taken as examples: the benefits to be derived
from the fisheries and the methods of encouraging them;
the value of the privileges of the East India Company and
other monopolies; the exportation of bullion and its supposedly evil effects upon the nation through loss of the precious metals.

Before Adam Smith, the English writers on economic
subjects do not at any time present the marks of a school.
The mercantilists most nearly approach this, but their
views were individual and independent.   However, wider
conceptions were held at this time than there had been before.   It was the nation now, rather than the craft or guild,
whose interests were considered.   Still, the majority of
writers were little conscious of a high national aim.   The
" hurtfull " trade generally was that of a rival company or
neighboring nation.   Much sharp reasoning was used, and
much information was brought to light, but it was not
organized as theory or science.   Nevertheless, during the
period under review, there were hundreds of writers on
economic themes.   Why with such an output of economic

[1] *The Cambridge History of English Literature,* vol. iv, p. 67.

thought a well organized branch of knowledge was not created, is thus explained by Palgrave:

1. With few exceptions the economic works of this period were written merely to advocate some definite object,—to urge the adoption of some scheme for the improvement of trade, to defend those whose interests were threatened by new developments, . . . or to protest against some abuse and to suggest a remedy. . . . This close relation of economic literature and the practical life of the nation was unfavorable to the development of economic doctrine. 2. Such being the objects of the writers, there is a strong bias in most of them in favour of the organization or project with which they happened to be identified. . . . 3. When once a controversy was concluded, no one endeavoured to develop and apply the general principles which may have been stated in the course of it. Thus the currency controversy of 1694, and the defense of the East India Company, led to a statement of the main outlines of the principle of the division of labor. . . . But it lay unregarded until Adam Smith made it one of the fundamental principles of the *Wealth of Nations.* 4. The early writers had to depend for the most part on their own knowledge and experience, to suggest or illustrate their arguments; trustworthy information on economic subjects was neither so copious nor so widely diffused as it is at the present time. Sir William Petty, John Graunt, Gregory King, and Charles Davenant, who laid the foundations of statistical science, all lived in the latter part of the seventeenth century. . . . 5. The early writers employed in their works the language of ordinary business. They had no scientific terminology. The language of the market-place is not characterized by scientific precision and their looseness of phrase gave rise to endless misunderstandings.[1]

We cannot therefore expect in these writings any uniformity, consistency and completeness which we would desire in scientific knowledge. Nevertheless, a beginning had been

[1] R. H. D. Palgrave, *Dictionary of Political Economy*, vol. i, p. 729.

made in economic writing and thinking, even if the subject
had not yet been formed into a science. Opinions which
might with the later generations be employed in science were
expressed, and as has been seen above, at the end of the
century statistics began largely to be collected which gave
promise of a science of political economy.[1]

To understand thoroughly the type of economic thought
held by the scholars of this period, it may be worth while to
review some of the theories and arguments advanced. No
illustration is more striking than the attack on and defense
of the monopolies held by the great trading companies. The
complaints raised and the reasons advanced why these
great enterprises should be suppressed bear an interesting
resemblance to attacks on American trusts. Many pamphlets were written both denouncing and defending the great
commercial corporations. The battle was particularly bit-
ter over the East India Company, as it possessed the monopoly of a trade which to the minds of many was detrimental
to the kingdom.

One of the ablest summaries of the evils alleged to exist
in connection with the chartered companies and their exclusive privileges is found in a seventeenth-century tract
called *Britannia Languens,* written by William Petyt. Its
arguments are mainly directed against the East India and
the African Companies which had " Pattents of the Sole
Trade of a great part of the World exclusive to the rest of
his Majesties Subjects." In the opinion of the author such
companies were injurious to English manufacturers and

---

[1] This fondness for collecting figures was shown by Sir William
Petty, who developed what he called "political arithmetic." He wrote
about his new study that "until this be done, trade will be too con-
jectural a work for any man to employ his thoughts about." Traill,
op. cit., vol. iv, p. 458. After Davenant and King had employed Petty's
methods with success John Willis placed the system of statistics as
then existent, upon a new basis. Macaulay, *op. cit.,* vol. i, p. 321.

exporters, " because by trading on a Joint-Stock they make but one buyer, and therefore have a Monopoly for all exportable goods proper only for the Foreign Nations within their pattents . . . . therefore will buy at their own prizes." For the same reason " they must be yet more injurious to home-Manufactures made of forreign materials; for first, they will sell the materialls as dear, and then buy the Manufacture in a trice, especially if made of forreign materials bought cheaper by forreign Manufacturers." Speaking of the benefits of real competition, he says that "underselling" is advantageous to the nations, " because when many wish to sell, some at least will be ready to come to terms with the customers and all of them will be anxious to do business and to turn to some new enterprise, thus they will beat each other down to a low price through competition." A very good example of how commercial monopoly might raise the price of imports and diminish the price of the domestic commodities that it exported is then given by the writer to support his conclusions. He shows how the African Company was no sooner established than it " raised the price of imported red-wood, which before was sold at £26 and £28 per Tun to £80 per Tun." This made English dyed cloths much dearer and proved to be so intolerable that the dyers began to use sandal-wood. Besides, after the formation of that company the prices of all goods used solely in the African trade were lowered at least 15 per cent, and not even a tenth part of those formerly sold to merchants trading to Africa was now disposed of to the new company.

According to Petyt, furthermore, since the companies have the local trade for a selling monopoly, they would impose such " arbitrary " prices that the merchants or reexporters who were compelled to buy at such high rates would be undersold by foreigners who have free trade in the place whence the commodity was imported. Another objection he raised was that the companies also having the monopoly of trade with the Orientals might sell " home-manufactures " at exorbitant prices and would profit more by disposing of a small quantity of goods at high rates, than by vending much larger amounts at lower prices. Besides, although the joint-stock was not sufficient to carry on the trade to its full extent, yet the investors would be satisfied with their returns, since these would be very great in proportion to the money invested. Thus they would trade with only a few ports where they could make great profits on their sales and purchases.[1]

Petyt declared that the East India Company in particular did not develop trade in the territories over which it had a monopoly to the extent that should have been the case in view of the favorable position it enjoyed. Although it controlled part of eastern Africa it did not trade there, and very little if any, with the Red Sea region. Its commerce with Persia might have been much more extensive. Even in India it was said that its traffic was carried on with only twenty or thirty ports, and woolen goods were taken to but three or four of them.[2]

The exclusive composition of the monopolistic companies, like their other characteristics, were also said to be illustrated by this company in which not more than sixty or eighty persons were " considerably concerned," although the stock was insufficient. It was pointed out that rather than sell more stock it borrowed £400,000 or £500,000 at interest.[3] It was charged, moreover, with exporting altogether too much bullion. Thus the author just quoted says that, although merchants other than the members of such

---

[1] William Petyt, " Britannia Languens, etc.," in McCulloch, *Collection, etc.* (London, 1856), p. 333, *et seq.*

[2] *Ibid.*, p. 339.

[3] *Ibid.*, p. 341.

a concern exported much treasure, they could not send it so easily, or in such great quantities as their monopolistic competitors, whose joint-stock having so great a credit enabled them to get as much money as they wanted.[1]   Therefore, much of the precious metals, which according to the mercantilists should have been kept in the kingdom, was being sent to the Orient to buy luxuries and was never recovered.

The answers to many of the complaints against the privileges of the East India Company and other corporations of the sort are equally interesting.   Thus to the objection that these monopolistic concerns purchased English goods for sale abroad at the lowest prices and sold the foreign goods they brought to England at the highest rates, Samuel Fortrey, another contemporary writer, while admitting that the contention was true to a great extent, urged that this was an advantage, as for inasmuch

they make their profit at home, so they make no less advantage abroad; for the whole commodity being in their hands, they will make the most that can be made of it; no one having the like commodities to undersell them: and the like advantage they have again in what they buy; whereby in truth, our own commodities are sold the dearer to strangers, and forein commodities bought much the cheaper [than] in a free trade; where each will undersel the other, to vent most; and also purchase at any rates, to prevent the rest [from gaining the advantage].

Besides, as the author points out, the trade was often entirely lost as individuals were too weak to maintain it. Moreover the company did not sell less goods than single persons would, for it always furnished as much as was demanded.   Therefore Fortrey contended that the companies

---

[1] Petyt, *op. cit.,* p. 336.

both sold English goods to the best advantage and bought from foreigners at the lowest rates the commodities the nation needed. The injury such concerns might do English workmen and shopkeepers was fully compensated for by the "clear profit they return to the publick; of which they are members as well as others." The author further declared that, if the stockholders' profits were thought too large, this evil might be lessened by admitting every one who so desired to an enjoyment of the advantages of the companies, "on fit and reasonable terms."[1]

Another contemporary, probably Child, answered the complaint that the East India stock was all taken by a few people, some owning £16,000 or £17,000 of it, by the assertion that the more stock an adventurer might have, the more he would be interested in finding out ways to promote the trade. Moreover he asserts that in the latter part of the century as many as 556 persons held stock in the East India Company, and that all could enter it who wished. Answering the accusation that the company did not trade with as many ports as might well be opened to English traffic, the same author declares that he believed others would not have more industriously enlarged English trade in the East. The Company through its endeavors to establish new centres of trade had lost as much as £100,000. The attempt to start commerce with Japan alone had caused a loss of £50,000 to the corporation. Besides, it was not necessary to found posts in every part of the country, for one factory would secure all the trade of the region. Thus "Surat shares in all the trade of the Red sea, as well as Moca." In many places a station was not desired, for the traffic could best be carried on through the natives. Again, the contention that, if the Company were not conducted on the

[1] Samuel Fortrey, "England's Interest and Improvement," in Mc-Culloch, *Collection* (1856), p. 244.

joint-stock principle, many more ships might be employed in India in the coasting trade, is met by the reply that it knew best what to do and was in need of " neither stock, or skill, or will, to employ as many ships as (it) can gain by . . . ." Indeed, it had almost doubled the amount of its stock and the tonnage of its ships within the ten preceding years.[1]

Locke stands in the forefront among his contemporaries in ability to deduce economic principles from the data furnished by the new enterprises. It may be well here to cite two illustrations. First, in discussing the question of the relative value of labor and land, to his mind labor was much the more important factor—in fact, the medium of value for everything. He went so far as to ascribe ninety-nine hundredths of all value to labor. To support this opinion he turns to America, of which he remarks:

There cannot be a clearer demonstration of any thing, than several nations of the Americans are of this, who are rich in land, and poor in all the comforts of life; whom nature having furnished as liberally as any other people, with the materials of plenty, i. e. a fruitful soil, apt to produce in abundance what might serve for food, raiment, and delight; yet, for want of improving it by labour, have not one hundredth part of the conveniencies we enjoy; and a king of a large and fruitful territory there feeds, lodges, and is clad worse than a day labourer in England. . . .

An acre of land, that bears here twenty bushels of wheat, and another in America, which, with the same husbandry, would do the like, are, without doubt, of the same natural intrinsic value: but yet the benefit mankind receives from the

---

[1] *A Collection of Scarce and Valuable Tracts . . . Selected from an infinite Number in Print and Manuscript, in the Royal, Cotton, Sion, and other Public, as well as private Libraries, particularly that of the late Lord Sommer's*, vol. iv, p. 51.

one in a year, is worth 5 l. and from the other possibly not
worth a penny, if all the profit an Indian received from it were
to be valued, and sold here; at least, I may truly say, not one
thousandth. It is labour then which puts the greatest part
of the value upon land, without which it would scarcely be
worth anything.[1]

A second excellent example is afforded by Locke's arguments against trying to determine the rate of monetary
exchange by government regulation. Thus:

Suppose fifteen to one be now the exact par between gold
and silver, what law can make it lasting; and establish it so,
that next year, or twenty years hence, this shall be the just
value of gold to silver; and that one ounce of gold shall be
just worth fifteen ounces of silver, neither more or less? It
is possible, the East India trade sweeping away great sums of
gold, may make it scarcer in Europe. Perhaps the Guinea
trade, and mines of Peru, affording it in greater abundance,
may make it more plentiful; and so its value, in respect of
silver, come on the one side to be as sixteen, or, on the other,
as fourteen to one. And can any law you shall make alter
this proportion here, when it is so every-where else, round
about you? If your law set it at fifteen, when it is at the free
market rate, in the neighbouring countries, as sixteen to one;
will they not send hither their silver to fetch away your gold, at
one sixteen loss to you?[2]

A further type of economic writing which illustrates the
thought of the time is afforded by the plans advanced.
Many projects and proposals were rife among Englishmen as to the possibilities of future advantage from the

---

[1] "Two Treatises of Government," no. 2, in *The Works of John
Locke* (London, 1794), vol. iv, pp. 362, 363.

[2] "Some Considerations of the Consequences of the Lowering of
Interest, and Raising the Value of Money" (1691) in *ibid.*, vol. iv,
p. 101.

colonies to be planted beyond the sea. In these as well as other thoughts which have been noticed above, there was much of the credulous and visionary, but as well, much hardheaded, critical planning. At first and for some time, the English like other European nations hoped to find immense stores of the precious metals ready to be carried away. Belief in the northwest passage, too, for a hundred years and more inspired numerous voyages. It was very difficult for the English to give up these early ideals and settle down to finding out what else of benefit might exist for them in the New World. It proved much easier, however, for a practical-minded race such as the Anglo-Saxon than it would have been for the Latin races, with their tendency to the emotional and visionary.

Many tracts and prospectuses, and even sermons, inspired by the colonizing and trading companies were written in the early seventeenth century. Most of them are characterized by their vivid and enthusiastic language, suggestive of the exaggerations of modern mining or western land-development circulars. Some, however, show a more careful study and a desire to reach a correct conclusion.

Nearly from the first the highest hopes were entertained regarding the future of commerce with America. It was even hoped that the new continent might become a second " Eden," and supply all the commodities that England could possibly desire to import and had been accustomed to buy from other nations:

Seeing that the Country is not unlike to equalize (though not India for gold, which is impossible yet), Tyrus for colours, Basan for woods, Persia for oils, Arabia for spices, Spain for silks, Narsis for shipping, Netherlands for fish, Benoma for fruit, and by tillage Babylon for corn . . . besides the abundance of mulberries, minerals, rubies, pearls, gems, drugs for physic, herbs for food, roots for colours, ashes for soap, timber for building, pastures for feeding, rivers for fishing, and whatsoever commodity England wanteth. . . . As also that Virgin country may in time prove to us, the farm of Britain, as Sicily was to Rome, or the garden of the World as was Thessaly, or the argosie of the world as is Germany.[1]

In a previous chapter attention has been called to the interest taken in the possibility of the New World affording a great supply of forest products, sorely needed in England for naval supplies.[2] Other conceptions that showed much foresight were the plans for the settlement and employment of the English poor in the colonies; the opportunity that the proposed settlements might afford for " a very liberal utterance of our English clothes into a maine Country, described to bee bigger than all Europe, the larger part whereof bending to the Northward, shall have wonderfull great use of our sayde English clothes after they shall come once to knowe the commoditte thereof; "[3] the construction of a great merchant marine through the prospective colonial trade, and the fisheries, which were capable of furnishing much profit to the kingdom and employment to the people.

The plan that appears the most fanciful, but which may have well seemed logical to the promoters of the period, was that of turning America into a great silk and wine growing country. Regarding this scheme it was said : "Our Frenchman assures us that no country in the world is more proper for vines, silk, olives and rice than Virginia. There be mulberry trees in wonderful abundance, and much excelling both in goodness and greatness those of the country of Languedoc." Accordingly King James I commanded the setting up of silk works and the planting of vines in Virginia, and the Treasurer and Council of the Virginia Com-

[1] Edward D. Neill, *Virginia Vetusta, etc.*, p. 46.
[2] *Supra.*
[3] Hakluyt, *op. cit.*, vol. viii, p. 140.

pany sent to their governor in the colony the following directions:

And if you shall finde any person, either through negligence or wilfulnesse, to omit the planting of Vines, and Mulberry trees, in orderly and husbandly manner, as by the Booke is prescribed, or the providing of convenient roomes for the breeding of Worms; we desire they may by severe censures and punishment, be compelled thereunto. And on the contrary, that all favour and possible assistance be given to such as yeelde willing obedience to his Highnesse commands therein. The breach or performance whereof, as we are bound to give a strict account, so will it also be required of you the Governor and Counsell especially. Herein there can be no Plea, either of difficulty or impossibility; but all the contrary appears, by the naturall abundance of those two excellent Plants aforenamed every where in Viriginia: neither will such excuses be admitted, nor any other pretences serve, whereby the businesse be at all delayed: and as wee formerly sent at our great charge the French Vignerons to you, to teach you their Art: so for the same purpose we now command this Booke unto you, to serve as an Instructor to every one, and send you store of them to be dispersed over the whole Colony, to every Master of a Family one, Silke-seede you shall receive also by this Ship, sufficient to store everyman: so that there wants nothing, but industry in the Planter, suddenly to bring the making of Silke to its perfection: which either for their owne benefit (we hope) they will willingly indevour, or by a wholesome and necessary severity they must be inforced.[1]

Silkworms had been sent over in 1614 and in a few months they had reached an extraordinary size. As they apparently flourished so well it was expected that silk growing would become a prominent industry. However, little was accomplished in this direction,[2] in spite of the high hopes entertained.

[1] Purchas, *op. cit.*, vol. xix, p. 156, *et seq.*
[2] Bruce, *op. cit.*, vol. i, p. 219.

That the New World and the conditions found there had their influence upon political philosophy is exemplified by Sir Thomas More in his *Utopia*. He wrote this famous treatise in 1516, when the imaginations of men were stirred by the sudden enlargement of their conceptions of the world. Many things which had hitherto not been dreamed possible were now found real. Why, therefore, should not the ideal which had not yet been practiced in the Old World now be possible in that other world where so much had been found true? Why should not the New World stand as a lesson to the Old? At least the corrupting life and works of European man had not been found there. Should there not then be a chance for the ideal life close to nature? The *Utopia*, it will be seen, is no mere imitation of Plato's *Republic*. Although the New World on the whole has little to do with its details, the possibilities suggested by America were largely responsible for this picture of a state of society so different from European life.[1]

The setting for More's famous work is what one might expect of one whose interest and imagination had been following the accounts of the voyages. In fact it is very plain that the accounts of Amerigo Vespucci's four voyages, appearing in 1507, gave More the stage setting for the *Utopia*.[2]

---

[1] *Cambridge Modern History*, vol. i, p. 58. As Sidney Lee remarks, " The *Utopia* is not merely a literary masterpiece; it is also a convincing testimony to the stirring effects on English genius of the discovery of an unknown, an untrodden world." Lee, *op. cit.*, p. 120.

[2] *The Utopia*, edited by George Sampson (London, 1910), p. 25, note. A book called *Cosmographiae Introductio* containing an account of the four voyages of Amerigo Vespucci was published in 1507. According to the story, on the fourth voyage twenty-four men were left in a fortress near Cape Bahia. This detail More used as a starting point. One of the twenty-four men called Raphaell Hythlodaye tells the story of Utopia. *The Utopia*, edited by George Sampson (London, 1910), pp. xxii, 25, note. More was staying in Antwerp and from there he brought back the first draft of the *Utopia*. One can well imagine

Raphaell Hythlodaye, a combination of just such a curious, garrulous voyager wise with experience as was beginning to be well known in western Europe and the Renaissance scholar conversant with Greek and Latin and the knowledge of past civilization,[1] sailing with Vespucci had wandered much farther instead of returning with this famous navigator. He succeeded in accomplishing just what so many of his day were anxious to succeed in doing, the feat of reaching Ceylon and Calicut through the western seas. Journeying to the westward from Brazil where he with other Portuguese had been left, he passed through many unknown lands, among them those which lay under " the equinoctiall." Here More gives a vivid portrayal of what was then supposed to be the state of the land near the equator.

For under the line equinoctiall, and on bothe sydes of the same, as farre as the Sonne doth extende his course, lyeth, great and wyde desertes and wildernesses, parched, burned, and dryed up with continuall and intollerable heate. All thynges bee hideous, terrible, lothesome, and unpleasaunt to beholde: All thynges out of fassyon and comelinesse, inhabited withe wylde Beastes, and Serpentes, or at the leaste wyse, with people, that be no lesse savage, wylde, and noysome, then the verye beastes theim selves be.[2]

how ideal were his surroundings in this great cosmopolitan, commercial centre of western Europe filled with the bustle of business created by other lands and throbbing with all manner of new thought. Here he made the acquaintance of Peter Giles, the great French scholar, with whom he had frequent discussions concerning contemporary and literary subjects. He pictures a conversation between his friend and a fictitious character, the old sailor, Raphaell Hythlodaye, lately returned from a voyage to America under Amerigo Vespucci. Hythlodaye tells of the strange isle of Utopia. Lee, *op. cit.*, pp. 28, 29.

[1] " For this same Hythlodaye is very well learned in the Latin tongue: but profounde and excellent in the Greke language." " He had given himself wholy to the study of Philosophy." *Utopia*, p. 24.

[2] *Ibid.*, p. 27.

However, More did not wish to follow the custom of that day of recounting marvelous tales of horrible monsters and the wonders of the newly discovered lands to please the popular taste. The conditions he described were to be the ideal ones which his mind conceived. There were no inquiries after monsters, " for nothyng is more easye to bee founde, then bee barkynge Scyllaes, revenyng Galenes, and Lestrigones devourers of people, and such lyke great, and incredible monsters." Instead the theme was rather one of institutions and governments, such as might convey a lesson to the serious men of the day. Hythlodaye " touched divers thynges that be amisse, some here and some there " and spoke " of suche wise lawes, and prudente decrees, as be established and used, bothe here amonge us and also there amonge theyme." [1] Such problems of the day were discussed, as the means of diminishing the number of thieves and robbers, the evils resulting from the enclosures to certain classes of the population etc.

The way was thus prepared for the consideration of the serious problems for which More desired to suggest the ideal solution. With the reader's mind thus alive to the possibilities of a land isolated from the conditions found in the Europe of his day, and situated in that far " western dreamland," where the wonderful had been constantly revealed to the startled vision of Europeans, he launches forth into an account of the ideal republic of " Utopia." Here the ideals suggested by Plato's *Republic,* and the fancies and the ideas which the New World furnished to his fertile brain, were both realized. All the evils and injustices which existed in the civilization of his day were to be corrected. There, in Utopia, free from the traditions of the past, existed a perfect society governed by just laws and whose rulers were chosen for their learning. There was absolute

[1] *Utopia*, pp. 28, 29.

toleration in religion.   Man was valued for his true worth rather than for his material riches and position.   All the follies and extravagances of the Old World were eliminated and a simple life was led close to nature.   Even in the matter of clothes, the outward evidence of an artificial civilization, this simplicity was observed.   While in

other places iiii or v clothe gownes of divers coloures, and as manye silke cootes be not enough for one man, yea and iff he be of the delicate and nyse sorte x be to fewe: where as there one garmente wyl serve a man mooste commenlye lj yeares.[1]

In Utopia there was to be no private property, but everybody had enough of all the necessities of life.   Every man was compelled to work, and since all did their share and every one's wants were simple, no one had to labor more than six hours a day.   The time thus saved was spent in a manner which would most please and develop the individual according to his tastes.   Much of this spare time was generally devoted to improving the mind through lectures.   The pleasures enjoyed were first, the physical ones derived from good wholesome food and drink, and from bodily health.   But "they imbrace chieflie the pleasures of the mind.   For them they counte the chiefist and most principall of all."

In considering certain aspects of the ideal presented, one may observe the influence of the New World in the idea of the bounty of nature that rewarded the labors of man, and in the description of the pleasures of a simple life led close to nature.   Everywhere in the accounts of the discoveries emphasis is laid on the lavishness of nature.   The thoughtful European of the time when More was writing, when the first glamour of the discoveries was still

[1] *Utopia, op. cit.*, p. 100.

vivid; before much was known of what lands might lie beyond the ken of the clear-visioned mariner; when Mexico
and Peru had still to be conquered; when a vision of the
luxuriant beauty of the western isles and of the simple-
hearted savages living in these ideal conditions rose before
him, may well have thought an ideal existence possible for
others endowed with the true virtues of the white race.
Here, if man could be in tune with nature, he could rise to
the ideal. Doubtless, part of More's thought was derived
from Greek philosophy, but one must likewise admit the
influence of the New World.

The philosophy which More advocates when he utters
his plea for searching the wonders of nature, may truly
be termed a " New World philosophy " in the double sense
of the word. He was in agreement in this conception with
that other great originator of an ideal commonwealth,
Francis Bacon, who carried the thought much further and
made it the corner stone of all of his philosophy. He was
in agreement likewise with the voyagers and scholars of
the sixteenth and seventeenth centuries. Evelyn, in the
century following the one in which More wrote his *Utopia*,
inspired by the wonders of the world about, utters nearly
the same plea for the nobility and worth of a life spent in
searching into the wonders of nature. Hitherto, during
the centuries which had preceded More's writing little encouragement had been given the searcher after the truths
of nature. In fact all was to be accepted as the ancient
scholars and writers of Holy Writ had interpreted it.
Therefore it was a new spirit which More breathed when
he said that God

beareth more good will and love to the curious and diligent
beholder and vewer of his work and marvelour at the same,
then he doth to him, which like a very brute beaste without

witte and reason, or as one without sense or moving, hathe no regarde to soo wonderfull a spectacle.[1]

It was an age, as has been seen above, when the New World was exciting the utmost curiosity and interest in ever changing phenomena, and it came to be thought legitimate to search and question the mysteries of God's earth, instead of accepting all on blind faith.

It is a fact that when one's soul is filled with the majesty and the beauty of surrounding nature, the artificial adornments and the false values of earthly wealth are despised. A longing is felt for the simple, the noble, the useful and inspiring, which will be worthy of the all-pervading presence that thrills. Thus one standing on the crest of a mountain, and beholding wave after wave of misty peaks fading into the distance, or again a wanderer on the shores of the sea, viewing the limitless expanse of waters, feels an appreciation and longing for the truly great. To More, living in a time when boundless seas, virgin isles, vast unexplored forests and streams were presented in amazing variety, splendor and vastness, the silly foibles and vices, the vain show, the greed for gold of European man, appeared small and utterly to be despised; whereas to the average man of his day the possibilities that the New World suggested were those of a material sort.

To More was granted the vision. He stood as the clear-eyed spiritual pilot, interpreting the appeal of universal nature to the noble life, warning the oncoming age of the folly of its material desires. The Utopians, filled with the great simplicity of nature, utterly despised gold and precious stones, as mere dross unworthy of the human touch. The ambassadors from other lands, coming like many a European decked in silks and rich jewels and the glitter of

[1] *Utopia*, p. 138, *et seq.*

gold, to the pristine isle, were held in derision by its simple inhabitants, who like the Indians whom the Europeans discovered held precious metals and jewels in small esteem. Here " of golde and sylver they make commonly Chamber pottes, and other vesselles, that serve for most vile uses," [1] and of them "make greate chaines, fetters, and gives where in they tie their bondmen." They likewise gathered " Pearles by the sea side, and Diamondes and Carbuncles upon certen rocks, and yet they seke not for them: but by chaunce finding them, they cut and polish them." With these they decked their children, who becoming proud of them in their childhood despised them when grown to manhood. [2]

More concludes this part of his ideal with the following splendid summary of the views he desires to present:

For they marveyle that any man be so folyshe, as to have delite and pleasure in the doubtful glistering of a lytil tryffelynge stone, which maye beholde anney of the starres, or elles the sonne it selfe. Or that aney man is so madde, as to count himselfe the nobler for the smaller or fyner threde of wolle, which selfe same wol (be it now in never so fyne a sponne threde) a shepe did ones weare: and yet was she all that time no other thing then a shepe. They marveile also that golde, whych of its owne nature is a thinge so unprofytable, is nowe amonge all people in so hyghe estimation, that man him selfe, by whome, yea and for the use of whome it is so much set by, is in muche lesse estimation, then the golde itselfe. In so muche that a lumpyshe blocke-hedded churle, and whyche hathe no more wytte then an asse, yea and as ful of noughtynes as of follye, shall have nevertheles manye wyse

---

[1] The popular play " Eastward Ho," published early in the seventeenth century, in its language is curiously reminiscent of this passage of the *Utopia:* " Eastward Ho," in *Dodsley's Old English Plays*, vol. iv, p. 249.

[2] *Utopia*, p. 115.

and good men in subjectyon and bondage, only for this, by-
cause he hath a greate heape of golde, whyche yf it should
be taken from hym by anye fortune, or by some subtyll wyle
and cautele of the lawe, (whyche no lesse then fortune dothe
bothe raise up the lowe, and plucke downe the highe) and be
given to the moste vile slave and abject dryvell of all his
householde, then shortely after he shal goo into the service of
his servaunt, as an augmentation or overplus beside his money.
But they muche more marvell at and detest the madnes of
them, whyche to those riche men, in whose debte and daunger
they be not, do give almost divine honoures, for none other
consideration, but bicause they be riche: and yet knowing them
to bee suche nigeshe penny fathers, that they be sure as longe
as they live, not the worthe of one farthinge of that heape
of golde shall come to them.[1]

The setting of the *New Atlantis,* written by Sir Francis
Bacon in 1624, is quite similar to that of the *Utopia,*
showing the unmistakable influence of the voyagers' tales.
The crew of the vessel whose mythical adventures Bacon
relates was sailing from Peru to China and Japan, when
" it came to pass that the next day about evening " they
saw before them what looked like " thick clouds," which
put them in hope of land as "that part of the South Sea
was utterly unknown, and might have islands or continents,
that hitherto were not come to light." All during the night
what appeared to be the shore of some island might be dis-
cerned on the misty horizon, and " in the dawning of the
next day " they plainly saw that it was " a land flat to
(their) sight, and full of boscage, which made it show all
the more dark." [2]

The first main theme of this treatise sets forth a fanciful
theory accounting for the American Indians, the sparseness

[1] *Utopia,* pp. 118-119.

[2] " New Atlantis," in *The Works of Francis Bacon* (Cambridge, 1863),
vol. v, pp. 359, 360.

of their number and reasons for their barbarous state of life, for the failure of the Europeans to have found them before and for the Indians having wandered in some way to the Old World. This is most interesting as it shows the speculations that were aroused by the New World and its inhabitants in one of the foremost minds of the time.[1]   An expedition from Mexico to Europe, as well as another from Peru to " New Atlantis," according to Bacon aroused the wrath of the gods, who accordingly destroyed most of the inhabitants·by a flood,—" those countries having, at this day, far greater rivers and far higher mountains to pour down waters, than any part of the Old World." As it happened, however, this inundation was not over forty feet deep. While it " destroyed man and beasts generally," a " few wild inhabitants of the wood escaped. Birds, also, were saved by flying to the high trees and woods." [2]   In Bacon's own words:

Marvel you not at the thin population of America, nor at the rudeness and ignorance of the people; for you must account your inhabitants of America as a young people; younger a thousand years, at the least, than the rest of the world; for that there was so much time between the universal flood and their particular inundation. For the poor remnant of human seed which remained in their mountains peopled the country again slowly, by little and little; and being simple and savage people, (not like Noah and his sons, which was the chief family of the earth,) they were not able to leave letters, arts, and civility to their posterity; and having likewise in their mountainous habitations been used (in respect of the extreme cold of those regions) to clothe themselves with the skins of tigers, bears, and great hairy goats, that they have in those parts; when after they came down into the valley, and found

---

[1] " New Atlantis," *op. cit.*, p. 376.

[2] *Ibid.*, p. 378.

the intolerable heats which are there, and knew no means of lighter apparel, they were forced to begin the custom of going naked, which continueth to this day. Only they take great pride and delight in the feathers of birds, and this also they took from those ancestors of the mountains, who were invited unto it by the infinite flights of birds that came up to the high grounds, while the waters stood below.[1]

The theory, however fanciful, is a remarkably interesting solution of the problem presented by the origin of the hitherto unknown Indian. The conception of degeneracy from type and decline from a formerly great civilization must have appeared quite logical to the Englishmen of that time, not yet removed from the influence of the Renaissance, and all it meant of the revival of a once splendid civilization after years of decline and degeneracy.

The other portion of the *New Atlantis* which serves in this connection is the concept of a great body of scholars: " Salomon's House, the noblest foundation that ever was upon the earth and the lantern of this kingdom," which made all possible kinds of experiments and collected all sorts of useful knowledge. The idea of it doubtless was suggested by the newly awakened curiosity and desire to investigate all interesting phenomena of nature. Both More in his *Utopia,* and Bacon in his *New Atlantis,* would seem to make this interest in the " New World philosophy " the supreme one in their ideal states.

Shakespeare, also, in his *Tempest,* gives evidence of holding similar philosophic ideas. Prospero, the man of wisdom living close to nature, and Miranda his daughter, the embodiment of what a pure life could be when free from the artificial world, may be cited as examples. Even an ideal commonwealth is pictured by Gonzalo:

[1] " New Atlantis," *op. cit.*, p. 379.

> " I' the commonwealth I would be contraries
> Execute all things; for no kind of traffic
> Would I admit; no name of magistrate;
> Letters should not be known; riches, poverty,
> And use of service, none; contract, succession,
> Bourn, bound of land, tilth, vineyard, none;
> No use of metal, corn, or wine, or oil
> No occupation; all men idle, all;
> And woman too, but innocent and pure,
> No sovereignty." [1]

Popular opinion regarding the characteristics of the state of nature, is excellently illustrated, moreover, by Caliban. He is pictured as:

' solitary, nasty, and brutish '; barely human, in fact but for his vices; living ' like a bear,' . . . grubbing roots, and plundering bees' nests; a prey to panic, haunted by the spirit of the power of the air, and instinctively appeasing him, as savages do, by abstinence, abasement, and offerings.

Doubtless traces of the gorilla as well as the wild man of medieval legend may be found in Caliban, but he is neither ape nor idiot, for he has his own moral code. In fact his resemblance to the current sixteenth-century description of " the feckless, passionate ' child of nature,' " particularly in his treatment of the invaders of his prosperity, is too great to be regarded as any thing else than an attempt to represent the natural man.[2]

As early as 1615 a clear evidence was given that the new discoveries were being used systematically for philosophic

---

[1] The *Tempest*, act ii, scene i, pp. 143, 160 (Hudson edition). Gonzalo's description of an ideal commonwealth was undoubtedly suggested by a chapter entitled " Of the Canniballes," in John Florio's translation of Montaigne's *Essays*.

[2] John Linton Myres, *The Influence of Anthropology on the Course of Political Science*, pp. 15, 16, in University of California Publications in History, vol. iv, no. 1.

ends. At that date a work entitled *The Estates, Empires, and Principallities of the World,* said to have been translated from the French by Edward Grimstone, was published in London. This consisted of a collection of studies of human societies. The scope of the book purported to include, besides the accounts of all European states,

the kingdoms of Tartary, China, Pegu, the Great Mogul, Calicut, Narsinge, and Persia; the Turkes Estate in Europe, Africke and Asia (including the ancient kingdomes of Egypt, Judaea, Arabia, etc.), the empire of Presbiter John, the Estate of the King of Monomotapa, the realms of Congo, and the Empire of Morocco.

Thus it dealt with much of the material made available by the travels and compilations of the day. America, however, was totally neglected, on the ground, presumably, that it had no political organization, since its inhabitants were in a pre-social state.[1]

Peter Heylin, the chaplain of Archbishop Laud, who wrote the standard English cosmography of the early seventeenth century, uses the same ideas and methods as those in Grimstone's treatise, although his book includes accounts of many parts of the world not touched upon by the latter. Particular attention is given to " the brutal kingships of western and southern Africa." It is evident likewise from Heylin's writings that the American Indian was commonly regarded " nearly, if not quite, in an unsocial state," [2] and this as will be seen later began to be used as an argument for annexation.[3]

Just as Bacon's enlargement of current ideas of scientific

[1] Myres, *op. cit.,* pp. 16, 20.

[2] *Ibid.,* pp. 21, 29, *note.*

[3] *Infra,* p. 270.

method was greatly influenced and inspired by interest in
the discoveries in America and the explorations made in
the Orient, it might be expected that Hobbes, for instance,
would incorporate in his *Leviathan* some traces at least, of
the current conceptions of what pre-social man must have
been like, as inferred from the contemporary voyagers' accounts of savages or semicivilized man. Now and then he
shows an interest in the reports of travelers and places considerable reliance upon them, even to the extent of being
misled, as in the case of his assertion that the people of
Asia, Africa and America never had such a thing as a
coat-of-arms. It is quite likely, moreover, that his contention in opposition to Aristotle that in the state of nature
the mother rather than the father controlled the child was at
least influenced to some extent by the discoveries in India,
Africa and America where these conditions prevailed.[1]
Heylin had indeed, already pointed out that female kingships were known in tropical climates.

Hobbes when he is dealing with the state of nature itself
makes a direct appeal to the evidence of discovery.

It may peradventure be thought [he says] there was never
such a time, nor condition of warre as this, and I believe it was
never generally so, over all the world: but there are many
places, where they live so now. For the savage people in many
places of America, except the government of small families,
the concord whereof dependeth on natural lust, have no government at all; and live at this day in that brutish manner, as
I have said before. Howsoever, it may be perceived what
manner of life there would be, where there were no common
Power to feare, by the manner of life, which men that have

[1] Myres, p. 23. Hobbes tells how the Amazons had the custom of
sending male children back to the tribe of their fathers and only re-
taining the female young, thus preserving the rule of the women over
the land. Thomas Hobbes, *The Leviathan* (Oxford, 1881), ch. xx,
p. 154.

formerly lived under a peacefull government, use to degenerate into a civill Warre.[1]

This shows that Hobbes was endeavoring to give the ideas of his time concerning man and was attempting to define and interpret the " new facts of human nature as they were revealed by the discoveries."

Hobbes found in the government of the English colonies in America an opportunity for discussing new political institutions in relation to the old ones. He says colonies may be of two sorts: either like those of the ancient Greeks independent of the mother land except for the honor and friendship they might show it, or those which are not commonwealths themselves but provinces of the nation which established them. In dealing with the latter type he believes a monarchical rather than a popular form of government the best, since the colonists could not be present in the mother country and therefore would prefer to commit their interests to one responsible authority rather than many. In case an assembly or council residing in England should be in charge of the colony, any debt contracted by that body, or any unlawful act would not be in force for any who dissented or were absent; likewise such an assembly could not seize the goods or persons of colonists for debt or other duty in any place except within the boundary of the colony itself, since they would have no jurisdiction within it.[2]

The philosophical works of John Locke are filled with a broad and comprehensive knowledge of all parts of the world. He was particularly interested in accounts of exploration and travel [3] where he could read of the manners of

[1] Hobbes, *op. cit.*, ch. xiii, p. 95.

[2] *Ibid.*, ch. xxii, p. 177.

[3] This is plainly shown at times in his *Essay on the Conduct of the Human Understanding*; it is also confessed in a striking passage of

savage or slightly civilized races. From this he sought
to penetrate into the causes which impel man from one
state of society to another. He was a zealous advocate of
venturing forth " into the great ocean of knowledge " which
was then being revealed to Europeans. He relates how it
was the fault of some scholars to live " mewed up within
their own contracted territories," failing to " look abroad
beyond the boundaries that chance, conceit, or laziness has
set to their inquiries." In this Locke most vividly compares
them to the inhabitants of the Mariana isles,

who, being separated by a large tract of sea from all com-
munion with the habitable parts of the earth, thought themselves the only people in the world. And though the strait-
ness of the conveniences of life amongst them had never
reached so far as the use of fire, till the Spaniards, not many
years since, in their voyages from Acapulco to Manila, brought
it amongst them; yet, in the want and ignorance of almost
all things, they looked upon themselves, even after that the
Spaniards had brought amongst them the notice of variety of
nations, abounding in sciences, arts, and conveniences of life,
of which they knew nothing; . . . as the happiest and wisest
people of the universe.[1]

In his *Essay on the Conduct of the Human Understanding,* when discussing the question of morality he is of the
opinion that " from their education, company, and customs
of their country" " men are persuaded that morals are

his *Thoughts concerning Reading and Study for a Gentleman;* and it
bears remarkable fruit in his *Introduction to Churchill's Collection
of Voyages,* published in 1704. Myres, *op. cit.,* p. 25. Locke, through
his close association with Lord Ashley, his position as secretary to
the proprietors of Carolina, and later to the Council of Trade and
finally as Commissioner of Trade and Plantations, was kept in constant
touch with oversea affairs. H. R. Fox-Bourne, *The Life of John
Locke,* vol. i, pp. 244, 287, vol. ii, pp. 347, 349.

[1] *The Philosophical Works of John Locke* (London, 1892), vol. i, p. 30.

binding on them." In a different age, or at a lower stage of civilization practices are committed without remorse which now would be considered dreadfully immoral. Thus:

Robberies, murders, rapes, are the sports of men set at liberty from punishment and censure. Have there not been whole nations, and those of the most civilized people, amongst whom the exposing their children, and leaving them in the fields to perish by want or wild beasts, has been the practice, as little condemned or scrupled as the begetting them? . . . The Caribbees were wont to geld their children, on purpose to fat and eat them. And Garcilasso de la Vega tells us of a people in Peru, which were wont to fat and eat the children. . . . The virtues whereby the Tououpinambos believed they merited Paradise, were revenge, and eating abundance of their enemies. They have not so much as a name for God, and have no religion, no worship. The saints who are cannonized amongst the Turks, lead lives which one cannot with modesty relate.[1]

Thus:

He that will carefully peruse the history of mankind, and look abroad into the several tribes of men, and with indifferency survey their actions, will be able to satisfy himself that there is scarce that principle of morality to be named, or rule of virtue to be thought on . . . which is not, some where or other, slighted and condemned by the general fashion of whole societies of men governed·by practical opinions and rules of living quite opposite to others.[2]

As regards religion Locke conceived the idea of God as not innate in the human being, citing as part of his proof a long list of tribes whose members are devoid of the idea of God:

[1] *The Philosophical Works of John Locke* (London, 1892), vol. i, pp 162, 163, 164.
[2] *Ibid.*, vol. i, p. 165.

Besides the atheists taken notice of among the ancients, and left branded upon the records of history, hath not navigation discovered, in these later ages, whole nations at the Bay of Soldania (in South Africa), in Brazil, in Boranday, and in the Caribbee islands, etc., amongst whom there was to be found no mention of God, no religion? [1]

In the same manner Locke, when he came to write his *Two Treatises of Government* in opposition to Sir Robert Filmer's *Patriarcha, or the Natural Power of Kings,* makes " an appeal to experience against authority; to modern discovery in the new worlds beyond the oceans, against traditional accounts of ancient societies." Filmer, on the contrary, had "with a thoroughness which would have delighted Aristotle," maintained the patriarchal theory of society, quoting all the ancient authorities, but entirely ignoring the evidence of America and other newly explored lands.[2] Locke to refute Filmer's claim that patriarchal rule is natural first refers to the fact previously mentioned,[3] taken from Garcilaso de la Vega's *History of the Incas,* concerning the Peruvians' systematic killing and eating of children. Elsewhere he tells us that there were " parts of America, where when the husband and wife part . . . the children are all left to the mother, follow her, and are wholly under her care and provision." [4]

Later in this same work he mentions conditions of government in America remarking that

if Josephus Acosta's word may be taken, he tells us, that in many parts of America there was no government at all. There

---

[1] *The Philosophical Works of John Locke* (London, 1892), vol. i, p. 184.

[2] Myres, *op. cit.,* pp. 28, 29.

[3] *Supra,* p. 266.

[4] "Two Treatises of Government," in *Works* (London, 1794), vol. iv, p. 374.

are great and apparent conjectures, says he, that these men, speaking of those of Peru, for a long time had neither kings nor commonwealths, but lived in troops, as they do this day in Florida, the Cheriquanas, those of Brasil, and many other nations, which have no certain kings, but as occasion is offered, in peace or war, they choose their captains as they please. . . . [They] commonly prefer the heir of their deceased king; yet if they find him any way weak, or incapable they pass him by, and set up the stoutest and bravest man for their ruler.[1]

Locke then says that this kind of sovereignty resembles that "of the first ages in Asia and Europe." Having absolute command in war time, at home when the land was at peace the king's rule was limited, his sovereignty moderate. It was the people in mass meeting or in council who generally decided as to peace or war.[2]

Passing from government to law, Locke gives a very forceful illustration of his theory regarding the rights of property as follows:

The fruit, or venison which nourishes the wild Indian, who knows no enclosure, and is still a tenant in common, must be his, and so his, i. e. a part of him, that another can no longer have any right to it, before it can do him any good for the support of his life. . . . Before the appropriation of land, he who gathered as much of the wild fruit, killed, caught, or tamed, as many of the beasts, as he could; he that so employed his pains about any of the spontaneous products of nature, as any way to alter them from the state which nature put them in, by placing any of his labour on them, did thereby acquire a propriety in them; but if they perished, in his possession, without their due use; if the fruits rotted, or the venison putrefied, before he could spend it; he offended against the

---

[1] *Works*, vol. iv, p. 397.

[2] *Ibid.*, vol. iv, p. 402.

common law of nature, and was liable to be punished; he invaded his neighbour's share, for he had no right, farther than his use called for any of them, and they might serve to afford him conveniences of life.[1]

Thus in primitive conditions, one had a right to as much as his needs required, or his labor supplied, provided always that he exercised careful stewardship and did not waste.

In the matter of contracts he turned to natural law and shows how it would be exercised in the American wilderness.

The promises and bargains for truck, &c., between the two men in Soldania, . . . or between a Swiss and an Indian, in the woods of America, are binding to them, though they are perfectly in a state of nature in reference to one another: for truth, and keeping of faith belongs to men as men, and not as members of society.[2]

It is likewise only by, and according to, the law of nature, that Europeans have the right to judge and punish Indians; since the latter do not recognize foreign jurisdiction.

Those who have the supreme power of making laws in England, France, or Holland, are to an Indian but like the rest of the world, men without authority: and therefore, if by the law of nature every man hath not a power to punish offenses against it, as he soberly judges the case to require, I see not how the magistrates of any community can punish an alien of another country; since, in reference to him, they can have no more power than what every man naturally may have over another.[3]

On this question of the authority of the law over the alien,

---

[1] *Works*, vol. iv, pp. 353, 360. See also *infra*, p. 271, for application of the principle of stewardship to arguments in favor of European possession of Indian lands.

[2] *Ibid.*, vol. iv, p. 346.

[3] *Ibid.*, vol. iv, p. 343.

Locke before long had the chance to make a practical application, for he was deputed to draw up a constitution for the new settlement of Carolina,[1] the first English settlement "which came into direct contact with communities of agricultural redskins of the Muscogean stock," and therefore one of the first to be confronted at all seriously with the problems of expropriation.[2]

These very questions as to the rights of Europeans taking possession of uncivilized lands are most interestingly discussed by an anonymous author, that of *Virginia's Verger,* previously quoted.[3] This writer held that there were several rights to the land. Christians, " such as have the Grace of the Spirit of Christ, and not the profession of his merit alone," held the world by superior tenure to that of " Hypocrites and Heathen." The latter could only claim a natural right which was given them by the law of nature. The author, however, did not deem it lawful for Christians " to usurp the goods and lands of Heathens; for they are villains not to us; but to our and their Lord." He then proceeded to deal with the question of the natural right Englishmen might have to Virginia and Summer Islands:

First as men, we have a naturall right to replenish the whole earth: so that if any Countrey be not possessed by other men, (which is the case of Summer Islands, and hath been of all

---

[1] The name given this instrument was " The Fundamental Constitutions of Carolina." The document as published in 1669 is printed in *Colonial Records of North Carolina,* vol. i, p. 187; *Cooper's Statutes of South Carolina,* vol. i, p. 43. See also Channing, *op. cit.,* vol. ii, pp. 19, 20 for comments and summary of contents.

[2] Myres, *op. cit.,* p. 29.

[3] *Supra,* p. 198. This pamphlet written in 1625, and included by Purchas in his collection of voyages, bears sufficient resemblance to certain arguments of Hobbes and of Locke to give the impression that these authors had at least read it. However, it has been impossible to throw more light upon the subject.

Countries in their first habitations) every man by Law of
Nature and Humanitie hath right of plantation, and not by
other after-comers to be dispossessed, without wrong to human nature. . . . Verginia hath roome enough for her own
(were their numbers an hundred times as many) and for
others also which wanting at home, seek habitations there in
vacant places, with perhaps better right than the first, which
(being like Cain, both Murtherers and Vagabonds in their
whatsoever and howsoever owne) I can scarcely call inhabitants.

Another right was that of trade, as the author remarks:

God in manifold wisedome hath diversified every Countries
commodities, so that all are rich, and all are poore; not that one
should be hungry and another drunken, but that the whole
world might be as one body of mankind, each member communicating with other for publike good. . . . It is therefore
ungodly, and inhumane also to deny the world men, or like
Manger-dogges (neither to eat hay themselves, nor to suffer
the hungry Oxe) to prohibite that for others habitation,
whereof themselves can make no use; for merchandise, whereby much benefit accreweth to both parts.[1]

Therefore, according to the author, Europeans had the
right of " mutual cohabitation and commerce." If the
natives opposed trade, they would lose their own natural
right, and thus give Europeans " another National right: "

their transgression of the law of Nature, which tieth Men to
Men in the rights of Natures commons, exposing them (as
forfeited bond) to the chastisement of that common Law of
mankind; and also on our parts to the severitie of the Law of
Nations, which tyeth Nation to Nation. And if they bee not
worthy of the name of a Nation, being wilde and Savage: yet
as Slaves, bordering rebells, excommunicates and out-lawes

---

[1] Purchas, *op. cit.*, vol. xix, p. 219, *et seq.*

are lyable to the punishments of Law, and not to the priviledges; So is it with these Barbarians, Borderers and Outlawes of Humanity: . . . If the Armes bee just, as in this case of vindicating unnaturall, inhumane wrongs to a loving and profitable Nation, entertained voluntarily, in time of greatest pretended amity. . . . That natural right of cohabitation and commerce we had with others, this of just invasion and conquest, and many others praevious to this, we have above others; so that England may both by Law of Nature and Nations challenge Virginia for her owne peculiar propriety, and that by all right and rites usuall amongst men, not those mentioned alone but by others also, first discovery, first actuall possession, prescription, gift, cession and livery of seisin, sale for price.[1]

As a further argument for the Englishmen's right of settlement and possession of Virginia, the author considers the land they take as just reward for redeeming the Indians from their savagery and converting them to Christianity:

All the rich endowments of Verginia, her Virgin portion from the creation nothing lessened, are wages for all this work: God in wisdome having enriched the Savage Countries, that those riches might be attractives for Christian suters, which they may sowe spirituals and reape temperals.[2]

Not only was political reasoning developed concerning the right to oversea territories, but the sea came in for its share of discussion, especially when great European countries began after the discoveries to compete for world commerce. At the time that Spain and Portugal embarked on their oceanic voyages, the principle of the freedom of the sea, which was later developed by Grotius, was unknown. The rule then was that the waters like the land belonged to the first occupant, and that the sea was closed to those who ventured

---

[1] Purchas, *op. cit.*, vol xix, p. 224.

[2] *Ibid.*, p. 232.

there after the first arrivals. Consequently one must consider the early enterprises of the Dutch and the English in the Orient as offenses against the international law of the time, and their advent in the East Indies as marking the inauguration of new progressive ideas regarding the rights of nations upon the ocean.

When, however, the English finally succeeded under Elizabeth and the earlier Stuarts in reaching into all parts of the world, and an ambition for a great maritime empire was born, a tendency on their part arose to support the theory of the closed sea. Considerable interest in this theory was aroused during the seventeenth century. In 1635 a treatise was written by John Selden, entitled *Mare clausum* and intended as a reply to Grotius' *Mare librum*. This attempted to demonstrate by many citations from the classics and the Bible that the sea could be considered as an object of ownership.[1]

---

[1] Paul Leroy Beaulieu, *De la Colonisation chez les peuples modernes* (Paris, 1908), vol. i, p. 62, *et seq.*; H. C. Morris, *The History of Colonization*, vol. i, p. 310; Paul Mantoux, *La Révolution industrielle au xviiie. siècle: essai sur les commencements de la grande industrie moderne en Angleterre,* p. 75.

CHAPTER X

Literature

There are times in the world's history, after an event of surpassing importance for the future has occurred, when men are stimulated to act, to speak and to write with a largeness of soul and broadness of vision, an enthusiasm and interest, which exert a profound influence upon the literature of the time. New scenes are portrayed, new deeds recounted, and comparisons and contrasts with the old state of society made. Such was the effect of the discoveries in the New World, the great thoughts and heroic endeavors, the views that delighted the eyes of the discoverers and colonists; and the romance of the whole adventure was strongly reflected in literature. Great deeds had been done, and still greater remained to be accomplished. Hakluyt's *Voyages'* and Purchas' *His Pilgrimes* were intended to be glowing accounts of the national heroes, showing them at the task of expanding England and turning her into a world power. These writings were a kind of English " Odyssey " whose heroes loomed large as the godlike men of old: first the valiant explorers of the North, Frobisher and Davis, Chancellor and Willoughby, then the bold rovers of the southern seas who bearded the haughty Spaniard in his richly stored lair, men inspired by religious zeal to deprive the hated Catholic of his spoils, as well as to heap their glittering treasures into their mother's lap, and spread her glory and power far over the western seas. Such were the men of those days, who dared to the utmost and surrounded England with visions of the future. To this were added the exploits of her greatest sea-hero, Sir Francis Drake. Then came the long list of pioneers in a new land, Somers and Smith, Lane and Miles Standish, not to mention many a colonist who ventured boldly and died bravely to found the English commonwealth in new lands, and to obtain a place of refuge from want or persecution. England loved to think of her brave adventurers in those days, to recount their deeds and to emulate them in heroic odes, in sermons and in accounts of voyages.

Many an example of these sentiments can be cited from the poets of the time. Thus Drayton's spirited ode, *To The Virginian Voyage,* written at the time Newport sailed for Virginia:

> You brave, heroic minds,
> Worthy your country's name,
> That honour still pursue,
> Goe and subdue:
> Whilst loit'ring hinds
> Lurk here at home with shame.
> Britons! You stay too long,
> Quickly aboord bestow you;
> And with a merry Gale
> Swell your stretch'd Sayle,
> With vows as strong
> As the winds that blow you.[1]

Raleigh's proposed colonization of Guiana was the occasion of George Chapman's *De Guiana Carmen,* written in 1596, which expresses British heroic aspiration:

> But you patrician spirits that refine
> Your flesh to fire, and issue like a flame
> On brave endeavours, knowing that in them
> The tract of heaven in morn-like glory opens;

[1] Neill, *The English Colonization of America during the Seventeenth Century,* p. 15; Alexander Brown, *Genesis of the United States, etc.,* vol. i, p. 86.

That know you cannot be kings of earth,
Claiming the rights of your creation,
And let the mines of earth be kings of you;
That are so far from doubting likely drifts,
That in things hardest y'are most confident:
You that know death lives where power lives unused,
Joying to shine in waves that bury you,
And so make way for life even through your graves,
That will not be content with horse to hold
A thread-bare beaten way to home affairs; . . . .
You that herein renounce the course of earth,
And lift your eyes for guidance to the stars,
That live not for yourselves, but to possess
Your honour'd country of a general store: . . .

.   .   .   .

You that are blest with sense of all things noble,
In this attempt your complete worths redouble.[1]

Drayton, also, in his *Poly-Olbion,* gives a Homeric recital of the deeds of English seamen:

And when our Civil wars began at last to cease,
And those late calmer times of olive-bearing peace,
Gave leisure to great minds, far regions to descry;
That brave advent'rous Knight, our Sir Hugh Willoughby,
Shipp'd for the Northern Seas, 'mongst those congeale'd piles,
Fashioned by lasting frosts, like mountains, and like isles,
(In all her fearfull'st shapes saw Horror, whose great mind,
In lesser bounds than these, that could not be confin'd,
Adventur'd on these parts, where Winter still doth keep;
When most the icy cold had chain'd up all the deep)
In bleak Arzina's Road his death near Lapland took,
Where Kegor from her site, on those grim Seas doth look.
Two others follow then eternal fame that won,
Our Chancellor, and with him compare Jenkinson:
For Russia both imbarqu'd, the first arriving there,
Entring Divina's mouth, up her proud stream did steer
To Volgad, to behold her pomp, the Russian State,
Moscovia measuring then, the other with like fate,
Both those vast Realms survey'd, then into Bactria past,
To Boghor's bulwark'd walls, then to liquid waste,

[1] *The Works of George Chapman, Poems and Minor Translations* (London, 1875), p. 51.

Where Oxus rolleth down twixt his far, distant shores,
And o'er the Caspian Main, with strong untired oars,
Adventur'ed to view rich Persia's wealth and pride
Whose true report thereof, the English since have tried.
With Fitch, our Eldred next, deserv'dly placed is,
Both travelling to see, the Syrian Tripolis.
The first of which (in this whose noble spirit was shown)
To view those parts, to us that were most unknown,
On thence to Ormus set, Goa, Cambaya, then,
To vast Zelabdim, thence to Echubar again
Cross'd Ganges' mighty stream, and his large banks did view,
To Baccola went on, to Bengola, Pegu;
And for Mallaccan then, Zeiten, and Cochin cast,
Measuring with many a step, the great East-India waste.
The other from that place, the first before had gone,
Determining to see the broad wall'd Babylon
Cross'd Euphrates, and row'd against his mighty stream;
Licia, and Gaza saw, with great Hierusalem,
And Our Dear Saviours seat, blest Bethlem, did behold,
And Jourdan, of whose waves, much is in Scriptures told.

    .   .   .   .

Then Windham who new ways, for us and ours trie,
For great Morrocco made, discovering Barbarie.
Lock, Towerson, Fanner next vast Guiney forth that sought,
And of her ivory, home in great abundance brought.
The East Indian voy'ger then the Lancaster,
To Buona Esperance, Gomera, Zanzibar
To Nicuba, as he to Gomerpolo went,
Till his strong bottom struck Mollucco's Continent:
And sailing to Brazeel another time he took
Olynda's chiefest Town, and Harbour Farnambuke,
And with their precious wood, sugar and cotton frought,
It by his safe return, into his country brought.
Then Frobosher, whose fame flew all the Ocean o'er,
Who to the North west sought huge China's wealthy shore,
When nearer to the North, that wand'ring seaman set,
Where he in our hott'st months of June and July met,
With snow, frost, hail, and sleet, and found stern winter strong,
With mighty isles of ice, and mountains huge and long
Where as it comes and goes, the great eternal Light,
Makes half the year still day, and half continual night,
Then for those bounds unknown, he bravely set again,
As he a Sea god were, familiar with the main.

> The noble Fenton next, and Jackson we prefer,
> Both voyagers, that were with famous Frobosher,
> And Davies, three times forth that for the north west made
> Still striving by that course, t'inrich the English Trade:
> And as he well deserv'd to his eternal fame,
> There a mighty sea immortalized his name, etc.[1]

No other English seaman of the Elizabethan Age was more honored in verse than Sir Francis Drake. The following lines were written by the scholars of Winchester School upon the celebration of Drake's return:

> On Hercules Pillars, Drake, thou maist
> Plus ultrà write full well,
> And say, I will in greatness that
> Great Hercules excell.
> Sir Drake, whom well the world's End knows,
> Which thou didst compass round,
> And whom both poles of Heaven once saw,
> Which North and South do bound;
> The Stars above will make thee known,
> If men here silent were:
> The Sun himself cannot forget
> His Fellow-traveller.
> Amongst the radiant stars to stand
> Thy ship well worthy were:
> Well worthy on the highest Top,
> Of Heaven a place to bear.[2]

Nearly the same sentiment is expressed in D'Avenant's play, *The Playhouse to be Let,* written in 1663:

> Great wand'rer of the sea,
> Thy walks still pathless be
> The races thou dost run
> Are known but to the Sun.[3]

[1] *The Complete Works of Michael Drayton* (London, 1876), vol. **iii**, pp. 9-12.

[2] William Camden, *The History of . . . Elizabeth*, p. 254.

[3] "The Play-house to be Let," act iii, sc. 2, in *The Dramatic Works of Sir William D'Avenant* (Edinburgh and London, 1872-74), vol. **iv**, p. 57.

An excellent example of the enthusiasm of the London crowds for brave deeds is a ballad which was printed in 1624, and sung in the streets of London, in celebration of a certain adventure of a Captain Madison who was serving in Virginia:

> And Captain Middisone like wise,
> With honor did proceed
> Who coming, tooke not all their corne, [referring to the Indians]
> But likewise took their king
> And unto James his Citty, he
> Did these rich trophies bring.[1]

As was only natural at such a period when patriotism and pride of race as well as imperialistic ambitions were aroused by the bold sea ventures, the national pulse was felt throughout its literature. Thus the dreams of a larger England broke forth in Spenser:

> . . . Rich Oranoky, though but knowen late;
> And that huge river, which doth beare his name
> Of warlike Amazons, which doe possess the same.
>
> Joy on those warlike women, which so long
> Can from all men so rich a kingdome hold!
> And shame on you, O men, which boast your strong
> And valiant hearts, in thoughts lesse hard and bold,
> But this to you, O Britons, most pertaines,
> To whom the right hereof it self hath sold;
> The which, for sparing little cost or paines,
> Loose so immortall glory, and so endless gaines.

Of Queen Elizabeth he recounts:

> In wildest ocean she her throne doth reare
> That over all the earth it may be seene. . . . [2]

[1] Edward D. Neill, *Virginia Carolorum*, p. 24.

[2] Edmund Spenser, " The Faerie Queene," bk. ii, canto iii, stanza xl; bk. iv, canto xi, stanza xxi, xxii, in *The Complete Poetical Works of Edmund Spenser*, Cambridge edition (Boston, 1908), pp. 244, 492.

Drayton continues in the same strain to give the English seaman's views:

> A thousand kingdoms will we seek from far,
> As many nations waste in civil war;
> Where the dishevelled ghastly sea-nymph sings,
> Our well-rigged ships shall stretch their swelling wings,
> And drag their anchors through the sandy foam,
> About the world in every clime to roam;
> And there unchristened countries call our own
> Where scarce the name of England hath been known.[1]

Milton's great work, *Paradise Lost,* echoes this same desire for conquest and the attainment of greater realms. Here it is the struggle of Satan to win the world and the soul of man whom God had made, " and for him built

> Magnificent this World, and Earth his seat,
> Him Lord pronounced, and O, indignity!
> Subjected to his service Angel-wings
> And flaming ministers, to watch and tend
> Their earthly charge.

Satan comments upon his intentions thus:

> Honour and empire with revenge enlarged
> By conquering this new World, compels me now
> To what else, though damned, I should abhor.

He returns triumphantly to hell and tells his subjects that, " Thrones, Dominations, Princedoms, Virtues, Powers " are to be theirs and that he will lead them forth " triumphant out of the infernal pit." Satan is termed the " great Adventurer " who went in " search of foreign worlds." [2]

It remained for Dryden, in his *Annus Mirabilis, The Year of Wonders, MDCLXVI,* written in 1667, to show

---

[1] *The Cambridge History of English Literature,* vol. iv, p. 101.

[2] " Paradise Lost," bk. ix, l. 152; bk. iv, l. 390; bk. x, l. 391, 440, 460 in *The Poetical Works of John Milton,* edited by David Masson, vol. i, pp. 225, 345, 389, 390.

how England through her vastly increased commerce would become the mistress of the world:

> The ebbs of tides and their mysterious flow,
> We as arts' elements shall understand,
> And as by line upon the ocean go,
> Whose paths shall be familiar as the land.

> Instructed ships shall sail to quick commerce
> By which remotest regions are allied;
> Which makes one city of the universe;
> Where some may gain and all may be supplied.

Again referring to England he says:

> Now, like a Maiden Queen, she will behold,
> From her high turrets, hourly suitors come;
> The East with incense, and the West with gold,
> Will stand like suppliants to receive her doom.

> The wealthy Tagus, and the wealthier Rhine,
> The glory of their towns no more shall boast,
> And Sein, that would with Belgian rivers join,
> Shall find her lustre stain'd, and traffic lost.

> . . . And, while this fam'd emporium we prepare,
> The British Ocean shall such triumphs boast,
> That those, who now disdain our trade to share,
> Shall rob like pyrats on our wealthy coasts.[1]

English drama also shows a strong nationalistic and imperialistic spirit. This is well exemplified in Shakespeare's plays. As Tilby remarks:

Even in Chaucer, living in the midst of the great French war, there are only the half-loving, half-cynical accounts of the people around him; there is no hint of the fierce love of country that breaks out in Shakespeare in such utterances as, " Come the three corners of the world in arms, and we shall shock them; nought shall make us rue, if England to herself do rest

[1] "Annus Mirabilis," stanzas, 162, 163, 298, 299, 302, in *The Poetical Works of John Dryden* (Cambridge edition).

but true," or " This precious stone set in the silver sea;" and
again in " Remember, sir, the natural bravery of your isle;
which stands as Neptune's park, ribbed and paled with rocks
unscaleable and roaring waters, with sands that will not bear
your enemy's boats, but suck them up to the topmast.[1]

The historical dramas of Shakespeare " paint England
true to herself, united against enemies, strong under one
king and ruled justly by him in coöperation with his
nobles." In *Henry VIII* there is a splendid illustration of
England's hopes of future greatness overseas. Cranmer
in his last speech, after telling of the fame that was to be
Elizabeth's, speaks thus of James I:

> " Wherever the bright sun of heaven shall shine,
> His honour, and the greatness of his name
> Shall be, and make new nations: he shall flourish,
> And, like a mountain cedar, reach his branches
> To all the plains about him: our children's children
> Shall see this, and bless heaven." [2]

Imperialism also appears in Ben Jonson's plays. Thus
in his *The Alchemist:*

> Come on, sir. Now, you set your foot on shore
> In novo orbe; Here's the rich Peru:
> And there within, sir, are the golden mines,
> Great Salomon's Ophir! . .
> I'll purchase Devonshire, and Cornwaile,
> And make them perfect Indies. . . .
> My meat shall all come in in Indian shells,
> Dishes of agate, set in gold, and studded,

---

[1] A. Wyatt Tilby, " The American Colonies (1583-1763)," p. 47, in
The English People Overseas, vol. i.

[2] *Henry VIII*, act v, sc. v. Prowse pictures Raleigh as expounding
with glowing eloquence to Shakespeare his vast schemes of the plantation in America and the building up of a greater England beyond the
seas. Prowse, p. 54. It is said that the leaders in the Virginia Company were friends and acquaintances of Shakespeare. Charles M.
Gayley, *Shakespeare and the Founders of Liberty in America*, p. 2.

> With emeralds, sapphires, hyacinths and rubies'.
> . . . . To be of power
> To pay an armie, in the field, to buy
> The king of France, out of his realmes, or Spaine,
> Out of the Indies.[1]

Nowhere may a deeper spirit of imperialism be found than that portrayed in Marlowe's works or in D'Avenant's *The Playhouse to be Let.* Marlowe speaks of the nation through his *Tamburlaine,* that modern Alexander who sighed for fresh worlds to conquer. As he is dying Tamburlaine calls his sons to his bedside and exclaims:

> Give me a map; then let me see how much
> Is left for me to conquer all the world,
> That these my boys, may finish all my wants.
>
> .   .   .   .
>
> Look here, my boys; see what a world of ground
> Lies westward from the midst of Cancer's Line,
> Unto the rising of this earthly globe;
> Whereas the sun, declining from our sight,
> Begins the day with our Antipodes!
> And shall I die, and this unconquerèd?
> Lo, here, my sons, are all the golden mines,
> Inestimable drugs and precious stones,
> More worth than Asia and all the world beside;
> And from the Antarctic Pole eastward behold
> As much more land, which never was descried,
> Wherein are rocks of pearl that shine as bright
> As all the lamps that beautify the sky!
> And shall I die, and this unconquerèd?[2]

The chorus in D'Avenant's *The Playhouse to be Let* utters these inspiring words calculated to stir the blood of Englishmen:

[1] Ben Johnson, *The Alchemist* (New York, 1903), act ii, scenes 1, 2.

[2] Christopher Marlowe, "Tamburlaine the Great," pt. ii, act v, sc. 3, in *Plays* (Mermaid Series), pp. 164, 165.

> This prophecy will rise
> To higher enterprise,
> The English lion's walk shall reach as far
> As prosprous valour dares adventure war,
> As winds can drive, or waves can bear
> Those ships which boldest pilots steer.[1]

Until the eighteenth century what is called romance was almost unknown to English literature.   Nevertheless, much that is romantic may be found in the narratives dealing with the sea and the exploits of seamen of the two centuries preceding, replete with exaggerations and marvelous tales that whetted the credulity of the age.   The accounts of the voyagers must have tended to arouse a desire to write fiction. Many of them, certainly, even when substantially truthful, were strange enough to have been pure romance.   The narrative of Peter Carder, who is said to have set out with Drake on his circumnavigation of the world, but to have become separated from the company, and after many strange adventures to have returned home nine years later, reads more like fiction than fact.   Captain John Smith's adventures, also, were highly romantic, and it has been proved that some at least of his marvelous tales were wholly fanciful.[2]

The sea stories of the time, notably those about shipwrecks, were vividly romantic.   Take for example the one on the Bermuda Islands, which is said to have furnished Shakespeare with most of the inspiration for his shipwreck scene in *The Tempest:*

> 'Tis true eleaven monthes and more,
> These gallant worthy wights
> Was in the shippe Sea-venture nam'd,
> Deprived Virginia's sight:

[1] "The Playhouse to be Let," act iii, sc. 4, in *The Dramatic Works of Sir William D'Avenant, op. cit.*, vol. iv, p. 62.

[2] Henry Adams, "Captain John Smith," in C. F. Adams and Henry Adams, *Chapters of Erie and other Essays*, p. 192, *et seq.*

And bravely did they glyde the maine,
Till Neptune 'gan to frowne,
As if a courser proudly backt
Would throwe his ryder downe.

The seas did rage, the windes did blowe,
Distressed were they then;
Their shippe did leake, her tacklings breake,
In daunger were her men,
But heaven was pylotte in this storme,
And to an iland nere,
Bermoothaws called, conducted them,
Which did abute their feare.

But yet these worthies forced were,
Opprest with weather againe,
To runne their ship between two rockes,
Where she doth still remaine;
And then on shoare the iland came,
Inhabited by hogges,
Some foule, and tortoyses there were,
They onley had one dogge.

To kill these swyne to yield them foode
That little had to eate,
Their store was spent, and all things scant,
Alas! they wanted meate.
A thousand hogges that dogge did kill,
Their hunger to sustaine,
And with such food, did in that ile
Two and forty weekes remaine. . . . [1]

Richard Clark is the hero of still another marvelous tale:

[He] was a most knowing pilot, and master of the ship
called the Delight, which anno 1583, went with Sir Humphrey
Gilbert for the discovery of Norembege. Now it happened
(without any neglect or default in the same Richard) that
ship struck on ground, and was cast away, in the year aforesaid, on Thursday, August 29th. Yet wave followed not wave

---

[1] R. Rich, "Newes from Virginia" (London, 1610), in Edward D.
Neill, *The Early Settlement of Virginia and Virginiola as noted by
Poets and Players*, p. 31.

faster than wonder wonder, in the miraculous preservation
of such as escaped this shipwreck. Sixteen of them got into
a small boat of a ton and a half, which had but one oar to
work withal. They were seventy leagues from land, and the
weather so foul, that it was not possible for a ship to brook a
course of sail. The boat being over-burdened, one of them,
Mr. Hedly by name, made a motion to cast lots, that those
four which drew the shortest should be cast overboard; provided, if one of the lots fell on the master, he notwithstand-
ing should be preserved, as in whom all their safety was concerned. Our Richard Clark their master disavowed any ac-
ceptance of such privilege replying, " they would live or
die together."

On the fifth day Mr. Hedly (who first motioned lot drawing) and another died, whereby their boat was somewhat alight-
ened. For five days and nights they saw the sun and the stars
but once; so that they only kept up their boat with their single
oar, going as the sea did drive it. They continued four days
without any sustenance, save what the weeds which swam in
the sea, and the salt water did afford. On the seventh day,
about eleven o'clock they had sight of, and about three they
came on the south part of Newfoundland. All the time
of their being at sea, the wind kept continually south (which
if it had shifted on any other point, they had never come to
land) ; but came contrary at the north within half an hour
after their arrival.

Being all come safe to shore, they kneeled down, and gave
God praise (as they justly might) for their miraculous deliver-
ance. They remained there three days and nights, having their
plentiful repast upon berries and wild peason. After five days
rowing along the shore, they happened on a Spanish ship of
Saint John de Lus, which courteously brought them home to
Biscay. The Visitors of the Inquisition, coming aboard the
ship, put them on examination; but, by the master's favour,
and some general answer, they escaped for the present. Fearing a second search, they shifted for themselves, and going

twelve miles by night, got into France, and so safely arrived
in England.[1]

A further source of romantic impulse was the buccaneer-
ing warfare carried on by the English with the Spanish.
The last fight of the " Revenge," described by Sir Walter
Raleigh in 1591, is a splendid illustration of this:

All the powder of the Revenge to the last barrell was
spent, all her pikes broken, fortie of her best men slaine and
the most part of the rest hurt. In the beginning of the fight
she had but one hundreth free from sickness, and four score
& ten sicke, laid in hold upon the Ballast. A small troup to
man, such a ship, & a weake garrison to resist so mighty an
army. By those hundred al was susteined, the voleis, boord-
ings, and entrings of fifteen ships of warre, besides those
which beat her at large. On the contrary, the Spanish were
always supplied with souldiers brought from every squadron:
all maner of Arms and powder at will. Unto ours there remained no comfort at all, no hope, no supply either of ships,
men or weapons; the Mastes all beaten overboard, all her
tackle cut asunder, her upper worke altogether raised, and
in effect evened shee was with the water, but the very foundation or bottome of a ship, nothing being left over head
either for flight or defence. Sir Richard finding himselfe in
this distresse, and unable any longer to make resistance, . . .
commaunded the Master gunner, whom hee knew to be a most
resolute man, to split and sinke the shippe: that thereby nothing might remain of glory or victory to the Spaniards': seeing
in so many houres fight, and with so great a Navie they were
not able to take her, having had fifteene houres time, above
ten thousand men, & fiftie and three saile of warre to per-
forme it withall; and perswaded the company, or as many as
hee could induce, to yeelde themselves unto God, and to the
mercie of none else, but as they had, like valiant resolute men,

---

[1] Fuller, *op. cit.*, vol. i, p. 459.

repulsed so many enemies, they should not nowe shorten the honour of their Nation, by prolonging their owne lives for a few houres, or a fewe dayes. . . . [1]

In no way did the discoveries influence literature more than by increasing the Englishman's power of description and his appreciation of the beauties of nature. While Shakespeare, Milton and other great authors of the day might not directly show the influence of the voyages by choice of plot for example, still when they desired a vivid or forceful simile they at once turned to that rich storehouse. Scattered here and there through these accounts, one discovers veritable pearls of expression. If reading of India, it may be a vision of untold opulence, of brilliant silks and the fragrant odors of spice and perfume; if of Virginia, the description of the great store of varied commodities, the natural wealth; if of the voyages to the northern ocean, the horrors of the grinding ice and dreadful fogs; while, again, it may be wild storms of the Atlantic. Thus Sir Thomas Roe, who was sent by King James I at the opening of the seventeenth century on an embassy to India, describes a birthday celebration of the Great Mogul: ›

The time was spent in bringing of his greatest Elephants before him, some of which being lord-Elephants, had their chaines, bels, and furniture of Gold and Silver, attended with many gilt banners and flags, and eight or tenne Elephants waiting on him, clothed in Gold, Silke, and Silver. Thus passed about twelve Companies most richly furnished, the first having all the Plates on his head and breast set with Rubies and Emeraulds, being a beast of a wonderfull stature and beautie. They all bowed downe before the King, making reverence very handsomely, and was a shew as worthy as ever

---

[1] Hakluyt, *op. cit.,* vol. vii, p. 45.

I saw any beasts onely. The Keepers of every chiefe Elephant gave a present.[1]

Again at the celebration of their New Year's Day the sovereign sat enthroned amidst great splendors:

The Prince, Sultan Coronne had at the left side a Pavilion, the supporters whereof were covered with Silver, as were some of those also neere the Kings Throne: the forme thereof was square, the matter wood, inlayed with mother of Pearle, borne up with foure pillers, and covered with cloth of Gold about the edge over-head like a valence, was a net fringe of good Pearle, upon which hung downe Pomgranates, Apples, Peares, and such fruits of Gold, but hollow; within that the king sate on Cushions, very rich in Pearles, in Jewels round about the Court; before the Throne the Principall men had erected Tents, which encompassed the Court, and lined them with Velvet, Damaske, and Taffatae ordinarily, some few with cloth of Gold, wherein they retired, and set to shew all their wealth: for anciently the Kings were used to goe to every Tent, and there take what pleased them; but now it is all changed, the King sitting to receive what New Yeeres gifts are brought to him. Hee comes abroad at the usuall houre of the Durbar, and retires with the same: here are offered to him by all sorts great gifts.[2]

How the conception of Oriental splendor affected Milton is evident in his picture of Satan:

> High on a throne of royal state, which far
> Outshone the wealth of Ormus and of Ind,
> Or where the gorgeous East with richest hand,
> Showers on her kings barbaric pearls and gold,
> Satan exalted sat.[3]

---

[1] Purchas, *op. cit.*, vol. iv, pp. 352-353.

[2] *Ibid.*, p. 332.

[3] " Paradise Lost," bk. ii, l. 1 in *Works*, vol. i, p. 158.

Lane, writing from Virginia to Hakluyt, says:

We have discovered the maine to be the goodliest soyle under the cope of heaven, so abounding with sweete trees, that bring such sundry rich and pleasant gummes, grapes of such greatnesse, yet wilde, as France, Spaine, nor Italie have no greater.[1]

Another writer of the time observes:

Nor is the present wildnesse of it without a particular beauty, being all over a naturall Grove of Oakes, Pines, Cedars, Cipresse, Mulberry, Chestnut, Laurell, Sassafras, Cherry, Plum trees, and Vines, all of so delectable an aspect, that the melanchollyest eye in the world cannot look upon it without contentment, nor content himself without admiration. No shrubs or underwoods choake up your passage, and in its season your foot can hardly direct itselfe where it will not be died in the bloud of large and delicious Strawberries. . . . [2]

So, too, a poem called *The Muse's Elizium*, written in 1630 by Drayton, vividly pictures a land which reminds one of the descriptions of Virginia:

> A paradise on earth is found
> Though far from vulgar sight
> Which with those pleasures doth abound
> That it Elizium hight.
>
> .   .   .   .
>
> Oft spreading vines climb up the cleeves,
> Whose ripen'd clusters there
> Their liquid purple drop, which drives
> A vintage through the year.

[1] Hakluyt, *op. cit.*, vol. vii, p. 319. It was said upon Amidas and Barlow's arrival in Virginia that the sea coast was "so full of grapes; as the very beating and surge of the sea overflowed them." John Smith, *op. cit.*, p. 2.

[2] Edward Williams, "Virginia: More especially the South part thereof, Richly and truly valued, etc.," The Second Edition, London, 1650, p. 11, in Force, *op. cit.*. vol. iii.

> Those cleeves whose craggy sides are clad
> With trees of sundry suits,
> Which make continual summer glad,
> Even bending with their fruits.
>
> Some ripening, ready some to fall,
> Some blossom'd, some to bloom,
> Like gorgeous hangings on the wall
> Of some rich princely room.
>
> Pomegranates, lemons, citrons, so
> Their laded branches bow,
> Their leaves in number that outgo
> Nor roomth will them allow.[1]

No part of the New World seemed to appeal to the English eye more than the Bermudas. Here was the scene, not only of romantic shipwrecks but of an earthly paradise. Just as Shakespeare introduced them to English drama, so Edmund Waller helped to make them famous in his *Battle of the Summer Islands.* Few poems can equal in descriptive power Andrew Marvell's

> Where the remote Bermudas ride,
> In ocean's bosom unespied;
>
> .   .   .   .
>
> He hangs in shades the orange bright,
> Like golden lamps in a green night,
> And does in the pomegranates close
> Jewels more rich than Ormus shows;
> He makes the figs our mouths to meet,
> And throws the melon at our feet;
> But apples plants of such a price,
> No tree could ever bear them twice;
> With cedars chosen by His hand,
> From Lebanon, He stores the land,
> And makes the hollow seas, that roar,
> Proclaim the ambergreese on shore; . . . [2]

[1] W. T. Young, *The Poetry of the Age of Shakespeare*, p. 179.

[2] *The Poems of Andrew Marvell* (London and New York, 1892), pp. 39-40. Marvell's " Bermudas " is descriptive of the experiences of friends of his who, in the days of Laud were exiled to these islands. *Cambridge History of English Literature*, vol. vii, p. 207.

Dryden pictures nature, as it was first seen by the Span-iards upon their landing in Mexico, in the following manner:

> Here nature spreads her fruitful sweetness round,
> Breathes on the air, and broods upon the ground:
> Here days and nights the only seasons be;
> The sun no climate does so gladly see;
> When forced from hence, to view our parts, he mourns,
> Takes little journeys, and makes quick returns.
> Methinks, we walk in dreams on Fairyland,
> Where golden ore lies mixt with common sand;
> Each downfall of a flood, the mountains pour
> From their rich bowels, rolls a silver shower.[1]

Contrast with these pleasing scenes the dread terror of the Arctic seas: " Here, in the place of odoriferous and fra-grant smels of sweete gums & pleasant notes of musicall birdes, which other Countreys in more temperate Zones do yeeld, wee tasted the most boisterous Boreal blasts mixt with snow and haile, in the moneths of June and July." There were ice along the coast like a " continuall bulwarke," high snow-clad mountains, and thick fogs. " There fell such a fogge and hidious mist that we could not see one another." [2] So when Milton wanted to make as dreadful a picture as possible of the stream which flowed from the mouth of hell, at once there flashed upon his mind the descriptions of the Arctic seas, which the English sailors had brought home, and in glowing language he portrays the terrors of the North East passage:

> Then both from out Hell gates, into the waste
> Wide anarchy of Chaos, damp and dark,
> Flew diverse, and, with power (their power was great)
> Hovering upon the waters, what they met

[1] John Dryden, " The Indian Emperor " (first acted in 1665), act i, sc. i, in *The Dramatic Works of John Dryden* (Edinburgh, 1882), vol. ii, p. 325.

[2] Hakluyt, *op. cit.*, vol. vii, pp. 214, 233.

> Solid or slimy, as in raging sea
> Tossed up and down, together crowded drove,
> From each side shoaling, towards the mouth of Hell,
> As when two polar winds, blowing adverse
> Upon the Cronian sea, together drive
> Mountains of ice, that stop the imagined way
> Beyond Petsora eastward to the rich
> Cathaian Coast.[1]

Once more the frozen seas must have been before the poet's vision when he wrote:

> Beyond this flood a frozen continent
> Lies dark and wild, beat with perpetual storms. . . . [2]

William Strachey, in his *A True Report of the Wreck and Redemption of Sir Thomas Gates Kt., upon the islands of Bermudas,* has given one of the most marvelous bits of description found anywhere in the literature of the time:

It was upon St. James day, July the twenty-fourth, 1609, . . . the cloudes gathering thicke upon us, and the windes singing, and whistling most unusually, (that) a dreadfull storme and hideous began to blow from out of the Northeast, which swelling, and roaring as it were by fits, some houres with more violence than others, at length did beate all light from heaven; which like an hell of darknesse, turned blacke upon us. . . . For foure and twenty houres the storme in a restlesse tumult, had blowne so exceedingly, as we could not apprehend in our imaginations any possibility of greater violence, yet did wee still finde it, not onely more terrible, but more constant, fury added to fury, and one storme urging a second more outragious than the former. . . . Sometimes strikes in our ship amongst women, and passengers, not used to such hurly and discomforts, made us looke one upon the other with troubled

---

[1] Milton, " Paradise Lost." The Petsora was a river in northern Russia; while the Cronian Sea refers to the Arctic Sea. *Works,* vol. i, p. 158.

[2] *Ibid.,* bk. ii, l. 587, vol. i, p. 175.

hearts, and panting bosomes: our clamours dround in the windes, and the windes in thunder. Prayers might well be in the heart and lips, but drowned in the outcries of the Officers: nothing heard that could give comfort, nothing seene that might incourage hope.[1]

Some writers were not merely concerned with describing the impressions that European voyagers gained from the new lands; they went further and attempted to picture the feelings of the Indians upon first seeing the white man and his ships.   Dryden in one of his plays has given a most interesting description of the arrival of Cortes in Mexico as it was seen supposedly through Aztec eyes.   Montezuma had sent one of his servants to the frontiers of his land to see whether an enemy was approaching.   This man, Guyomar by name, came rushing back with the following tale:

> I went, in order, sir, to your command,
> To view the utmost limits of the land:
> To that seashore where no more world is found,
> But foaming billows breaking on the ground;
> Where, for a while, my eyes no object met,
> But distant skies, that in the ocean set;
> And low-hung clouds, that dipt themselves in rain,
> To shake their fleeces on the earth again.
> At last, as far as I could cast my eyes
> Upon the sea, somewhat, methought, did rise,
> Like bluish mists, which, still appearing more,
> Took dreadful shapes, and moved towards the shore.
>
> . . . The object, I could first distinctly view,
> Was tall straight trees, which on the waters flew;
> Wings on their sides, instead of leaves, did grow,
> Which gathered all the breath the winds could blow:
> And at their roots grew floating palaces,
> Whose outblowed bellies cut the yielding seas.

Montezuma   What divine monsters, O ye gods, were these,
> That float in air, and fly upon the seas!
> Came they alive, or dead, upon the shore?

[1] Purchas, *op. cit.*, vol. xix, p. 6, *et seq.*

Guyomar   Alas, they lived too sure : I heard them roar.
    All turned their sides, and to each other spoke;
    I saw their words break out in fire and smoke.
    Sure 'tis their voice, that thunders from on high, . . . [1]

The wide ocean furnished many a descriptive phrase, many a character to dramatists and poets. It was the symbol, also, of limitless space, of the deeper and less easily expressed truths and experiences of life. Thus Dryden used the ocean to portray depth of mind :

    Like the vast seas, your mind no limits knows,
    Like them, lies open to each wind that blows. . . . [2]

Again depth of anger is represented by the poet through sea terms :

    'Twere vain to own repentance, since I know
    Thy scorn, which did my passions once despise,
    Once more would make my swelling anger flow,
    Which now ebbs lower than your miseries. . . . [3]

Shakespeare fully appreciated the sea's appeal of power and tempestuous unrest, though he seldom deals with it directly. Throughout his works are scattered similes, desscriptive illustrations, words and phrases suggested by the sea.[4] Venus when Adonis breaks from her is compared to to

    One on shore
    Gazing upon a late embarked friend,
    Till the wild waves will have him seen no more,
    Whose ridges with the meeting clouds contend.[5]

[1] Dryden, " Indian Emperor," act i, sc. i, in *Works*, vol. ii, p. 331.

[2] Dryden, " Indian Queen," act i, sc. i, in *Works*, vol. ii, p. 231.

[3] *Ibid.*, act ii, sc. i, p. 239.

[4] Shakespeare undoubtedly studied Hakluyt's accounts and derived inspiration concerning sea life from them. Hakluyt's *Principall Navigations* were published in the first edition in 1589. *The Cambridge History of English Literature*, vol. iv, p. 92.

[5] *Venus and Adonis, Lucrece and other Poems* (edited by Rolfe), p. 76.

Salarino, in *The Merchant of Venice,* struck a personal chord with many of his auditors at the Globe Theatre when he delivered his speech:

> Your mind is tossing on the ocean;
> There, where your argosies with portly sail,
> Like signiors and rich burghers of the flood,
> Or, as it were, the pageants of the sea,
> Do over peer the petty traffickers,
> That curt'sy to them, do them reverence,
> As they fly by them with their woven wings.

Salarino then confesses freely that, if he had placed his money in such an adventure, his mind would be filled with anxiety for the issue:

> I should be still
> Plucking the grass, to know where sets the wind;
> Peering in maps for ports, and piers, and roads:
> And every object, that might make me fear
> Misfortune to my ventures, out of doubt:
> Would make me sad.[1]

Many members of the East India Company must have experienced feelings similar to those ascribed by the poet to Antonio's friend, who had invested his money in a voyage to the Orient, and could not so much as gaze upon the running sands in an hour-glass without thinking

> Of shallows and of flats;
> And see my wealthy Andrew dock'd in sand
> Vailing her high-top lower than her ribs,
> To kiss her burial. Should I go to church,
> And see the holy edifice of stone,
> And not bethink me straight of dangerous rocks?
> Which, touching but gentle vessel's side,
> Would scatter all her spices on the stream;
> Enrobe the roaring waters with my silks;
> And, in a word, but even now worth this,
> And now worth nothing? [2]

[1] *Merchant of Venice,* act i, sc. 1.
[2] *Ibid.*

" I would have," says the clown in *Twelfth Night,* " men of
such Constancy put to sea, that their business might be every
thing and their intent everywhere: for that's it that always
make a good voyage of nothing." In this passage there is
given almost word for word the gist of the East India Company's instructions to its servants.[1] The king in *Henry
IV,* speaking of sleep, presents a marvelous picture of sea-
life:

> Wilt thou upon the high and giddy mast
> Seal up the ship-boy's eyes, and rock his brains
> In cradle of the rude imperious surge
> And in the visitation of the winds,
> Who take the ruffian billows by the top,
> Curling their monstrous heads and hanging them
> With deafening clamor in the slippery clouds,
> That with the hurling death itselfe awakes?
> Canst thou, O partial sleep, give thy repose
> To the wet sea-boy in an hour so rude,
> And in the calmest and most stillest night,
> With all appliances and means to boot,
> Deny it to a king? Then, happy low lie down!
> Uneasy lies the head that wears the crown.[2]

In *King Richard III* there is a most vivid picture of the
bottom of the sea:

> Lord, Lord! methought, what pain it was to drown!
> What dreadful noise of waters in mine ears!
> What ugly sights of death within mine eyes!
> Methought I saw a thousand fearful wrecks;
> Ten thousand men that fishes gnawed upon;
> Wedges of gold, great anchors, heaps of pearl,
> Inestimable stones, unvalued jewels,
> All scattered in the bottom of the sea:
> Some lay in dead men's skulls; and in those holes
> Where eyes did once inhabit, there were crept,

[1] Beckles Willson, *Ledger and Sword, or the Honourable Company of
Merchants of England trading to the East Indies,* p. 75.

[2] *King Henry IV*, act iii, sc. I.

As 'twere in scorn of eyes, reflecting gems,
Which woo'd the slimy bottom of the deep,
And mock'd the dead bones that lay scattered by.[1]

Many sea terms are used by Shakespeare. *In Twelfth Night,* act iii, scene 2, Maria says to Malvolio that " he doth smile his face into more lines than there are in the new map with the augmentation of the Indies." This was the map published in Hakluyt's *Voyages* bearing the marks of Davis's hand. Again in act i, scene 6, Viola answers Malvolio's rudeness, " Will you hoist sail, sir? " with the idiom, " No good swabber, I am to hull here a little longer." In act v, scene 1, the Duke speaks of Antonio as captain of a " bawbling vessel for shallow draught, and bulk, unprizable; " in modern terms, a small privateer that played such havoc with the enemy's fleet that " very envy and the tongue of loss cried fame and honor on him." Shakespeare must have had Drake in mind when he wrote this.[2] In *Romeo and Juliet,* the metaphor " high top gallant of joy," and the sea term " tackled stair " are used, while in *As You Like It* is the expression, "dry as the remainder biscuit after a voyage." [3] As Alfred Noyes remarks:

It is in his use of sea music, of sea imagery, to bring his readers into touch with the thoughts that would otherwise be beyond the reach of the soul, that we are to find his greatest sea poetry. He uses the sea sometimes as an image for the universe itself, for all that is outside the bounds of the individual soul. He does this, for instance in Hamlet, where

[1] *King Richard III,* act i, sc. 4. Many other sea pictures from Shakespeare might be quoted did space permit. For further illustrations see Alfred Noyes, " Shakespeare and the Sea " in *The New York Times,* March 19, 1916.

[2] Frank T. Bullen, " Shakespeare and the Sea," in *A Sack of Shakings,* p. 55.

[3] *The Cambridge History of English Literature,* vol. iv, p. 91.

he debates whether he shall "take arms against a sea of troubles," and in Pericles where he cries:

> Put me to present pain:
> Lest this great sea of joys rushing upon me
> O'erbear the shores of my mortality
> And drown me with their sweetness.[1]

Milton perhaps more than any other English poet was influenced by the imagery of the vast reaches of the mysterious ocean, as when he writes:

> Before their eyes in sudden view appear
> The secrets of the hoary Deep—a dark
> Illimitable ocean, without bound,
> Without dimension; where length, breadth, and highth,
> And time, and place, are lost; where eldest Night
> And Chaos, ancestors of Nature, hold
> Eternal anarchy, amidst the noise
> Of endless wars, and by confusion stand.[2]

One has only to compare Milton's conception of the universe with Dante's to realize how much greater nature and the God who ruled it had become to the English sage, whose mind fired with the magnitude of the discoveries of his age sought to realize all creations both spiritual and worldly in the new light which had just been presented. His words are full of the power and spaciousness of the seas over which his countrymen were voyaging:

> Witness this new made world, another Heaven
> From Heaven's gate not far, founded in view
> On the clear hyaline, the glassy sea;
> Of amplitude almost immense, with stars
> Numerous, and every star perhaps a world
> Of destined habitation. . . . [3]

[1] Noyes, *op. cit.*
[2] "Paradise Lost," bk. ii, l. 891, *et seq.* in *Works*, vol. i, p. 181.
[3] *Ibid.*, bk. vii, l. 617, p. 318.

> When I behold this goodly frame, this world,
> Of Heaven and Earth consisting and compute
> Their magnitudes—this Earth, a spot, a grain,
> An atom, with the Firmament compared
> And all her numbered stars, that seem to roll
> Spaces incomprehensible. . . . [1]

A vast sea panorama is presented in Book Seven when the poet pictures how

> Heaven opened wide
> Her ever during gates, harmonious sound
> On golden hinges moving, to let forth
> The King of Glory, in his powerful Word
> A Spirit coming to create new worlds.
> On Heavenly ground they stood, and from the shore
> They viewed the vast immeasurable Abyss,
> Outrageous as a sea, dark, wasteful, wild,
> Up from the bottom turned by furious winds
> And surging waves, as mountains to assault
> Heaven's highth, and with the center mix the pole.[2]

In book two may be seen another stormy sea scene, when Milton in beautiful language compares the applause of the assembly of spirits to the boisterous ocean which many an English seaman had experienced:

> He scarce had finished, when such murmur filled
> The assembly as when hollow rocks retain
> The sound of blustering winds, which all night long
> Had roused the sea, now with hoarse cadence lull
> Seafaring men o'erwatched, whose bark by chance,
> Or pinnace, anchors in a craggy bay
> After the tempest.[3]

However, not every mariner was safe in port. Some, like those men in Dominican or Franciscan garb who attempted to enter Heaven, were driven far from their course:

[1] " Paradise Lost," bk. viii, l. 15, p. 320.

[2] *Ibid.*, bk. vii, l. 205, p. 306.

[3] *Ibid.*, bk. ii, l. 284, p. 166.

And now Saint Peter at Heaven's wicket seems
To wait them with his keys, and now at foot
Of Heavens ascent they lift their feet, when lo!
A violent cross wind from either coast
Blows them transverse ten thousand leagues awry,
Into the devious air.[1]

Milton had a philosophical interpretation of those winds which roam over the pathless deep filling the sailor's heart with dread. Before Adam's fall the universe had been perfect, but

At that tasted fruit,
The Sun, as from Thyestean banquet, turned
His course intended; else how had the world
Inhabited, though sinless, more than now
Avoided pinching cold and scorching heat?
These changes in the heavens, though slow, produced
Like change on sea and land-sideral blast,
Vapour, and mist, and exhalation hot,
Corrupt and pestilent. Now from the north
Norumbega, and the Samoed shore,
Bursting their brazen dungeon, armed with ice,
And snow, and hail, and stormy gust and flaw,
Boreas and Caecias and Argestes loud
And Thrascias rend the woods, and the seas upturn;
With adverse blasts upturns them from the south
Notus and Afer, black with thunderous clouds
From Serraliona; thwart of these, as fierce
Forth rush the Levant and the Ponent winds,
Eurus and Zephyr, with their lateral noise,
Sirocco and Libecchio.[2]

The ocean is not always boisterous, and far away on the southern seas there are often gentle breezes which softly waft the craft to the spicy shore. Milton had depicted chaos before the creation as a stormy sea; when on the contrary he wished to picture the gentle zephyrs from paradise he thought of the Indian Ocean:

[1] " Paradise Lost," bk. iii, l. 487, p. 205.

[2] *Ibid.*, bk. x, l. 687, p. 397.

> . . . Now gentle gales,
> Fanning their odoriferous wings, dispense
> Native perfumes, and whisper whence they stole
> Those balmy spoils. As, when to them who sail
> Beyond the Cape of Hope, and now are past
> Mozambic, off at sea north east winds blow
> Sabean odours from the spicy shore
> Of Araby the Blest, with such delay
> Well pleased they slack their course, and many a league
> Cheered with the greatful smell old Ocean smiles;
> So entertained those odorous sweets the Fiend. . . . [1]

Another beautiful sea scene is used to describe Satan calmly flying toward hell:

> As when far off at sea a fleet descried
> Hangs in the clouds, by equinoctial winds
> Close sailing from Bengala, or the isles
> Of Ternate and Tidore, whence merchants bring
> Their spicy drugs; they on the trading flood,
> Through the wide Ethiopian to the Cape,
> Ply stemming nightly toward the pole: so seemed
> Far off the flying Fiend. [2]

In book one Milton utilizes one of the seamen's tales of the monsters of the deep. Satan is described as talking to his nearest mate

> With head uplift above the wave, and eyes
> That sparkling blazed; his other parts besides
> Prone on the flood, extended long and large,
> Lay floating many a rood, in bulk as huge
> As whom the fables name of monsterous size,
> Titanian or Earth-born, that warred on Jove,
> Briareos or Typhon, whom the den
> By ancient Tarsus held, or that sea-beast
> Levianthan, which God of all his works
> Created hugest that swim the ocean-stream.
> Him, haply slumbering on the Norway foam,
> The pilot of some small night foundered skiff,

[1] " Paradise Lost," bk. iv, l. 156, p. 218.

[2] *Ibid.*, bk. ii, l. 636, p. 177.

Deeming some island, oft, as seamen tell,
With fixed anchor in his scaly rind,
Moors by his side under the lee, whilst night
Invests the sea, and wished morn delays.
So stretched out huge in length the Arch-Fiend lay.... [1]

Satan's narrative of his adventures upon his voyage to
the earth and of the dangers and hardships he had to un-
dergo might well have been that of some bold navigator of
Milton's age:

Thrones, Dominations, Princedoms, Virtues, Powers!
I call ye, and declare ye now, returned,
Successful beyond hope, to lead ye forth
Triumphant out of this infernal pit
Abominable, accursed, the house of woe,
And dungeon of our tyrant! Now possess,
As lords, a spacious World, to our native Heaven
Little inferior, by my adventure hard
With peril great achieved. Long were to tell
What I have done, what suffered, with what pain
Voyaged the unreal, vast, unbounded Deep
Of horrible confusion—over which
By Sin and Death a broad way now is paved,
To expedite your glorious march; but I
Toiled out my uncouth passage, forced to ride
The untractable Abyss, plunged in the womb
Of unoriginal Night and Chaos wild,
That, jealous of their secrets, fiercely opposed
My journey strange, with clamorous uproar
Protesting Fate supreme; thence how I found
The new created World, which fame in Heaven
Long had foretold, a fabric wonderful.[2]

The boisterous sea-going population and the tales of their
adventures are often met with in English plays. Perhaps
no illustration will better serve our purpose, than a play of
Thomas Haywood's printed in 1633, and called *The English
Traveler*. In the second act the manner of making great

1 "Paradise Lost," bk. i, l. 193, *et seq.*, p. 139.
2 *Ibid.*, bk. x, l. 460, *et seq.*, p. 390.

fortunes through distant trading voyages and great dangers
and risks, and the easy spendthrift habits of the time are
commented upon thus:

Old Wincott   " Wife, it grieves me much
                Both for the young and old man: the one graces
                His head with care, endures the parching heat
                And biting cold, the terrors of the lands,
                And fears at sea, in travel, only to gain
                Some competent estate to leave his son.
                Whiles all that merchandise through gulfs, cross tides,
                Pirates, and storms, he brings so far, the other
                Here shipwrecks in the harbour." [1]

Then there follows an humorous account of an imaginary
shipwreck showing the boisterous life of the times:

In the height of their carousing, all their brains
Warmed with the heat of wine, discourse was offered
Of ships and storms at sea: when suddenly,
Out of his giddy wildness, one conceives
The room wherein they quaffed to be a pinnace,
Moving and floating: and the confused noise
To be the murmuring wind, gusts, mariners,
That their unsteadfast footing did proceed
From rocking of the vessel: this conceived,
Each one begins to apprehend the danger,
And look out for safty. " Fly," saith one,
" Up to the maintop, and discover," he
Climbs the bedpost to the tester, there
Reports a turbulent sea and tempest towards,
And wills them, if they'll save their ship and lives,
To cast their lading overboard; at this
All fall to work, and hoist into the street,
As to the sea, what next come to hand
Stools, tables, trestles, trenches, bedsteads, cups,
Pots, plate, and glasses; here a fellow whistles,
They take him for the boatswain; one lies struggling
Upon the floor, as if he swum for life;
A third takes the bass-viol for the cockboat,
Sits in the belly on't, labours and rows,

[1] " The English Traveler," act i, sc. i, in *Thomas Heywood's Plays*
(Mermaid Series), edited by A. Wilson Verity, p. 77.

His oar the stick with which the fiddler played;
A fourth bestrides his fellows, thinking to scape
As did Arion on the dolphins back,
Still fumbling on a gittern.[1]

There are periods in the life of a country when many words and phrases hitherto unfamiliar are suddenly brought into its language and retained there. Sometimes these accessions have imparted much additional richness and beauty of expression; at other times new words have naturally accompanied new thoughts and new conditions. Again, the linguistic innovations may tend to corrupt and detract from the beauty of the original language. When one turns to a consideration of the elements of the English language not derived from old Saxon, Norman or Latin two historical facts of great importance are met with. First, these words, with comparatively few exceptions, came in after the year 1500; second, they flowed in from two entirely different channels: (a) colonization and commerce, (b) the study of foreign literatures.[2] The former is the one of special concern, although the latter also must have been greatly promoted and enlarged by colonization and commerce, for, with the expansion of activities that attended them, and the acquaintance made with other nations, came likewise an interest in their literature.

The Dutch, as the English nation's masters in nautical matters, furnished them with many of their maritime terms of which the following are examples: avast, boom, dock, hull, skipper, flyboat, rover, sloop, schooner, yacht, dogger, lubber, tafferel, smuggle, stiver. A few nautical terms appear to have been derived from the Spanish, such as cargo, commodore, embargo, flotilla and armada.[3]

[1] Verity, *op. cit.*, p. 79.

[2] *The New Websterian Dictionary*, p. xxv.

[3] Henry Bradley, *The Making of English*, p. 102; Richard C. Trench, *English Past and Present*, p. 17. George P. Krapp, *Modern English, its Growth and Present Use*, p. 258.

The chief source of supply for Eastern wares, after the discovery of the cape route to Asia, until the English and Dutch began to make successful voyages to the East in the later sixteenth and early seventeenth centuries, was the Portuguese trade carried on with the rest of Europe through Lisbon. Naturally many Portuguese words were picked up in this traffic. These were mostly names for Eastern commodities. The following is a partial list of such words: albatross, Gentoo, mandarin, marmalade, moidore, palanquin, yam, verandah, caste, Madeira, molasses, pimento, tank, coco, peon and port.[1]

The Spanish, as they had taken possession of the New World so long before the English went there, and had first become acquainted with the Indians and the native commodities in America, naturally had much to do with giving European terms to many products whose native names were unpronounceable by European tongues, and with passing on those of the Indian appellations which could be pronounced in their original form. The English, reading Spanish accounts translated by their zealous countrymen like Hakluyt, and trading with their ports, came to know hitherto unfamiliar commodities through their Spanish names. This was the case with the following words now commonly used in the English language: alligator, armadillo, buffalo, cigar, cochineal, indigo, merino, sarsaparilla, vanilla, canary, negro, mosquito, mulatto, mustang, olio, soda, sherry. Other words which were introduced through intercourse with the Spanish were those taken from their language itself. The following will serve as illustrations: albino, sierra, sombrero, barricade, bastinado, bravado, caracole, carbonado, desperado, don, duenna, el dorado, fandango, gala, grandee, grenade, guerilla, infanta, maroon, maravedi,

---

[1] W. W. Skeat, *An Etymological Dictionary of the English Language*, p. 771.

jennet, palaver, parado, paragon, parasol, parroquet, pas-
sadillo, picaroon, poncho, stampede, and tornado.[1]

Other words may be mentioned as originally formed by
the Indians and then used by the Spanish and passed on by
them in their original form to the English. Among these
are included the following: barbecue, tobacco (which was
sometimes said to get its name from the pipe in which it
was smoked, while others claimed the name came from the
island of Tobago), potato, maize, cacique, cannibal, canoe,
guava, iguana, hurricane. paw-paw, savannah, manateè,
yucca, cacao, chocolate, copal, tomato, alpaca, coca, condor,
guano, oca, pampas, vicuna.[2]

Through the French accounts of voyages and the English intercourse with them in the colonies, new words came
into the English language. The most interesting and commonly used was the word "buccaneer." This word came from
the habit of some lawless French settlers on the northern
coast of Hayti of smoking their meat. These same men
later became pirates and were called buccaneers. The words
cavy, colibri and quinine (French, Spanish, Peruvian) are
examples of native words introduced through French influences.[3]

There were many Indian words directly introduced into
the English language. The following will serve as illustrations: caucus, hickory, hominy, manito, moccasin, moose,
musquash, opossum, pemmican, persimmon, raccoon,
skunk, squaw, toboggan, tomahawk, totem, wampum, wig-
wam.[4]

Considering now the influence of the direct intercourse
with Asiatic countries, it is evident that when the ocean

[1] Trench, *op. cit.*, p. 17.
[2] Skeat, *op. cit.*
[3] *Ibid.*
[4] *Ibid.*; Krapp, *op. cit.*, p. 258; *The New Websterian Dictionary.*

route by the Cape was discovered and trade was opened directly with the East, accessions were made to the English language of Arabic, Persian, Hindu, Chinese, Japanese and Malay words.   The following are some of them introduced during the centuries under discussion: shrub, mohair, salaam, coffee, henna, vizier, harem (Arabic); divan, caravan, durbar, caravansary, firman, bazar, khan (Persian); mandarin (Portuguese, Malay, Sanskrit); calico (East Indian); rupee (Sanskrit); toddy (Hindustani-Persian); amuck, bamboo, cockatoo, crease, gorg, orang-outang, proa, rattan, sago, (Malay) tea, chinaware (Chinese); soy, japanware (Japanese).[1]

The intercourse with the East promoted the study of Eastern languages and thus made the English familiar with Asiatic words as well as in some cases with the literature. Several examples of men in the employ of the Levant Company displaying interest in this subject may be cited to illustrate this statement.   Edward Pococke, the chaplain at Aleppo in 1630 translated several Arabic books, assisted the editors of the Polyglot Bible by collecting the Arabic Pentateuch and published a good account of the literature and history of the East.   Robert Huntington, chaplain at the same place in 1670 interested himself in the discovery and purchase of valuable Oriental manuscripts.   He corresponded with the learned men of every nation relative to his studies.   He made his researches in a number of places in the Orient, among them Samaria, where he examined "the famous copy of the Pentateuch belonging to the Samarians at Naplosa."   He journeyed to Cyprus to see the library of Hilarion, Archbishop of Justiniana, and then explored the ruins of Palmyra.   In Egypt he collected many valuable manuscripts and saved for European scholars

---

[1] Skeat, *op. cit.*

several important copies of the gospels, Church Fathers, Councils' reports etc. Edmund Chishull, chaplain at Smyrna, "discovered the Teïan Dirae, and ascertained the mode of reading the singular inscription on the Sigaean marble." He published also *Inscriptis Sigaea Antiquissima.* A number of others in the Company's employ were interested in these studies.[1]

[1] Robert Walsh, *Account of the Levant Company*, p. 39, *et seq.*

CHAPTER XI

ART

THE chief influence of oversea expansion upon the art and artistic conceptions of the English people up to the close of the seventeenth century appeared in the realm of decorative design for silverware and jewelry. Many of the earliest models were furnished by the ocean and its denizens. In the latter part of the sixteenth century sea-monsters, dolphins, shells and ocean waves were popular as ornamentation for silver. Lord Swaything's ewer, bearing the London hall-mark for the year 1596, had " its body divided into three sections," the upper " embossed with festoons of drapery interspersed with snails and insects; the middle with marine monsters and bulrushes on a background of waves, and the base with erect acanthus leaves on a matted ground." " In the Maye rose-water dish made in 1583 another example of marine decoration appeared. Upon its band divided into three oval panels were pictured "dolphins amidst waves." [1] Other good examples of such design were found in the old English plate of the imperial family of Russia. One of the most interesting pieces in this collection was a vase whose covers and feet were decorated "with grotesque figures representing sea waves and sea-monsters in high relief." The handles were formed of " large intertwined serpents; " while the spouts were large dragons and the thumb-pieces, lions.[2] Indeed, in its wealth of beautiful

[1] James Jackson, *An Illustrated History of English Plate. Ecclesiastical and Secular*, vol. i, p. 198.

[2] E. Alfred Jones, *The Old English Plate of the Emperor of Russia*, p. 20.

[310

design the silver of this period seems to have expressed the pride and the exaltation of the nation in its maritime successes and in its ability to meet Spain, the strongest nation of the time.[1],

As evidences of the desire for unusual objects suggested by oversea ventures, standing cups made of ostrich eggs, cocoanuts or nautilus shells, all " exquisitely mounted in pierced and chased silver," were very popular. Although some of them appear to have been known in England as early as the fifteenth, it was during the following century that they seem to have been in vogue. Cocoanut cups with English mounts are preserved at Cambridge and at Oxford, the former dating from the end of the fifteenth century, while the latter was made in 1600. The plate of Charles I contained an ostrich-egg cup, " garnished with enamelled gold," the cover of gold and the handle a green enameled serpent.[2] Another cup formed of an ostrich egg made in England in 1593 had an ornamented base enriched with mouldings of sea-monsters in relief.[3]

Some curious knops for spoons were made in England in the latter part of the sixteenth century. One type is that of a figure with " arms beneath the breast," but " the legs and feet bent behind," where they can be seen at the back in a somewhat distorted position. This form of knop, which bears the year-mark of 1561-2, has been described in catalogues as the figure of Buddha. Other examples of this design, are two " late sixteenth century Plymouth-made " silver spoons. These bear resemblance to images of Oriental

[1] *The Burlington Magazine for Connoisseurs*, vol. ix, p. 3.

[2] E. L. Lownes, *Chats on Old Silver*, p. 189; E. H. Jones, *Catalogue of the Gutmann Collection of Plate, now the Property of J. Pierpont Morgan Esquire*, pp. xi-xii.

[3] John E. Foster and Thomas D. Atkinson, *An Illustrated Catalogue of Plate exhibited in the Fitzwilliam Museum*, May, 1895, p. 22.

deities in the British Museum. The choice of such designs may have had some connection with the trade that was carried on between England and the East in the sixteenth century. Although the prevailing opinion among antiquaries favors the view that the knops were "mere variants of the apostle and maidenhead design,"¹ the unnaturally bent position of the feet and legs of the image on the first one mentioned would seem to be more appropriate to the representation of an Oriental deity than that of an apostle. The features of the image certainly have a Hindu or Chinese cast rather than a Semitic one.

Toward the close of the reign of Charles II the decoration of plate "with engraved landscapes, foliage and figures, in the Chinese style," became very fashionable. The designs were most likely copied from the Nanking porcelain jars and lacquer work imported from the East about that time, and made popular by the East India Company. This style of decorating was employed for the ornamentation of silver during a very short period. It was abandoned, probably because, while it was effective enough for the adornment of small objects, it was altogether unsuitable for large pieces of plate. "The same kind of pattern depicted in colors on porcelain was effective at a considerable distance, but merely engraved on silver it was, at an equal distance, almost unnoticeable."²

While the fashion lasted, this kind of ornamentation was engraved on all sorts of objects, such as cups, tankards, bowls, vases and candle-sticks; but it most frequently was found on articles for the toilet table. A good example of the latter is an octagonal-shaped toilet box, five inches wide, with vertical sides upon which exotic foliage is traced. Its cover has a " boldly moulded edge and a similarly engraved

¹ Jackson, *op. cit.*, vol. ii, p. 490, *et seq.*
² *Ibid.*, vol. i, p. 255, *et seq.*

convex member ascending to the flat top," which is ornamented with " the figure of a soldier attired in Eastern costume, armed with sword and halberd, standing beneath."
Another toilet casket of the latter years of Charles II is decorated with Chinese flowers and fruit.[1]

Silver jars for chimney pieces were of large size and were
copied from the imported Oriental ones.[2]   " A jar-shaped
vase of 1685-6 was reproduced both as to form and decoration from a ginger-jar of Oriental porcelain, as nearly
as porcelain might be practicably imitated in silver. Candle-
sticks also were engraved with sprays of Chinese foliage and
birds.[3]

One of the most elaborately adorned pieces of the time
is an oval dish on which a Chinese scene is depicted.   " In
the foreground is a personage of high rank attended by
armed men, and a boy with a sunshade; on the right is a
high rectangular pillar; and on the left is a pedestal, on
which is a vase containing a fruit-bearing plant; " while in
the background " a pagoda within a boundary wall with
high arched openings " may be seen. " A mounted spear-
man appears to have come from the enclosure, and is gallop_
ing away in the distance; the whole is surrounded by a
raised rim embossed with a series of simple mouldings."

There are many examples of jugs, tankards, and cups
with Chinese decorations. A jug, bearing London hall-
marks for 1583-6, is decorated with Chinese boys at play
groups of fruit, toys, birds and scrolls. A tankard made
in 1683 is " chased with designs like those on early Nanking
jars." The design is " composed of Oriental trees, and
fruit-bearing plants, with large birds and insects walking

[1] *Ibid.*; Lownes, *op. cit.*, p. 236.

[2] *Lownes*, op. cit., p. 237.

[3] Jackson, *op. cit.*, vol. i, p. 256, *et seq.*

and flying amidst the foliage." [1] A gold porringer made
in 1685 is the only existing example of a piece of old English gold plate decorated in the Chinese taste. This style
of porringer or cup is never found at a later date than 1690.[2]

The influence of oversea voyages is even more interestingly displayed in the designs of jewelry than in the plate of
the time. Interest in the sea is particularly shown in the
jewelry of the Elizabethan period. Silver whistles resembling boatswains' pipes were worn as pendants. These were
often ornamented with a mermaid, siren or seahorse and
were also frequently worn as watch charms. A pendant
jewel in the form of an anchor, and another in the form of
a dolphin, are found among Elizabeth's jewels.[3]

The ship-jewel was a favorite in England. Among the
queen's ornaments was " a jewel of golde, being a shippe,
sett in a table dyamond, of fyve sparcks of dyamonds, and
a smale perle pendaunt," and another " a juell, being a shippe
of mother-of-pearle, garneshed with small rubys, and 3 small
diamonds." One of the most important Hudson heirlooms
at Berkeley Castle is a pendant in the form of a ship, which
was presented to Elizabeth by Sir Francis Drake. It is
supposed to represent the famous " Golden Hind " in which
Drake circumnavigated the world.

The hull, which is of ebony, is set with a table diamond;
the masts and rigging of gold are enriched with blue, white,
green and black opaque enamels, and set with seed pearls. In
the ship is a seated figure of victory blowing a horn, and behind
is a cherub crowning her with a wreath. The small boat suspended below is enameled blue.[4]

[1] Jackson, *op. cit.*, vol. ii, pp. 678, 720, 766, 780, 865, 806.
[2] E. Alfred Jones, *Old English Gold Plate*, p. 9; Lownes, *op. cit.*, p. 199.
[3] H. Clifford Smith, *Jewelry*, p. 250, *et seq.*
[4] *Ibid.*, p. 252, *et seq.*

The jewels produced after the defeat of the Spanish Armada, whereon England is figured as an ark floating securely and tranquilly on a troubled sea, surrounded by the motto " Saevas Tranquila per Undas " display a most charming symbolism. A jewel of this class, which is undoubtedly English, is now in the Poldi Pezzoli Museum at Milan. It has in its center a mother-of-pearl medallion with the ark carved in low relief, surrounded by the inscription in gold, " Saevas Tranquila per Undas," on white enamel, and encircled by a band of table-cut rubies. The edge is enameled with translucent red and green, and opaque white enamel. The ark floating tranquilly amid violent waves is emblematic of the fortunes of England, or possibly of Elizabeth, who according to the legend " Per Tot Discrimina Rerum," which appears on the back of the jewel, had sailed triumphantly through many dangers.[1]

Another jewelled pendant which has been associated with Sir Francis Drake is preserved, with other relics of the great navigator, at Nutwell Court, Devon. " It is set in front with a fine Renaissance cameo in Oriental sardonyx representing two heads, a negro in the upper and dark layer, and a classical head in the light layer of stone. Behind is a miniature of Elizabeth, dated 1575." [2] The negro's head as a design was used in other countries of Europe, and of course showed oversea influence in its conception.

The enhanced supply of jewels from America and the East, coupled with the increased wealth and the desire for brilliant display which had been so characteristic a consequence of expansion in the sixteenth century, led to new ideas in the production of artistic effects. This was shown in the fashion of setting many small stones so as to form glittering lines of masses, instead of employing them as pre-

[1] Smith, *op. cit.*, p. 256.
[2] *Ibid.*, p. 253.

viously had been done for the sake of their color, or to act as a focus of interest within the gold work and enamel.[1] As the seventeenth century approached, a more refined taste in jewelry is noticeable. It had an open lace-like character, suitable for the display of precious stones. The ruby, sapphire and emerald were employed at first, but soon the diamond entirely supplanted them. In Renaissance ornaments this latter gem had played only a secondary part, being employed solely for the sake of contrast; but it now appeared as the chief object in view. All other parts of the jewel, the setting and possible addition of other stones, were wholly subordinated to it. This change in taste may be attributed to the opening up of the diamond fields on the borders of the state of Hyderabad, India, the products of which were cut and polished at Golkonda.[2]

The earliest decorative ideas used in the manufacture of china, which, as has been seen, started during the seventeenth century as an infant industry in England, were drawn from Oriental sources. The detail as well as the method of decoration is due to Chinese influence. The Oriental blue and white pieces were frequently imitated. In some cases Oriental designs were copied as closely as it was possible to do.[3] Tiger-ware jugs, having a mottled surface were also made at the Fulham pottery. These were said to imitate the Chinese " splash ware." [4]

Another example of Oriental influence on decorative design is shown in English tapestry and wall-paper. A company was established in 1625 which made tapestry " equal to whatever the Attalic Court could anciently boast," representing Indian figures, history and landscapes.[5] A set

---

[1] MacIver Percival, *Chats on Old Jewelry and Trinkets*, p. 113.

[2] Smith, *op. cit.*, p. 277.

[3] W. Burton, *A History and Description of English Porcelain*, p. 26.

[4] Lownes, *op. cit.*, p. 194.

[5] Scott, *op. cit.*, vol. iii, p. 119.

of four very beautiful tapestries in Indo-Chinese style, woven in England toward the end of the seventeenth century, and formerly belonging to Elihu Yale, founder of Yale University, may be seen in Glenham Hall, Norfolk. Upon them are pictured Oriental figures, ponds of water, ornamental bridges and shrubbery.[1] A blue wall-paper manufactory was started in England in 1691. Its product is described as " Japan and India figured hangings, and another sort, consisting of large Japanese subjects and forest work, also imitation wainscot." [2]

The wood-carving of the seventeenth century also shows some traces of oversea influence. The elaborate work of Grindley Gibbons represents animals, fruit, foliage and shells. In one carving ears of maize are shown.[3] In the same connection may be mentioned the fad about the middle of the seventeenth century for lead images and statues used in garden decoration, representing all sorts of foreign and domestic fauna among which ostriches figure.[4]

Except for some water-color drawings of Virginian subjects by John White,[5] a few paintings of Indians brought

[1] W. R. Thomson, *A History of Tapestry from the Earliest Times until the Present Day*, p. 344.

[2] Scott, *op. cit.*, vol. iii, p. 72.

[3] H. Avery Tipping, *Grindley Gibbons and the Woodwork of His Age*, *passim*.

[4] Lawrence Weaver, *English Leadwork, its Art and History*, p. 194; W. R. Lethaby, *Leadwork, Old and Ornamental and for the most part English*, p. 102.

[5] White accompanied Sir Richard Grenville with the intention of illustrating the events of the voyage and life in Virginia, when the latter sailed in 1585 from Plymouth. He was among the company left on Roanoke Island which returned to England in 1586 with Sir Francis Drake. In *Additional Manuscript* 3270, now in the print room of the British Museum, may be found some of these drawings by White. *Dictionary of National Biography*, vol. lxi, p. 54.

to England,[1] some crude signs made to advertise shows of
natural objects from beyond the seas, and several pictures
of pine-apples, oversea voyages had little effect upon painting
in England during the period under review.   The portraits
of Indians, however, can hardly be classed as English art,
since Cornelius Kettell, a Dutchman, who came to England in 1573, and returned to Amsterdam in 1581, was the
artist who was responsible for them.   Paintings of an
Indian man and woman, whom Frobisher had brought as
curiosities, are known to have been made for the queen and
sent to Hampton Court.   One of them represented an Indian
in his native dress, another, in English apparel, and still
another, nude.   In the inventory of Charles the First's
personal effects sold after his death, mention is made of a
picture of " A Cataia, or Island Man," with " a Cataia
Woman." [2]

At Kensington Palace a curious picture of King Charles
II receiving a pine-apple from his gardener, who is pre-
senting it on his knees, is on exhibition.   A painting by
Netscher may be seen in the Fitz-William Museum of Cambridge of a landscape in which is a pineapple.   It is stated
on the picture that the fruit which it represents was the first
ever grown in England.[3]

On the illustration of English books during the sixteenth and seventeenth centuries the effect of oversea influence was much less marked than in the case of continental productions.   Neither Hakluyt's *Voyages* or Purchas'
His Pilgrimes was illustrated.   In fact, Thomas Hariot's
Brief and True Report of the new found land of Virginia,
published in 1588, and Captain John Smith's *Generall His-*
torie of Virginia, New England, and the Summer Isles,

[1] Rye, *op. cit.*, pp. 18, 205, 206.

[2] *Ibid.*, pp. 18, 205, 206.

[3] Phillips, *Pomarium, etc.*, p. 294.

in 1624, are the only editions of English voyages which were illustrated. The former was also published in Frankfort by Theodore De Bry in 1590. The Frankfort edition was illustrated by 23 copper plates from drawings by John White, including a *Carte of all the coast of Virginia,* which formed the basis of the subsequent *Map of Virginia* by John Smith in 1612. The drawings are almost entirely concerned with the Indians and their mode of life. Smith's *Generall Historie of Virginia, New England and the Summer Isles,* had a frontispiece consisting of a map of Virginia about which are grouped Virginian scenes.[1] Indeed, the maps of this period are usually fantastic in their pictorial embellishments. Their " wavy seas are alive with ships in deadly combat and the fabulous monsters of the deep; their tracts of country are dotted with wild animals that would puzzle zoologists, and armies waging battle; fleshly nymphs emerge from serpenting rivers, and dryads are sportive among the disproportionate trees; while sometimes even the devil himself will appear in fearful places of haunted repute."[2]

That other Europeans were far ahead of the English in the illustration of scientific works is shown by the fact that less than one per cent, or sixteen, of the 1800 woodcuts in Gerard's *Herball* are original; the rest are from Tabernaemontanus' *Eicones.* Parkinson's *Paradisus Terrestris* of 1629 contains a considerable proportion of original figures of no great merit, besides others borrowed from previous writers. The engravings were made in England by Switzer. His illustrations in the *Theatrum Botanicum,* however, are of no importance, since they were chiefly copied from Gerard.[3]

[1] Frank Weitenkampf, *American Graphic Art,* p. 51; *Dictionary of National Biography,* vol. lxi, p. 54; John Smith, *op. cit., passim.*

[2] Salamon, *op. cit.,* pp. 3, 4.

[3] Agnes Arber, *Herbals, their Origin and Evolution, a Chapter in the History of Botany,* 1470-1670, pp. 109, 115, 197; Green, *op. cit.,* p. 39.

CHAPTER XII

POLITICAL DEVELOPMENT

TURNING to a consideration of the influence of oversea expansion in the broadest political sense, namely, how England was through it made a greater nation, and its citizens individually aroused to patriotic zeal and to pride in their country's growth in prestige, it is evident that by the seventeenth century it was fast becoming through its new commercial ventures a great world power. Most truly did Lewis Roberts remark of his native land:

It is not our conquests, but our commerce; it is not our swords, but our sayls, that sped the English name in Barbary, and thence came into Turkey, Armenia, Muscovia, Arabia, Persia, India, China, and indeed over and about the world; it is the traffike of their Merchants, and the boundlesse desires of that nation to eternalize the English honour and name, that hath induced them to saile, and seek into all corners of the earth.[1]

The aspiration to become a great nation and engirdle the world with English sails and English possessions was born in Elizabeth's day, and has constantly grown ever since. The little island ruled by the Virgin Queen had been suddenly aroused from the dull lethargy of the preceding reign which politically hung over the country like a cloud. The nation could look back on nothing but defeat and humiliation, no military victories, no great increase of trade. With

---

[1] Lewis Roberts, " The Treasure of Traffike," in McCulloch, *Collection* (1856), p. 108.

the fall of Calais, all aspiration for territorial expansion in Europe, which had been gradually waning during the preceding reigns, was extinguished, and the prestige of the country suffered by the contraction of its continental power. It had even witnessed the spectacle of seeing its queen neglected by Philip II of Spain, who had hoped through his marriage with Mary to bring back the heretical isle into the fold of the Catholic church, to employ its resources, and make it dependent upon Spain. Never, indeed, was a nation more depressed and humbled than was England during Mary's reign.

With Elizabeth's accession quite suddenly all was changed. The New World opened to the view of Englishmen a splendid vision of future commercial and territorial greatness. Then came those daring voyages to discover a passage by the northeast and northwest to the riches of the East, and those bold warlike expeditions to secure England's share of the treasure of America from the " all-devouring Spaniard," with which now a chance was found to redeem the nation's prestige, and strike at the same time the enemy of its faith. Glorious dreams were aroused of an imperial power in the vast reaches of the New World, which should rival that of Spain's; and who knew but that English coffers would be flooded with America's riches in the same manner as those of its rival, and that the little isle might step forth before the world a mighty nation without peer! Such were the political enthusiasm, the national pride, and the hopes for the future which had metamorphosed England and its people.

Thus during the Elizabethan period there arose among Englishmen an ambition to create out of their land an empire which should fill a more important place in the world's history. English sovereigns had in the past entertained thoughts of extensive domains in France, but their idea was that of their ancestors' estates. A greater England was far from their conception. Doubtless, the Plantagenets would gladly have relegated England to a secondary position, if instead they could have become the rulers of France. Elizabeth, on the contrary, sovereign of a country whose numerous enemies she skillfully withstood, had come to feel as an English ruler the desire to create such a power that it would triumph over all dangers. Now with the inspiration of the New World before them, her subjects felt as they never had before a desire for national exaltation. It was no longer merely the sovereign who followed a foreign policy, it was the nation which led the way. It was no longer an Edward or a Henry who plotted and schemed, and then took his subjects to the continent. Instead it was a Drake, Raleigh, Hawkins, Davis or a Frobisher who was in the vanguard of the nation's advance. The realm was no longer the sovereign's, it was the people's, and this they one and all felt more and more, as through individual effort on the tossing seas wealth and power flowed to the mother land. Thus the Englishman's pride in his state, and his eagerness for its future glory was born, not like other nations in continental strife, but on the broad ocean and upon far distant strands.

Hakluyt in Queen Elizabeth's time, exultantly exclaimed that England excelled all nations and peoples of the world:

For, which of the kings of this land, before her Majesty, had theyr banners ever seen in the Caspian sea? which of them hath ever dealt with the Emperor of Persia, as her Majesty hath done, and obtained for her merchants large & loving privileges? who ever saw, before this regiment, an English Ligier in the stately porch of the Grand Signor of Constantinople? who ever found English Counsuls & Agents, at Tripolis in Syria, at Aleppo, at Babylon, at Balsara, and which is more, who ever heard of Englishmen at Goa before now? what

English shippes did heeretofore ever anker in the mighty river
of Plate? passe and repasse the unpassable (in former opinion)
straight of Magellan, range along the coast of Chili, Peru, and
all the backside of Nova Hispania, further than any Christian
ever passed, travers the mighty bredth of the South sea, land
upon the Luzon in despight of the enemy, enter into alliance,
amity, and traffike with the princes of the Moluccaes, & the isle
of Java, double the famous Cape of Bona Speranza, arive at the
isle of Santa Helena, & last of al, returne home most richly
laden with the commodities of China, as the subjects of this now
flourishing monarchy have done? [1]

The same splendid spirit of national pride and ambition
is evidenced in the governor of Virginia's message to the
adventurers, which is included in a pamphlet called " News
from Virginia," published in 1610:

> Be not dismayed at all,
> For scandall cannot doe us wrong,
> God will not let us fall.
> Let England knowe our willingnesse,
> For that our work is good,
> Wee hope to plant a nation,
> Where none before hath stood. . . . [2]

Not only were the aspirations of Englishmen aroused,
but their characters through the oversea ventures were
welded in a sturdy and resolute mold and thus adapted to
the tasks before them. " Walled towns, stored arsenals
and armouries, goodly races of horses, elephants, ordnance,
artillery, and the like all this," said Lord Bacon, " is but
sheep in a lion's skin except the breed and disposition of
the people be stout and warlike." [3]   Through the voyages
made by the sailors of Bristol into the unknown West in

[1] Hakluyt, *op. cit.*, vol. i, p. xx.

[2] Neill, *The Early Settlement of Virginia and Virginiola, etc.*, p. 133.

[3] Edwin Goadby, *The England of Shakespeare*, p. 11.

search of O Brazil before even Columbus had ventured across the Atlantic,[1] through the hazardous journeys of the Cabots and their successors into the frozen north amid the grinding ice and fogs, through the bold fishermen in their fragile barks going to Greenland, Iceland and New-foundland, through many a daring venture of wayfarer on the oceans, the best that was in the Englishman was trained and brought into being. Years of battling with mighty seas had created that bold and strenuous personage, the English mariner, who during the Elizabethan period became the nation's ideal. As a contemporary exclaims:

Hee will hazard a life in the whirlewind without feare, rather than lose the benefit of his fare. The bredth of an inch-board is betwixt him and drowning, yet hee sweares and drinks as deeply, as if hee were a fathom from it. His familiarity with death and danger hath armed him with a kind of dissolute security against any encounter.[2]

Again it was said:

A sailor is a pitcht peece of reason calckt and tackled, and onely studied to dispute with tempests. . . . His sleepes are but repreevals of his dangers, and when he wakes, 'tis but next stage to dying. His wisdome is the coldest part about him, for it ever points to the North; and it lies lowest, which makes his valour every tide ore-flow it. In a storm 'tis disputable, whether the noise be more his, or the elements, and which will first leave scolding. . . . [3]

[1] Weare, *op. cit.*, pp. 58, 59.

[2] Richard Brathwaite, *The Whimzies, or a New Cast of Characters, from the original edition published in 1631*, edited by James O. Halliwell (London, 1859), p. 35.

[3] *The Miscellaneous Works in Prose and Verse of Sir Thomas Overbury*, edited by Edward F. Rimbault (London, 1890), p. 75.

How great the dangers from the seas encountered by the daring mariners were, one can only realize when the size of many of

With such a courageous character it is not surprising
that year after year, amid terrible hardships and disappointments, the English should have persisted in their attempts
to find the northeast and northwest passages to Asia, and
continued to engage in their bold encounters with the Spaniard for a share in the wealth of the New World.   Davis,
after three voyages, all total failures from a financial point
of view, and none of which was successful in reaching the
desired goal, still believed in the passage to India and had
lost none of his dauntlessness.[1]   For more than a hundred
years voyage after voyage was sent to the frozen north on
this vain quest.   What a training in persistence, resolution,
and stubborn resistance to all hardships!   The English national character gained much in these years of disappointment.   As Sir James Mackintosh remarks : " The patience
under suffering, and the perseverance after disappointment,
the hardihood and skill, the calmness displayed by these
early mariners, throw the strongest light on the value of that
school in which the commanders and seamen of the English navy were then formed." [2]   And since it had been for
nearly a century a " prevalent passion among men of all
ranks, including the highest, to become members of associations framed for the purpose of discovery, colonization and
aggrandisement," much of this spirit must have been communicated to the best of English society.

the ships is noted.   The " Squirrel," which took Sir Humphrey
Gilbert across the Atlantic, was only of ten tons burden.   Martin
Frobisher's fleet, when he set out to discover the northwest passage to
China, consisted of two twenty-four ton vessels, and a pinnace of ten
tons.   Sir Francis Drake circumnavigated the globe with five vessels
of which the largest was less than a hundred tons.   Goadby, *op. cit.,*
p. 47.

[1] Fox-Bourne, *English Seamen under the Tudors,* vol. i, p. 273.

[2] James Mackintosh, *The Cabinet History of England, Scotland and
Ireland,* vol. iii, pp. 175, 179.

Thus the English nation passed through a period of preparation in which its seamen gained the requisite skill, hardihood and confidence in themselves; the nation's fighting spirit was aroused, and its coffers were filled through the daring encounters of its buccaneer captains and crews with the proud Spaniard, then master of the western seas, and during which her statesmen were awakened to the ultimate need of meeting the power of Spain on a great scale. How necessary this preparation was may readily be understood. Before the Elizabethan period, the English navy was scanty and ill-manned. The vessels were hardly equal to medium-sized coasters of today, and were armed with primitive cannon of short range. Many of them were unseaworthy, except for a short distance from the coast. Recourse often had to be made to a foreign nation to supply the few ships there were. English seamen had had little experience in navigating far seas and meeting a foe on water. Now, during Elizabeth's reign. although its navy was not large, much had been added to the nation's maritime strength by the famous 'fighting ships' of its buccaneers, and by the barks of the adventurers and traders to the distant parts of the earth, whose number had increased by a third in fifty years.[1]

It was not, however, so much the number or size of her ships which enabled England to meet the crisis which soon confronted the nation. It was rather the spirit and skill of her seamen. When the Spanish Armada was at hand the best ships were given to Hawkins, Frobisher, Drake and other mariners, who in voyages of commerce, piracy and discovery had acquired experience, and displayed that spirit of enterprise characteristic of the skilled sailors of the time. The hope and the confidence of England lay in the fleet. If

[1] F. P. G. Guizot, *A Popular History of England from the Earliest Times to the Reign of Queen Victoria*, vol. ii, p. 362.

Spain had destroyed this defence, what could have retarded Spanish victory?

Could recruits hastily levied and led by the conspicuous incapacity of Leicester have successfully opposed the genius of Parma, and the disciplined soldiers of Spain? While Philip's fleet was very powerful, his army was the most formidable in Europe. It had been led to victory by a succession of illustrious chiefs, and was composed mainly of an infantry then the terror of the world.[1]

This glance at the history of England during the reign of Elizabeth will suffice to show how necessary the nation's maritime trading and the development of the mercantile spirit were, not only for the national prosperity, but even for very existence. Spain had taken the lead in maritime discovery and had been enriched by the treasure of America, and as a consequence was enabled to fit out an armada, which at that time might well have struck English hearts with terror. Thus, if England had not previously taken advantage of the opportunities afforded for adventurous voyages of discovery, trade or plunder, the utmost she could have done in such a crisis as the Armada presented would have been "to await the uncertain issue of an invasion, by which she would have been thrown back for a century at least in progress, even if she had been finally victorious." [2]

[1] *Documents from Simancas relating to the Reign of Elizabeth 1558-1568*, translated from the Spanish by Spencer Hall, pp. ix, 21.

[2] *Ibid.*, pp. ix, 21, 22, 243. In later years the East India trade was defended for the saltpetre it furnished and the large ships it employed, which in time of need might be turned into warships. In nearly all the great naval battles of the sixteenth and early part of the seventeenth century more than half the fighting was done by merchantmen. London alone in the reign of Charles I possessed a hundred vessels which might easily be converted into warships. Philopatris, p. 6; Fox-Bourne, *English Merchants, etc.*, p. 91.

Besides furnishing fighting ships and trained sailors to meet the Spanish attack, the development of English commerce and buccaneering had helped to provide England with the financial resources needful to aid her allies, and thus postpone the attack until she was ready for the bold stroke she dealt the Spaniards. By subsidizing the Dutch with half a million pounds, which the thrifty London traders contributed, Elizabeth helped to keep Spain occupied for a time in suppressing the revolt of its subjects in the Netherlands. Drake's expedition, while furnishing the queen with further sums for loans to the Dutch to carry on their struggle against the Spanish monarchy, is said to have deprived Philip II of from one third to one fourth of the whole annual produce of the American mines at a time when his finances were in an embarrassed condition. The annual damage caused about the year 1567 to Spain through the attacks of English privateers was as much as 300,000 ducats. The aid rendered by Elizabeth to Philip's revolted subjects had been somewhat offset by the support which the king gave the Catholic Irish; but when England seized upon privateering as a new weapon of offense, the leak in Philip's finances was so great that he was forced into his attempt to invade England.[1]

How wealth derived from oversea development proved the source of England's political power is visible also in the century that followed the coming of the Armada. The nation, indeed, was led to expand to the distant parts of the earth for political, as well as social and economic reasons. To have left the field of colonial endeavor to other countries would have meant the stifling of oversea commerce;

[1] Scott, *op. cit.*, vol. i, pp. 49, 82, 85. Elizabeth also found this money useful for loans to the Duke of Alençon and to other friends, thus keeping up opposition to her enemies until she was ready to strike. *Ibid.*, vol. iii, p. 503.

for English trade with their dominions was not tolerated by foreign states. This would have proved disastrous politically to the extent that the colonies and factories and their trade, first in the case of Spain and Portugal, then in that of the Dutch, French and English, came to be recognized as sources of national power. From them came wealth and, as the mercantilists soon saw, money paid for ammunition, arms and soldiers.[1] Thus John Evelyn writes:

The blessings of navigation and visiting national climes does not stop at traffick only: but (since 'tis no less perfection to keep than to obtain a good) it enables us likewise with means to defend what our honest industry has gotten, and if necessity and justice require, with inlarging our dominions too, vindicating our rights, repelling injuries, protecting the oppress'd, and with all the offices of humanity and good nature. . . .

This was true, because "whoever commands the ocean, commands the trade of the world, and whoever commands the trade of the world, commands the riches of the world, and whoever is master of that, commands the world itself." [2] Sir Josiah Child likewise well understood this fact, and warned his countrymen that, " while the Spaniards had Portugal and with it the Trade of India, they were able to invade England with a Navy, by them called the Invincible." He further says:

The Dutch since the Portugals sunk in the East India Trade, have grown so potent in and by the Trade of the Indies, that they have in three great and bloody wars, contended with us for the Dominion of the Sea; and yet secretly do not allow us the predominancy. . . . [However], he that looks no further than into the bare force of Ships and Men now employed by the Company, do not see the tenth part of the way into this great

[1] E. J. Payne, *Colonies and Colonial Confederations*, p. 4.
[2] *Literary Remains of John Evelyn*, p. 635.

Business: For if we should throw off the East India Trade, the Dutch would soon treble their strength and power in India. . . .

They would become " sole Masters of all those rich and necessary Commodities of the East," and by making the European world pay five times more for them than they were doing, they would " so vastly encrease their Riches, as to render them irresistible." Then follows a statement of facts by Child which have proved only too true in the recent European conflict as well as in the remoter past: "All wars at Sea, and in some sense Land-wars, since the Artillery used is become so chargeable, being in effect but dropping of Doits; that Nation that can spend most and hold out longest, will carry the Victory at last with indifferent counsels." He declares, further, that a nation having sufficient money can get foreigners to man its fleet, if there are not enough of its own countrymen ready to serve:

If it be said, where shall they have Men? I answer, If they have Trade and Money enough, they cannot want Men. Seamen are Inhabitants of the Universe; and where-ever they are bred, will resort to the best Pay, and most constant Employment; especially in a Countrey where they cannot be prest or compelled into any Service against their Wills.[1]

Petyt, the author of " Britannia Languens," continues in the same strain as Child and asserts that the nation

which hath the greatest Treasure, will finally have the Victory, and probably with little or no fighting. . . . For being enabled by their Treasure to keep themselves in a posture of War, they will oblige their Enemies to the like Expense, till their Enemies' Treasures are exhausted, and then their Armies and also their Councils will dissipate. . . . But since the Wealth of the Indies came to be discovered and dispersed more and more, Wars are

---

[1] Philopatris, *op. cit.*, pp. 25, 26.

managed by much Treasure and little Fighting, and therefore with little hazard to the richer Nation.[1]

The East India Company may well be quoted here as an excellent example of how trade contributed to the war funds of the nation. At many times it made large loans to the government and besides was able to pay an annual tribute of £400,000 to the treasury.[2] Davenant, also, states that the rise in the general rental in England due to trade had made " the kingdom stronger, more powerful and abler to wage war in 1688, than it was in 1600." [3]

Some consideration may be given to the effect the New World and the East had upon the foreign policy of England. The great national enemy during Elizabeth's reign was Spain. For the first seventeen years of her rule nominal peace existed between the two nations, which however did not according to the customs of the time preclude the possibility of strife in America and the East. As has already been noted, it was the English adventurers who took the lead in determining the national policy of expansion. They could not bear to let their ardor be curbed by Spanish or Portuguese monopolies of oversea wealth, but through their smuggling and privateering forced their nation forth on its world career. Elizabeth, tempted by the wealth acquired by these means and by the weakening effects of their losses upon the enemy, encouraged her subjects to undertake such enterprises. She then sought to shield herself from the consequences of her attitude by asserting that she was not responsible for her subjects' deeds.[4] Philip II of Spain feared for the safety of his lands and trade, upon which

---

[1] " Britannia Languens," in McCulloch, *Collection* (1859), p. 293.

[2] Earl of Cromer, *Ancient and Modern Imperialism*, p. 43.

[3] Davenant, *op. cit.*, vol. i, p. 362.

[4] Arthur Lyon Cross, *A History of England and Greater Britain*, p. 392.

the prosperity of his empire depended. He sought to check Elizabeth's aggressions by seizing the English ships when they appeared in Spanish waters. Upon this Elizabeth issued letters of reprisal and sent privateers to the scene of activity. After the simultaneous action of Leicester in aiding Philip's revolting subjects in the Netherlands and Drake's expedition in 1585 to Spain and the West Indies, Philip was led to plan for the invasion of England. This planning resulted in the fitting out and the sailing of the Armada in 1588.[1]

Upon the defeat of the Armada, the younger generation of Englishmen thirsted for further exploits. They went so far as to aspire to break up Spanish dominion beyond the seas and set up English rule in its place. Essex and Raleigh, the leaders of this party, managed to override the queen's older, and more cautious councilors, and launched an expedition in 1589 for driving out the Spanish from Portugal and restoring Don Antonio to the throne of that nation. Elizabeth approved of this enterprise and went so far as to furnish some ships and money, although Drake and Norris bore the main expense. Some years later, in 1596, further evidence was given of this policy of crushing Spanish power when an English fleet sacked Cadiz and destroyed the shipping there.[2]

One of the early reasons advanced for founding English colonies in the New World was that they might prove an obstacle to Spanish dominance of the western hemisphere. Although it was during their reign that England's first colonies were founded, the early Stuarts apparently failed to grasp their importance for their country's future. Turning from the policies of Elizabeth's reign they regarded the Old World rather than the New. However, with the Com-

---

[1] Cross, *op. cit.*, p. 393.

[2] *Ibid.*, p. 397.

monwealth [1] the foreign policy once more became oceanic, like that of the later years of Elizabeth.   One of the three cardinal points of Cromwell's policy was the development of England's colonial and commercial power.   He was probably influenced by the success of Holland in procuring national wealth and importance through her eighty years of war with Spain as well as by his zeal for making Protestantism victorious throughout the world.[2]   Besides, Spanish religious and commercial policy was still unbearably exclusive.   Not only was the Inquisition rigorously enforced against Englishmen in the Spanish dominions, but English settlements in the West Indies were harassed, and their vessels were constantly intercepted in Caribbean waters.   France and Spain at the time were both contending for an alliance with Cromwell's government.   Accordingly England allied itself with France and commenced an attack upon the Spanish dominions.   Still clinging to the old tradition that no peace existed beyond the line, Cromwell like Elizabeth believed that he could war on Spain in the Indies and remain at peace in Europe.   This time however the contention proved false.   As of old it was planned to aim a blow at the Spanish Indies to break Spain's colonial monopoly and strike at the same time the great enemy of Protestantism.   An attack made in 1655 on Hispaniola resulted in failure; but in May of the same year Jamaica was captured.   In June Admiral Blake received orders to seize the treasure ships on their way to Spain as well as vessels containing troops and supplies for the West Indies.   Cromwell so kept to the traditional Elizabethan policy that it was not until October 26, 1655, some months after these

---

[1] The English merchants who supported Cromwell's cause and mostly belonged to the Puritan Party doubtless contributed largely to this result.

[2] Seeley, *The Expansion of England*, p. 112.

attacks upon Spanish colonies and ships, that he declared war.[1]

From this time forward the navy was the great instrument of England's power.

The army though it is more highly organized than ever before, and has in fact usurped the government of the country and placed its leader on the throne: this army falls and is devoted to public execration, but the navy from this time forward is the nation's favorite. Henceforward it is the maxim that England is not a military state, that she ought to have either no army or the smallest army possible, but that her navy ought to be the strongest in the world.[2]

From the defeat of the Armada to the end of the seventeenth century one finds as Spain's strength declined that England and Holland, the two Protestant countries which had successfully resisted her, grew in importance and power. A maritime group of states, united and divided mainly by commercial interests, now appeared by the side of the old European group of nations which had been held together by royal marriages and successions as well as by a common religion. Old feudal England was rapidly being changed into a wealthy commercial and industrial country. It was steadily building up the resources which made it the strongest financial and political power in Europe. While France was led to spend its resources in useless campaigns to strengthen the French frontiers and win glory for its kings; while Spain became weakened because of poor social, economic and political conditions; while Portugal " fell under the yoke of Spain " and her world-wide commerce and dependencies were dragged down and made a scapegoat to Spanish ambitions; while Holland after eighty years of war with

[1] Cross, *op. cit.*, pp. 519, 520.
[2] Seeley, *op. cit.*, p. 113.

Spain was afflicted by a great naval struggle with England and a war with France, the greatest military power of the time,[1] hardheaded English merchants were constantly storing up wealth. They gained an ascendency in governmental affairs which was unknown in other European countries, outside of the Netherlands, and thus were able, on the one hand, to direct the national policy into just those very channels which might add to the opportunities for commercial gain, and on the other to avoid the entangling alliances and ambitions which led other countries into wasteful wars.

Commercial interests from now on began to have so important an influence on foreign policy that the former friendship for the Dutch as religious and political allies was lost in wars for the control of oversea trade. The Commonwealth and Protector, " though they had risen up against Popery, ... understood that in their age the struggle of the Churches was falling into the background, and that the rivalry of the maritime Powers for trade and empire in the New World was taking its place as the question of the day." [2] If, indeed, the Reformation had been the dominating force in the policies of these countries during the sevententh century, they would have been in permanent alliance instead of at arms. The rivalry arose over the spice trade from the East Indies and over the Dutch carrying trade to the English colonies, which took away much of the mother land's profits from the trade with its possessions. The first of these causes of dispute led to the Amboyna massacre, 1623, which precipitated the struggle that ultimately ended in the crowding out of the English traders from the Dutch isles; the second caused the passage of the Navigation Act of 1651, which excluded the Dutch from

[1] Seeley, *op. cit.,* pp. 92, 93.
[2] *Ibid.,* p. 117.

trade with the colonies and provoked a war between the two countries.[1]

During Charles the Second's reign commercial interests continued to exert the most important influence in determining foreign policy. Probably the main reason why Charles took a Portuguese princess for his bride, and thus allied England with Portugal, was the cession by Portugal of Tangier in Morocco and Bombay, India, to England, together with the extensive commercial privileges with Portuguese possessions granted to English merchants. Again, the Second Dutch War, 1665-1667, was chiefly caused, on the one hand, by the Dutch seizure of ships and the English spice isle of Pularoon; on the other hand, by the capture in 1663 of Dutch ships off the coast of Africa and the seizure in 1664 by Colonel Nicolls of New Netherland.[2] Later, when Charles forced war upon the Dutch in 1672-1674, by ordering an attack on the Dutch East India fleet as it passed up the Channel, he was following precedents set by the Commonwealth and Cromwell, since one had waged war with Holland and the other had formed an alliance with France. Accordingly many statesmen of the day supported Charles in this war, who might not have done so if they had also understood his Catholic designs. Anthony Ashley Cooper went so far upon this occasion as to quote the old words " Delenda est Carthago," implying that since Holland was England's great trade rival, it should be destroyed though it was a Protestant power, and that the English should not scruple to use the help of France, a Catholic power, to accomplish this worthy end.[3] The king, although he does not express them, may well have had some of the same sentiments upon the question.

[1] Cross, *op. cit.*, p. 519; Woodward, *op. cit.*, p. 128.

[2] Cross, *op. cit.*, pp. 540, 541.

[3] Seeley, *op. cit.*, p. 117.

Good relations between England and the Netherlands were restored and a long rivalry brought to a close, at the end of the seventeenth century, by the accession to the English throne of William of Orange. The long period of one hundred and twenty-seven years of strife, mainly caused by commercial and colonial rivalry, with France, did not begin until the seventeenth century was drawing to a close. While this succession of wars may seem to have no unity of cause or result, England was interested in a single issue: the securing of " an unrivaled commercial ascendancy and vast colonial possessions, chiefly at the expense of France." During King William's War, 1689-1697, the only one of this series which comes within the present period of study, these issues were not yet plainly in evidence, although the crippling of French resources exerted an important influence upon the subsequent struggles.[1] Thus, whatever foreign wars England had in the seventeenth century were caused in the main by commercial rivalry, and it was commerce likewise which finally created a world empire, and has influenced English foreign policy ever since.

Noticing now some of the effects of expansion on the government of England, it may be said that the country underwent a transformation from absolute monarchy and the aristocratic institution of feudalism under the Tudors and Stuarts into a constitutional monarchy and a semblance at least of democracy through two causes: the weakening of the power of the king and landed aristocracy, and the rise to wealth and power of the great middle class. When the wealth of England was chiefly its lands, the king and his nobles with their large estates possessed all the power in the kingdom. With the discovery of the New World, as al-

---

[1] Cross, *op. cit.*, pp. 617, 618.

ready observed, changes took place which increased the
resources of the farmer who rented the land, and that of the
growing industrial and commercial class.   The king and
the landed proprietors who had helped to support his power
never recovered for long the preponderant position which
they had lost at this time.   Elizabeth, the last Tudor sovereign, succeeded in keeping all her powers through her tact
and skill in meeting at the same time her own and her
people's desires.   However, she only refrained from pressing her subjects for money, because of rigid frugality and
abstinence from wars.   Her immediate successors were met
with an ever-increasing lack of funds, due largely to a sta-
tionary revenue that was depreciating in value, and a vastly
increased cost of living,[1] as well as to their own carelessness
and extravagance.   What did they do to adjust matters?
The story of their failure will be found in the events leading to the Civil War.

The financial situation which confronted James I was
significant.   The king found that his court expenses were
from £500,000 to £600,000 a year, and that his revenue to
meet them was so insufficient that he was incurring an annual
deficit of from £50,000 to £150.000.[2]   What was he to do?
He thought at once of the possibilities of English commerce.
The regulation of trade with foreign countries by the imposition of duties at the ports, and the grant or sale of trading monopolies quite naturally were invested in the crown,
as English commerce first became important under Tudor
and Stuart absolutism, and as these sovereigns rather than
Parliament had the power to sanction and encourage such
enterprises.   Here perhaps was a way in which the king
could replenish his purse without troubling about Parliament.

[1] *Supra*, p. 164.

[2] George M. Trevelyan, *England under the Stuarts*, p. 107.

which he dreaded as likely to limit his absolute power. The ever-increasing volume of English trade gave him good hopes that he might in time derive a large and independent revenue from this source. Accordingly he went about the matter in a thorough manner, and issued a " book of rates " which systematized the import duties upon many articles.

Evidently the regularity of the collection of these duties was soon felt, for a merchant named Bate, chafing at what he regarded as exactions, offered resistance to them. He brought the whole question of the collection of the custom duties, or " impositions " as they were called, before the judges. They at once took the side of the king, and there the matter rested for a while. But in 1610 the House of Commons began to realize that trade was increasing so rapidly that the king would soon be independent of Parliament, if he were allowed to continue to control the duties, and it would lose the power of the purse.[1]

At this time, side by side with the controversy over impositions, a friendly negotiation was being conducted to put the whole financial system on a new footing. Both parties were anxious to commute the antiquated and vexatious feudal rights of the crown into a permanent settlement of £200,000 a year. Both were anxious to come to such terms as would at once supply the financial needs of England and put an end to the use of royal power for raising money without the consent of Parliament. At the last minute, however, religious and political misunderstandings prevented this financial arrangement, and the difficulty continued in the next reign to keep dissatisfaction with the royal government alive, particularly among the rising class of English business men.[2]

[1] Trevelyan, *op. cit.*, p. 108.
[2] *Ibid.*, p. 108.

Under Charles I the situation was complicated by foreign wars. Here again American silver entered on the side of the Hapsburgs, who were thus financially backed for the struggle with Protestantism which ensued in the Thirty Years War. The English ran up their expense account with subsidies to the Danish king, who was induced to oppose Wallenstein. Charles I, accordingly, resorted to a forced loan as a method to collect money. Much opposition was aroused without financial satisfaction. In 1629 the House of Commons had come to fear so much for its powers, that it passed a resolution by which anyone voluntarily paying tonnage and poundage was branded as a " betrayer of the liberty of England." In obedience to this injunction the whole body of London merchants preferred to give up buying and selling goods, rather than submit to the payment of these duties to the king. Here was a most decided evidence of the existence and solidarity of a great new party of the middle class, which had constantly grown in power as English commerce had increased.[1]

According to outward appearances, the Parliamentary party failed to follow commercial interests when at a somewhat later date it opposed the collection of ship-money. It seems probable, however, that the king was to blame for this attitude, since he was not frank in revealing the great necessity for spending the money and therefore leading his opponents to surmise that he intended to employ this as a means of escape from Parliamentary control of taxation. An urgent problem doubtless confronted Charles. Since the Dutch had become the leading commercial power of Europe, and even carried half the goods to and from English ports, and also possessed the finest navy in the world and were upon the point of allying themselves with the French,

---

[1] Trevelyan, *op. cit.*, pp. 158, 159.

the deplorable condition of the English navy endangered the nation's future prosperity. A more immediate cause for action was furnished by the Channel pirates. With this grave situation facing him, Charles first attempted to get the aid of the Spanish fleet in return for helping that nation to recover the Palatinate. Failing in this, he acted upon the advice of his attorney-general and turned to the practice of collecting money for the fleet from towns throughout the kingdom. This method of taxation, although very infrequently employed, had already been practiced by the Stuart kings, for in 1619 James had secured money for an expedition against Algiers, and Charles had in 1612 raised a fleet in the same way.[1]

Not fully appreciating the situation and aroused to action through former attempts of the king to raise an independent revenue, the opposition, especially after the king in 1637 had made a fourth levy, felt it had just grounds for fearing the tax might become a permanent and general one, which might upon occasion be applied to other purposes. Besides, they saw no reason for its continuance since the country was then at peace. Thus, since the king's government deprived of popular support could not expect to gain control of the sea, it was necessary " if only for the sake of external power," that choice should soon be made between popular government and despotism.[2]

However, the questions of taxation were only the immediate cause of friction. On such a question alone it is very doubtful whether the country would have been driven to war. In reality it was the clash of the nobles and the older landed gentry with the newly rising commercial class which drew the issue. The former were displeased with the transference of the sovereign's dependence upon his

[1] Cross, *op. cit.*, pp. 466, 467.
[2] Trevelyan, *op. cit.*, .p 183.

council of nobles to reliance on the administrative capacity of the middle class. Thus, when the crown became embroiled with that class over matters of taxation, the nobility thought their opportunity had arrived. They had hopes of recovering their old position and reviving and extending the council's power. When the middle class discovered the intentions of its opponents, it decided to throw off its policy of " subtle permeation to places of influence and assume a bold frontal attack." If a struggle must come between the court and the middle classes, then everything which could not be made a middle-class institution must be eliminated.[1]

As time went on the breach ever widened between the king and old-fashioned aristocracy on the one hand, and the newly enriched yeomen and merchants on the other, whose interests politically, religiously and economically were so diverse. At length the Civil War broke out, and when the strength of each side came to be reckoned, it was found that the very section of England which supported the Parliamentary party had the business interests, trading vessels, fleets and wealth under their control, to whom was opposed the remainder of landed England.[2] Thus had the power and wealth shifted within a few years from king and aristocracy to the great middle class, which had been so largely formed by the changed conditions brought about by English expansion. Here, perhaps, for the first time, it was brought forcefully home that patriotism backed by wealth and other resources wins.

Through the Puritans, who had emigrated from England to New England in a time of religious and political oppression, and who in their American haven of refuge had found much opportunity to develop freely their religious and political ideals, the New World exercised a direct in-

[1] R. H. Gretton, *The English Middle Class*, pp. 122, 123, 126.

[2] Trevelyan, *op. cit.*, pp. 234, 241.

fluence toward promoting the English revolution and the constitutional changes which resulted from it. It is quite evident that the Parliamentary party in England was strengthened in its political and religious beliefs by the support and coöperation of the Puritans of New England. How far this influence extended is difficult to judge, since so many family papers of those connected with the resistance to the king were destroyed.

The following facts would lead to the conclusion that the Puritans in New England had considerable influence upon the ideas of their party in England.[1] Soon after the Long Parliament commenced its reformation of ecclesiastical affairs, a letter from five peers and thirty-four members of the House of Commons was sent to Cotton of Boston, Hooker of Hartford and Davenport of New Haven, urging them to come over to give help " for the settling and composing the affairs of the Church." When the quarrel between the king and his last Parliament arose, Hugh Peters of Salem, Thomas Welde of Roxbury and William Hibbens, a merchant of Boston, were selected " to go to England upon some weighty occasions for the goode of the country." One of the magistrates, John Winthrop, Jr., also accompanied this commission.

What the business of the commission was, can only be surmised as their instructions have not been preserved. However, on the trial of Hugh Peters, which took place after the Restoration, a witness testified to having heard him say, that he had been sent from New England, " to promote the interest of the Reformation by stirring up war, and driving it on." At any rate, it is known that Peters was for twenty years active in the revolutionary movements of the time.[2]

[1] Palfrey, *op. cit.*, vol. i, p. 580, *et seq.*

[2] *Ibid.*, p. 580.

The list of New Englanders who became very prominent on the Parliamentary side is a long one. Sir Harry Vane, one of the governors of Massachusetts, may well head the list. He it was whom Milton described as " young in years, but in sage council old." His natural ability made him one of the most prominent parliamentary leaders of his time. It was he that dared vigorously to oppose even Cromwell when the latter dissolved the Rump Parliament by force. He was considered so important an opponent of the Stuart kings that together with Hugh Peters he was one of the twelve leaders executed by the king's government upon the Restoration.[1] Stephen Winthrop, son of the governor, became one of the Parliamentary major generals, Robert Sedgwick, of Charlestown, one of Cromwell's generals, and John Leverett, afterward governor of Massachusetts, was one of his subalterns. Other New Englanders who held Parliamentary commands were Stoughton, the Massachusetts leader in the Pequot War, and George Fenwick, of Saybrook. Samuel Desborough, of Guildford, was made Keeper of the Great Seal of Scotland by the Protector; while Edward Hopkins, governor of Connecticut, became a member of Parliament, warden of the fleet and commissioner of the navy and admiralty. Edward Winslow, of Plymouth, was created one of the commissioners in command of the naval force sent by Cromwell to Jamaica. George Downing, one of the first nine graduates of Harvard, became scoutmaster-general of the English army in Scotland, and afterwards ambassador to the Netherlands. Among the noted chaplains in the Parliamentary service who came from New England were Hugh Peters, Benjamin Woodbridge, chaplain of Charles II when he pretended to have renounced episcopacy, John Woodbridge, chaplain of the

[1] Cross, *op. cit.*, pp. 476, 515; Trevelyan, *op. cit.*, p. 332.

commissioners of Parliament, William Hook, a chaplain of Cromwell's and Hoodley, chaplain to the garrison of Edinburgh.[1] From the facts just stated it is quite apparent that much of the thought and inspiration as well as leadership was afforded by New England to the Parliamentary cause.

Turning to the Restoration it is evident that it was largely determined by middle-class considerations. When its own government of the Commonwealth carried on war, disturbing trade and even closing the ports for the more rigorous enforcement of customs dues, which might no longer be evaded by corrupting court officials, the middle class realized the mistake it had made and welcomed a return to the ancient form of government. Surrendering the attempt to create a middle-class state, it admirably succeeded in making the state middle class.[2] It was willing to tolerate an immoral court which otherwise would have been directly opposed to its principles, because it found Charles II willing to listen to the new conceptions of policy which it advocated. He it was who appointed a committee of the Privy Council for trade and plantations, and who concluded treaties upon a commercial basis with foreign countries.[3]

Again, the new commercial class helped along the Revolution of 1688, for it knew that, while morals made very little difference to trade, religion could make a great deal. England through James the Second's policies seemed on the point of being brought back into that " particular form of relation with foreign countries which the middle class had succeeded in supplanting by a new one." Instead of treaties of commerce the country would be making alliances on quite a different basis. Foreign policy would again be " in-

[1] Palfrey, *op. cit.*, vol. i, p. 580.

[2] Gretton, *op. cit.*, p. 127.

[3] *Ibid.*, p. 142.

volved with the territorial interests of Rome;" and national affairs, which under the influence of the middle class had been brought to the position "of being controlled by considerations of revenue rather than those of power," would pass out of the control of the commercial interests. The popular fear of Catholicism had to be aroused by those interested in inciting it if it were to be effective. It was the middle class led by anxiety for its commercial interests which furnished the stimulus to action.[1]

[1] Gretton, *op. cit.*, p. 143.

CHAPTER XIII

CONCLUSION

THE essential traits and characteristics of individual and national life and thought which are distinctly modern were largely formed at the time and under conditions narrated in the preceding chapters. Hitherto civilization and the ideals which had prompted them had come from the East or westward; now an entirely new spirit, that of the New World, was to sweep eastward over the seas and, along with new forces generated from active and regular contact with the Orient, transform and revivify Europe. Its essence was essentially that of materialism, of worldly comforts and interests, of boundless freedom and assertion of individuality, of an unquenchable thirst for knowledge of the natural world which would not be satisfied with mere authority, of a bold spirit of adventure which stopped at nothing to reach the most distant goal, of an awakened imperialism which embraced the whole world in its scope.

In the material realm alone what would Europe be today without such creature comforts as potatoes, maize, sugar, tea, coffee and chocolate; without cotton cloth; without many such luxuries as the silks, perfumes and jewels of every-day commerce, without the aid of numerous exotic drugs so valuable to medical science. Picture a chinaless table and a garden deprived of most of the beautiful shrubs and plants now cherished, and a landscape without many a tree that graces the countryside.

Turning the leaves a little further, a small isle, beat upon by the restless seas, inhabited by a rather coarse, provincial, and conservative people appears. England without floating possessions, without its far-flung colonies, is hard for a man of this generation to conceive, so intermingled have the three realms become in the vision which the name Britain conjures up. It takes considerable imagination to picture England of the pre-discovery period catered to by the ships of other nations, whose coasts were infested with swarms of pirates, a country of staid landed gentry moderately rich from the wool sold to the more enterprising Flemings, a country of industries insignificant in comparison with many other European nations. Here was a land free from the stir of industrial and commercial life and likewise saved the strain and stress of foreign invasion. Its political ambitions, save for the dynastic aspirations of its kings, were on the whole mediocre and confined to domestic interests.

One needs but a few words to recall that second picture of England, the growing sea-power, whose people were favored with all the latest discovered products, and objects of interest from the farthest corners of the earth, whose commerce had encircled the globe and was pouring untold treasures into the nation's coffers. Indeed, it is the inspiring glimpse of a people that had just awakened under the stimulus of new and exhaustless possibilities. Enterprise was everywhere in the air. Great colonial and trading ventures were launched to all parts of the earth. Industries were arising to satisfy new as well as the old demands, and to provide wares for barter in distant oversea lands. Everything was tending to create wealth both public and private, and soon money was lavishly spent, and a new, luxurious, materialistic civilization arose.

What, it may be asked, had become of the spiritual strivings, the stress and strain, to desert the earthly life and attain to the heavenly joys of another existence which characterized the preceding period? One has to admit that the world had placed its coarse thumb upon life, had made men more greedy for riches than ever before, more careless of how they were attained. At the same time a broader, more tolerant and wholesome outlook upon the religious life was slowly seeping into society. Moreover, the church as well as the state was affected by imperialistic ideas. It looked to lands beyond the seas to add to Christ's kingdom. Its work was no longer to consist in merely settling doctrinal points, and ministering to the home flock, for to it was presented the vision of countless savages in need of salvation. Here, too, were lands where a broad religious toleration might exist, and a pure undefiled life might be led close to nature.

Perhaps most interesting of all and most general in its application to the Old World, was the limitless intellectual empire presented by a generous nature. Men's minds were fired by a zeal for new discoveries, by a curiosity, an enthusiasm for learning the utmost about the new and the strange, a craving to see and examine things for themselves, which led to the creation of large collections of curiosities and botanical gardens. Then came a fad in England for experimentation and, in the seventeenth century, for accurate trade statistics. From these various steps arose the first traces of a modern experimental science. Indeed, certain sciences such as geography, navigation, economics, botany, zoology, geology and medicine were the first to feel the impulse from the New World, but the methods which were largely an outgrowth of the interest aroused by the discoveries were soon communicated to other sciences.

Turning from the scientific to the philosophical, as might be expected the revelation of totally different races of men living in strange lands where primitive conditions prevailed caused some Europeans to wonder whether at last the world had not been found where ideal life free from the enervating influences of an artificial civilization might exist. Much speculation of the past was discredited and a new field opened where the mind might rove for many a day free from the restraint of tradition, without coming to the limits of new discovery. Why, since so much which before had seemed problematical was now found to be true, should not the ideal as well as the material have a place in the universe? Was not the safest course after all completely to throw off the mantle of the past and accept with boundless credulity the new possibilities which lay before one's eyes or which imagination led one to believe might exist. Again the philosopher turned to the more practical task of utilizing what was discovered to point out the lessons it taught concerning the foundation of an ideal state and society, the interest which should be displayed in the wonders of nature and the impulse they might give to the deeper life. He even condescended to attempt to settle the problem of the right of European possession of the new lands and the contentions of rival colonial powers for dominion of the seas.

The literature and art of the period were given the impress of the dominant events. A lofty heroic and imperialistic strain was imparted to English literary productions. They were vivified by the rush of the great ocean, and the loud, harsh accents of the sailors might be heard above the quiet pastoral life of the conservative squires of the countryside. Bright flashes of color, of verdant tropical forests, of luscious fruits, of the bleak white stillness of an Arctic world, of the gorgeous splendors of an Asiatic court, meet the eye of the reader when he scans the writings of the great authors of the period. Men were no longer contented with simple narration or description; now all must be filled with the throbbing pulse of a new life. The extravagant, the unreal, the romantic was in demand. Not only literature, but the language, was enriched by many phrases and foreign words gathered in distant countries and upon the high seas. Although England showed far less of this influence in its art than other countries, still some interesting examples of silverware, jewelry and pictures which bore traces of it in their design or conception have been cited.

In the field of political and constitutional history oversea expansion was of vital importance. Because of the preparation this afforded, the nation was able to meet the threat of a Spanish invasion which might have meant disaster for many years to come. Likewise English policy was given that stamp of imperialism which it has ever since kept. A middle class, created by the growing commerce, henceforth was to direct foreign affairs into the path of colonial and commercial aggrandizement. England soon through the weight of her commerce, industry and money power proved to be a most weighty factor to be reckoned with in anything which concerned her interests. In brief, the nation was made wealthy and powerful, her people were given large imperial aims and aspirations for national greatness and her government was placed in the hands of those interested in promoting these very things. Still further, her very constitutional development was made possible, largely because the new mercantile class, filled with the aggressive, independent spirit of adventure, had risen to importance in the state.

BIBLIOGRAPHY

Among the classes of authorities found particularly helpful in writing this treatise, the following may be mentioned: collections of voyages, particularly those of Hakluyt and Purchas; the various state papers; the Acts of the Privy Council, and to a less extent, the Journals of the House of Commons, and of the East India Company, together with the correspondence of the latter with its factors; contemporary herbals and botanical works; special treatises on potatoes, sugar, beverages, tobacco, etc.; sixteenth and seventeenth century trade tracts, particularly the McCulloch collections of 1856 and 1859; histories of the great commercial companies; Evelyn's and Pepys' Diaries; contemporary literature and histories of literature and of art. The histories of England, and even those of colonization, were of little assistance in either suggesting material or in giving information upon the matter.

SOURCES

A Calendar of the Court Minutes... of the East India Company, 1635-1654, edited by E. B. Sainsbury. 4 vols. Oxford, 1907-13.

A Clear and Evident Way for Enriching the Nations of England and Ireland and for setting very great numbers of Poore on Worke, by F. D. London, 1650.

A Collection of Scarce and Valuable Tracts on the most Interesting and Entertaining Subjects. . . . Selected from an infinite Number in Print and Manuscript, in the Royal, Cotton, Sion, and other Public, as well as private Libraries: particularly that of the late Lord Sommer's. 13 vols. London, 1748.

Acts of the Privy Council: Colonial Series, vols. i and ii, 1613-1720, edited by W. L. Grant and James Munro. Hereford, 1908.

Ancient British Drama, printed for William Miller. 3 vols. London, 1810.

An English Garner; Social England Illustrated, a Collection of XVII Century Tracts, edited by Thomas Seccombe. Westminster, 1903.

A Short and True Relation concerning the Soap Business. London, 1641.

Astley, Thomas, *A New General Collection of Voyages and Travels*, consisting of the most esteemed relations... hitherto published and selected from the most authentic travellers foreign as well as English. 4 vols. London, 1745-47.

A Treatise Concerning the East India Trade, wrote at the instance of Thomas Papillon. London, 1680.

Aubrey, John, *Letters written by Eminent Persons in the Seventeenth and Eighteenth Centuries to which are added Hearne's Journeys to Reading and Whaddon Hall and Lives of Eminent Men.* 2 vols. London, 1813.

Bacon, Francis, *The Works of Francis Bacon*, collected and edited by James Spedding, Robert Leslie Ellis and Douglas Denon Heath. 15 vols. Cambridge, 1863.

Brathwaite, Richard, *The Whimzies, or a New Cast of Characters*, from the original edition published in 1631, edited by James O. Halliwell. London, 1859.

Brown, Alexander, *The Genesis of the United States... 1605-1616* through a series of historical manuscripts now first printed, together with a re-issue of rare contemporaneous tracts, accompanied by bibiliographical memoranda, notes and brief biographies. 2 vols. Boston and New York, 1890.

Browne, Thomas, *Works, including his Life and Correspondence*, edited by Simon Wilkin. 4 vols. London, 1852.

Burton, Robert, *The Anatomy of Melancholy*, what it is, with all the kinds, causes, symptomes, prognostickes or severall cures of it, etc. 2 vols. New York, 1889.

Calendar of Letters and State Papers relating to English Affairs, preserved principally in the Archives of Simancas, 1558-1603, edited by Martin A. S. Hume. London, 1892.

Calendar of State Papers and Manuscripts, Relating to English Affairs, existing in the Archives and Collections of Venice, and in other Libraries of Northern Italy, 1527-1629, edited by Rawdon Brown and Allen H. Hinds. London, 1871.

Calendar of State Papers, Colonial Series, 1513-1698 . . preserved in the Public Record Office, edited by W. Noel Sainsbury and J. W. Fortescue. London, 1892.

Camden, William, *The History of the most renowned and victorious Princess Elizabeth late Queen of England.* London, 1675.

Chapman, George, *The Works of George Chapman, Poems and Minor Translations.* London, 1875.

Child, Josiah, *A New Discourse of Trade.* London, 1698.

Churchill, John and Churchill, Awnsham, *Collection of Voyages and Travels*, collected and revised by Sir C. Whitworth. 6 vols. London, 1704-32.

Coke, Roger, *Reflections upon the East Indy and Royal African Companies.* London, 1695.

Colin, Antoine, *Histoire des Drogues, Epiceries, et de Certains Medicamens Simples qui naissent des Indes & en Amérique.* Lyons, 1619.

Collection of Voyages and Travels from the Library of the Earl of Oxford, printed for Thomas Osborne. 2 vols. London, 1745-47.

Collins, John, *A Discourse about the Several Ways of Making Salt in England.* London, 1882.

Crook, William, *A Treatise of Wool and the Manufacture of It.* London, 1685.

Davenant, Charles, *Political and Commercial Works.* 5 vols. London, 1771.

D'Avenant, William, *The Dramatic Works of Sir William D'Avenant.* 5 vols. Edinburgh and London, 1872-74.

Deacon, John, *Tobacco Tortured, or the Filthie Fume of Tobacco Refined.* London, 1616.

Documents from Simancas relating to the Reign of Elizabeth, 1558-1568, translated from the Spanish by Spencer Hall. London, 1865.

Dodsley's Old English Plays, second edition with notes, vol. iv. London, 1780.

Drayton, Michael, *The Complete Works of Michael Drayton,* with introduction and notes by Rev. Richard Hooper. 3 vols. London, 1876.

Dryden, John, *The Dramatic Works of John Dryden,* edited by George Saintsbury. Edinburgh, 1882.

——, *The Poetical Works of John Dryden.* Cambridge edition. Boston and New York, 1908.

England's Advocate—Europe's Monitor, being an Intreaty for Help in Behalf of the English Silk-weavers and Silk Throsters. London, 1699.

England's Danger by Indian Manufacturers. London, 1690.

English Factories in India, 1618-1654: a Calendar of Documents in the India Office, British Museum and Public Record Office, edited by W. Foster. 9 vols. Oxford, 1906-1915.

English Reprints, edited by Edward Arber, No. 19. London, 1870.

Evelyn, John, *Memoirs, Comprising his Diary from 1641-1706, and a Selection of his familiar Letters* . . . edited by William Bray. 5 vols. London, 1827.

——, *Literary Remains of John Evelyn,* edited by William Upcott. London, 1834.

Everaerdts, Regidius, *Panacea, or The Universal Medicine, being A Discovery of the Wonderfull Vertues of Tobacco, etc.* London, 1659.

Force, Peter, *Tracts and Other Papers, Relating principally to the Origin, Settlement, and Progress of the Colonies in North America from the Discovery of the Country to the Year 1776.* 4 vols. Washington, 1836-46.

Fuller, Thomas, *The History of the Worthies of England,* a new edition containing the notices of the most celebrated worthies of England . . . since the time of Fuller; with notes . . . by P. Austin Nuttall. 3 vols. London, 1840.

Gee, Joshua, *The Trade and Navigation of Great Britain.* London, 1731.

Gerard, John, *The Herball; or Generall Historie of Plantes,* enlarged by Thomas Johnson. London, 1636.

Gilbert, Humphrey, *A Discourse to Prove a Passage to the Northwest.* (The Prince Society Publications). Boston, 1903.

Hakluyt, Richard, *The Principall Navigations, Voyages Traffiqúes and Discoveries of the English Nation.* 12 vols. Glasgow, 1904.

Hakluyt Society Publication, 1st. Series, no. 7. London, 1854.

Hale, Thomas, *New Invention of Mill'd-Lead for Sheathing of Ships against the Worm, etc.* London, 1691.

Harleian Miscellany: or a Collection of scarce, curious, and entertaining Pamphlets and Tracts, as well in Manuscript as in print, found in the late Earl of Oxford's Library. 12 vols. London, 1808-11.

Harris, John, *Navigantum atque itinerantum bibliotheca, or Complete Collection of Voyages and Travels.* 2 vols. London, 1705.

Harrison, William, *Description of England,* edited by Frederick J. Furniwell. London, 1877.

Heywood, Thomas, *Thomas Heywood's Plays* (Mermaid Series), edited by A. Wilson Verity. London, 1902.

Hobbes, Thomas, *The Leviathan.* Oxford, 1881.

Jonson, Ben, *The Alchemist,* edited by C. M. Hathaway. New York, 1903.

——, *The Works of Ben Jonson.* London, 1816.

Josselyn, John, *An Account of Two Voyages Made during the Years 1638, 1663 to New England.* 2 vols. London, 1675.

Journals of the House of Commons, the first thirteen volumes, 1547-1702. London, n. d.

Lamb, Samuel, *Seasonable Observations Humbly Offered to his Highness Lord Protector.* London, 1657.

L'Estrange, R., *The Ancient Trades Decayed, Repaired Again: wherein are declared the several Abuses that have utterly impaired all the Ancient Trades in the Kingdom, etc.* London, 1678.

Letters received by the East India Company from its servants in the East; transcribed from the Original Correspondence Series of the India Office Records. 6 vols. London, 1896-1901; vols. 3-6, edited by W. Foster.

Lignon, Richard, *A True and Exact History of the Island of Barbados.* London, 1657.

Locke, John, *The Philosophical Works of John Locke,* edited by J. A. St. John. 2 vols. London, 1892.

——, *The Works of John Locke,* vol. iv, London, 1794.

Luttrell, Narcissus, *A Brief Historical Relation of State affairs from September 1678 to April 1714.* 6 vols. Oxford, 1857.

Marlowe, Christopher, *Marlowe's Plays* (Mermaid Series). London, 1887.

Marvell, Andrew, *The Poems of Andrew Marvell.* London and New York, 1892.

McCulloch, J. R., *A Select Collection of Early English Tracts on Commerce from the Originals of Mun, Roberts, North and Others.* London, 1856.

——, *A Select Collection of Scarce and Valuable Tracts on Commerce from the Originals of Evelyn, Defoe, Richardson, Tucker, Temple, and Others.* London, 1859.

Middlesex County Records, edited by John C. Jeaffreson. 4 vols. London, 1889.

Milton, John, *Poetical Works*, edited by David Masson. 3 vols. London, 1874.

More, Thomas, *The Utopia of Sir Thomas More; Ralph Robinson's Translation*, edited by George Sampson. London, 1910.

Mun, Thomas, *A Discourse of Trade from England unto the East Indies.* London, 1621.

Overbury, Thomas, *The Miscellaneous Works in Prose and Verse of Sir Thomas Overbury*, edited by Edward F. Rimbault. London, 1890.

Parkinson, John, *Paradisi in Sole Paradisus Terrestris or The Garden of Pleasant Flowers.* Faithfully reprinted from the edition of 1629. London, 1904.

——, *Theatrum Botanicum: The Theater of Plants or An Herball of a Large Extent.* London, 1640.

Pepys, Samuel, *The Diary of Samuel Pepys*, edited by Henry B. Wheatley. 9 vols. London, 1893.

Pett, P., *The Happy Future State of England;* also the obligation resulting from the oath of supremacy to assist and defend the pre-eminence or prerogative of the dispensing power belonging to the king. London, 1688.

Petty, William, *Several Essays in Political Arithmetic.* London, 1735.

Philopatris (Josiah Child), *A Treatise wherein is demonstrated: That the East India trade is the most National of all foreign trades. . . .* London, 1681.

Philosophical Transactions of the Royal Society of London . . . to 1800, etc., abridged by Charles Hutton, George Shaw and Richard Pearson, vol. iii. London, 1809.

Physiologus, Philotheos, Friendly Advice to the Gentlemen Planters of the East and West Indies. London, 1684.

Purchas, Samuel, *Hakluytus Posthumus, or Purchas His Pilgrimes*, containing a History of the World in Sea Voyages and Lande Travells by Englishmen and Others. 20 vols. Glasgow, 1905.

Rea, John, *Flora, seu De Florum Cultura or a Complete Florilege.* London, 1676.

Records of the Virginia Company, Court Book 1619 to 1622, edited by Susan Myra Kingsbury. 2 vols. Washington, 1906.

Robinson, Henry, *England's Safety in Trades Encrease.* London, 1641.

Rye, W. B., *England as Seen by Foreigners in the Days of Elizabeth and James the First.* Comprising translations of the Journals of the two Dukes of Wurtemberg in 1592 and 1610. London, 1865.

Smith, John, *The Generall Historie of Virginia, New England and the Summer Isles.* London, 1624.

Some Considerations Humbly Offered to Both Houses of Parliament concerning the Sugar Colonies, and Chiefly the Island of Barbados. London, 1701.

Some General Considerations offered relating to our present Trade. London, 1698.

Spenser, Edmund, *The Complete Poetical Works of Edmund Spenser,* Cambridge edition. Boston, 1908.

Stevens, Henry, *The Dawn of British Trade to the East Indies;* as recorded in the court minutes of the East India Company, 1599-1603. London, 1886.

Story of the Pilgrim Fathers, 1606-1623, edited by Edward Arber. London, 1897.

Stubbes, Philip, *Philip Stubbes' Anatomy of the Abuses in England in Shakespere's Youth, A. D. 1583,* pt. i, collated with other editions in 1583, 1585, and 1595, edited by F. J. Furniwell. The New Shakespere Society Publications, Series vi, nos. 4 and 6. London, 1877-9.

The British Merchant, containing the sentiments of the most eminent and judicious merchants of London concerning the trade and commerce of these kingdoms . . . , published by Charles King, now republished compleat with improvements. London, 1748.

The Groans of the Plantations, or a True account of their Grievous and Extreme Sufferings by the Heavy Impositions upon Sugar. London, 1689.

The Present State of England—part iii and part iv, printed for William Whitwood. London, 1683.

Thorius, Raphael, *Hymnus Tabaci: a Poem in honour of Tobaco,* translated by Peter Hausted. London, 1651.

Travers, Joseph, *An Essay to the Restoring of our Decayed Trade,* wherein is Described the Smuglers, Lawyers, and Officers Friends. London, 1678.

Vaughan, William, *The Golden Fleece Divided into three parts, under which are discovered the Errors of Religion, the Vices and Decayes of the Kingdome, and lastly the wayes to get wealth, and to restore Trading so much complayned of.* London, 1626.

Venner, Tobias, *A Briefe and Accurate Treatise,* concerning the taking of the fume Tobacco, which very many in these dayes doe too licentiously use. London, 1621.

Whitbourne, Richard, *A Discourse and Discovery of Newfoundland,* with many reasons to prove how worthy and beneficiall a plantation may there be made. London, 1620.

Winthrop's Journal, 1630-1649, edited by J. K. Hosmer (Original Narratives of Early American History). New York, 1908.

Wood, William, *Survey of Trade;* together with considerations on our money and bullion. London, 1719.

Young, Alexander, *Chronicles of the First Planters of the Colony of Massachusetts Bay, 1623-1636.* Boston, 1846.

Young, W. T., *The Poetry of the Age of Shakespeare.* Cambridge, 1910.

SECONDARY WORKS

Abhandlungen der K. K. Geographischen Gesellschaft in Wien, vol. iv. Vienna, 1902.

Academy, September 5, 1885, vol. 28.

Adams, C. F. and Henry, *Chapters of Erie and other Essays.* New York, 1886.

Aiton, William, *Hortus Kewensis or, A Catalogue of the Plants Cultivated in the Royal Botanic Garden at Kew.* 5 vols. London, 1810.

American Historical Review, October, 1896, vol. ii.

Anderson, A., *Historical and Chronological Deduction of the Origin of Commerce, from the earliest accounts.* 6 vols. Dublin, 1788-99.

Andrews, C. M., and Davenport, F. G., *Guide to the Manuscript Material for the History of the United States to 1783, in the British Museum, in minor London Archives, and in libraries of Oxford and Cambridge* (Carnegie Institution), Washington, 1908.

An Encyclopaedia of Plants, Comprising the Description of...all the Plants indigenous, cultivated in or introduced to Britain, edited by J. C. Loudon. London, 1829.

Apperson, G. L., *Bygone London Life, Pictures from a Vanished Past.* New York, 1904.

Arber, Agnes, *Herbals, their Origin and Evolution, a Chapter in the History of Botany, 1470-1670.* Cambridge, 1912.

Aria, E., *Costume: Fanciful, Historical and Theatrical.* London, 1906.

Baines, Edward, *History of the Cotton Manufacture in Great Britain; with a notice of its early history in the East, and in all quarters of the Globe.* London, 1835.

Ballagh, J. C., *White Servitude in the Colony of Virginia* (Johns Hopkins University Studies in Historical and Political Science). Baltimore, 1895.

Barrera, A. De, *Gems and Jewels.* London, 1860.

Bean, W. J., *Trees and Shrubs Hardy in the British Isles.* 2 vols. New York, 1915.

Beer, George Louis, *The Commercial Policy of England toward the American Colonies.* New York, 1893.

——, *The Old Colonial System, 1660-1754.* 2 vols. New York, 1912.

——, *The Origins of the British Colonial System, 1578-1660.* New York, 1908.

Besant, Walter, *London in the Time of the Stuarts.* London, 1904.

——, *London in the Time of the Tudors.* London, 1903.

Bigbee, J. M., *Cocoa and Chocolate* (Publications of the Baker Company), Dorchester, 1886.

Billings, E. R., *Tobacco: Its History, Varieties, Culture, Manufacture and Commerce, with an Account of its Various Modes of Use, from its first Discovery until Now.* Hartford, 1875.

Birch, Thomas, *History of the Royal Society of London.* 4 vols. London, 1756-57.

Birdwood, George C. M., *Report on the Old Records of the India Office,* with supplementary notes and appendices. London, 1891.

Blake, W. O., *The History of Slavery and the Slave Trade, Ancient and Modern.* Columbus, 1861.

Blanqui, J. A., *History of Political Economy in Europe,* translated from the fourth French edition by E. J. Leonard. New York, 1880.

Boas, F. S., *Shakespeare and his Predecessors.* New York, 1908.

Bradley, Henry, *The Making of English.* New York, 1904.

Bradley, Richard, *New Improvements of Planting and Gardening.* London, 1718.

Brothers, Samuel, *Wool and Woolen Manufactures of Great Britain.* London, 1859.

Brown, Alexander, *The First Republic in America*: an Account of the Origin of this Nation, written from the Records then (1624) concealed by the Council rather than from the Histories then licensed by the Crown. Boston, 1898.

Bruce, John, *Annals of the Honourable East India Company from their Establishment by the Charter of Queen Elizabeth 1600 to the Union of the London and English East India Companies, 1707-8.* 3 vols. London, 1810.

Bruce, Philip A., *The Economic History of Virginia in the Seventeenth Century, an Inquiry into the Material Condition of the people; based upon Original and Contemporaneous Records.* 2 vols. New York, 1896.

Brushfield, T. N., *Raleghana,* reprinted from the Transactions of the Devonshire Association for the Advancement of Science, Literature, and Art, vol. xxx.

Bryce, George, *The Remarkable History of the Hudson's Bay Company, including that of the French Traders of Northwestern Canada and of the North West, X Y, and Astor Fur Companies.* New York, 1900.

Bullen, Frank T., *A Sack of Shakings*. London, 1901.

Burlington Magazine for Connoisseurs, vol. ix.

Burton, W., *A History and Description of English Porcelain*. London, Paris and New York, 1911.

Cadbury, Richard, *Cocoa, all about It*. London, 1896.

Cambridge History of English Literature. 12 vols. Cambridge, 1907-15.

Cambridge Modern History, vol. i, ch. ii. New York, 1903.

Campbell, Douglass, *The Puritan in Holland, England and America:* an Introduction to American History. 2 vols. New York, 1892.

Campbell, John, *Considerations on the Nature of the Sugar Trade*. London, 1763.

Candolle, Alphonse de, *Origin of Cultivated Plants*. New York, 1865.

Carey, John, *Discourse on Trade*. London, 1745.

Cawston, G. and Keane, A. H., *The Early Chartered Companies, A. D. 1296-1858*. London, 1896.

Chalmers, George, *An Estimate of the Comparative Strength of Great Britain during the present and four preceding reigns, and of the Losses of her trade from every war since the Revolution, with an introduction of previous history*; new edition corrected and continued to 1810. London, 1810.

——, *Political annals of the present united colonies, from their settlement to the peace of 1763*; compiled chiefly from records and authorized often by the insertion of state-papers. London, 1708.

Chambers, Robert, *The Book of Days, A Miscellany of Popular Antiquities in Connection with the Calendar*. 2 vols. Edinburgh, 1863.

Channing, Edward, *A History of the United States*. 4 vols. New York, 1908-1911.

Charnock, John, *A History of Marine Architecture of all Nations*. 3 vols. London, 1801.

Chatterton, Edward Keble, *The Old East Indiamen*. London, n. d.

——, *Ships and Ways of Other Days*. London, 1913.

Cheyney, Edward, *A History of England from the Defeat of the Armada to the Death of Queen Elizabeth; with an Account of English Institutions during the Sixteenth and early Seventeenth Centuries*. 2 vols. New York, 1914.

Cooke, John Esten, *Virginia: a History of the People*. Boston, 1883.

Cooley, Arnold J., *The Toilet and Cosmetic Arts in Ancient and Modern Times, etc.* London, 1866.

Cromer, Earl of, *Ancient and Modern Imperialism*. New York, 1900.

Cross, Arthur Lyon, *A History of England and Greater Britain*. New York, 1916.

Cunningham, William, *The Growth of English Industry and Commerce in Modern Times*, pt. i, The Mercantile System. Cambridge, 1907.

Dictionary of National Biography, edited by L. Stephen and S. L. Lee. Vols. xxi, xxiii, xli. London, 1887, 1890, 1895.

Dowden, Edward, *Shakespere: A Critical Study of His Mind and Art.* New York and London, 1880.

Drake, Nathan, *Shakespeare and His Times; including the Biography of the Poet; Criticisms of his Writings; . . . and a History of . . . his Age.* 2 vols. London, 1817.

Eden, Frederick, *State of the Poor.* London, 1797.

Egerton, Hugh Edward, *The Origin and Growth of the English Colonies and of their System of Government.* Oxford, 1903.

Edwards, Bryan, *History Civil and Commercial of the British Colonies in the West Indies.* 2 vols. Dublin, 1793.

Ellis, Ellen D., *An Introduction to the History of Sugar as a Commodity* (Bryn Mawr College Monographs), Philadelphia, 1905.

Elze, Karl, *Essays on Shakespeare,* translated by Dora Schmitz. London, 1874.

Emerson, Edward R., *Beverages, Past and Present.* 2 vols. New York, 1908.

English Illustrated Magazine, vol. xxiii. London, 1900.

Epstein, M., *The English Levant Company, its Foundation and its History to 1640.* London, 1906.

Fairholt, F. W., *Tobacco: Its History and Associations;* including an account of the plant and its manufacture, with its modes of use in all ages and countries. London, 1859.

Fincham, John, *A History of Naval Architecture.* London, 1851.

Fiske, John, *The Beginnings of New England, or The Puritan Theocracy in its Relations to Civil and Religious Liberty.* Boston and New York, 1899.

Foster, John E. and Atkinson, Thomas, *An Illustrated Catalogue of Plate exhibited in the Fitzwilliam Museum, May, 1895.* Cambridge, 1896.

Fox-Bourne, H. R., *English Merchants; Memoirs in Illustration of the Progress of British Commerce.* London, 1896.

——, *English Seamen under the Tudors.* 2 vols. London, 1869.

——, *The Life of John Locke.* 2 vols. New York, 1876.

Froude, A., *History of England from the Fall of Wolsey to the Death of Elizabeth.* 12 vols. London, 1865-75.

Gardiner, Samuel Rawson, *History of the Commonwealth and Protectorate, 1649-1660.* 3 vols. New York and Bombay, 1897.

Gayley, Charles M., *Shakespeare and the Founders of Liberty in America.* New York, 1917.

Genty, M. l'Abbé, *L'Influence de la Découverte de l'Amérique sur le Bonheur du Genre Humain.* Paris, 1786.

Geographical Journal, vol. xlvi, no. 3, Sept. 1915.

Gerson, A. J., *The Organization and Early History of the Muscovy Company* (University of Pennsylvania Studies in the History of English Commerce in the Tudor Period). New York, 1912.

Gibbins, H. de B., *Industry in England*. Second Edition. New York, 1898.

Goadby, Edwin, *The England of Shakespeare*. London, 1881.

Green, J. R., *A History of Botany in the United Kingdom from the Earliest Times to the End of the Nineteenth Century*. London, Toronto and New York, 1914.

Gretton, R. H., *The English Middle Class*. London, 1917.

Guizot, F. P. G., *A Popular History of England from the Earliest Times to the Reign of Queen Victoria*. 4 vols. Boston, 1886.

Hackwood, Frederick, *Inns, Ales and Drinking Customs of Old England*. London, 1909.

Hahn, Victor, *The Wanderings of Plants and Animals from their First Home*. London, 1888.

Hayes, Carlton J. H., *A Political and Social History of Modern Europe*. 2 vols. New York, 1916.

Heward, Edward V., *St. Nicotine of the Peace-Pipe*. London, 1909.

Hewins, W. A. S., *English Trade and Finance chiefly in the Seventeenth Century*. London, 1892.

Hoefer, J. C. F., *Histoire de la Botanique, de la Minéralogie et de la Géologie*. Paris, 1882.

Hough, James, *The History of Christianity in India*. 2 vols. London, 1839-45.

Houssaye, J. G., *Monographie du Thé; Description botanique, Torrefaction, Composition chemique, Propriétés hygiéniques de cette Feuille*. Paris, 1843.

Humboldt, Alexander von, *Oeuvres*. 11 vols. Paris, 1811.

Hunt, William, *Bristol*. London, 1889.

Hunter, William Wilson, *The Indian Empire: its People, History, and Products*. Third edition. London, 1893.

Jackson, James, *An Illustrated History of English Plate, Ecclesiastical and Secular; in which the Development in the Silver and Gold work of the British Isles from the Earliest known Examples to the Latest of the Georgian Period is Delineated and Described*. 2 vols. London, 1911.

Jacob, William, *An Historical Inquiry into the Production and Consumption of the Precious Metals*. 2 vols. London, 1831.

Jewitt, Llewellyn, *The Ceramic Art of Great Britain from Prehistoric Times down to the Present Day, being a History of . . . Pottery and Porcelain Works of the Kingdom. . . .* 2 vols. London, 1878.

Jones, E. Alfred, *Catalogue of the Gutmann Collection of Plate*, now the Property of J. Pierpont Morgan, Esquire. London, 1907.

——, *Old English Gold Plate*. London, 1907.

——, *The Old English Plate of the Emperor of Russia*. London, 1909.

Keltie, J. Scott and Howarth, O. J. R., *History of Geography*. New York and London, 1913.

Krapp, George P., *Modern English, its Growth and Present Use.* New York, 1909.

Laut, Agnes, C., *The Conquest of the Great Northwest.* 2 vols. New York, 1908.

Lecky, William E. H., *A History of England in the Eighteenth Century.* 8 vols. New York, 1878-90.

Lee Sidney, *Great Englishmen of the Sixteenth Century.* New York, 1904.

Lenygon, Francis, *Furniture in England from 1660 to 1760.* London, 1914.

Leonard, E. M., *The Early History of the English Poor Relief.* Cambridge, 1900.

Leroy-Beaulieu, Paul, *De la Colonisation chez les peuples modernes.* 2 vols. Paris, 1908.

Lethaby, W. R., *Leadwork, Old and Ornamental and for the most part English.* London and New York, 1893.

Lewis, George R., *The Stannaries: a Study of the English Tin Miner* (Harvard Economic Studies). Boston and New York, 1908.

Lindsay, W. S., *A History of Merchant Shipping and Ancient Commerce.* 4 vols. London, 1874-76.

Lodge, Henry Cabot, *A Short History of the English Colonies in America.* New York and London, 1900.

Long, E., *History of Jamaica.* London, 1774.

Lownes, E. L., *Chats on Old Silver.* London, 1909.

Macaulay, Thomas Babington, *History of England from the Accession of James the Second.* 5 vols. New York and London, 1899.

Mackintosh, James, *The Cabinet History of England, Scotland and Ireland.* 3 vols. London, 1830-38.

Macpherson, David, *Annals of Commerce, Manufactories, Fisheries and Navigation.* 4 vols. London, 1805.

——, *The History of European Commerce with India;* To which is subjoined a review of the arguments for and against the trade with India, and the management of it by a Chartered Company; with an appendix of authentic accounts. London, 1812.

Mantoux, Paul, *La Révolution industrielle au xviiie siècle: essai sur les commencements de la grande industrie moderne en Angleterre.* Paris, 1906.

Markham, Clements R., *A Memoir of the Lady Ana de Osorio, Countess of Chinchon and Vice-Queen of Peru.* London, 1874.

Meller, Henry J., *Nicotina or the Smoker's and Snuff-taker's Companion, Containing the History of Tobacco.* London, 1833.

Milburn, William, *Oriental Commerce.* 2 vols. London, 1813.

Morris, Henry C., *The History of Colonization.* 2 vols. New York, 1908.

Myres, John Linton, *The Influence of Anthropology on the Course of Political Science* (University of California Publications in History, vol. iv, no. i). Berkeley, 1916.

Neal, Daniel, *History of New England; Containing an impartial Account of the Civil and Ecclesiastical Affairs of the Country to the Year 1700, to which is added the Present State of New England with a new and accurate Map.* 2 vols. London, 1720.

Neill, Edward Duffield, *The Early Settlement of Virginia and Virginiola, as noticed by Poets and Players.* Minneapolis, 1878.

——, *The English Colonization of America during the Seventeenth Century.* London, 1871.

——, *Memoir of Patrick Copeland, Rector Elect of the First Projected College in the United States: A Chapter of the English Colonization of America.* New York, 1871.

——, *Virginia Carolorum: the Colony under the Rule of Charles the First and Second, A. D. 1625–A. D. 1685, based upon Manuscripts and Documents of the Period.* Albany, 1886.

——, *Virginia Vetusta, during the Reign of James I:* Containing Letters and Documents never before printed, A Supplement to the History of the Virginia Company. Albany, 1885.

Newton, Arthur P., *The Colonising Activities of the English Puritans.* New Haven and London, 1914.

New York Times, March 19, 1916.

Notes and Queries, Sixth Series, vol. x, London, 1850.

Oldmixon, John, *The British Empire in America.* 2 vols. London, 1708.

Oppenheim, M., *A History of the Administration of the Royal Navy and Merchant Shipping in relation to the Navy, 1509-1660.* London, 1896.

Ornstein, Martha, *The Rôle of the Scientific Societies* (Columbia University Studies in History, Economics and Public Law), New York, 1913.

Osgood, Herbert L., *The American Colonies in the Seventeenth Century.* 3 vols. New York and London, 1904-1907.

Palfrey, John Gorham, *History of New England during the Stuart Dynasty.* 5 vols. London, 1859.

Palgrave, R. H. I., *Dictionary of Political Economy.* 3 vols. London, 1894.

Payne, Edward J., *Colonies and Colonial Confederations.* London, 1904.

——, *History of European Colonies.* London, 1877.

——, *History of the New World called America.* 2 vols. London, 1892.

Penn, W. A., *The Soverane Herbe: A History of Tobacco.* London, 1902.

Percival, MacIver, *Chats on Old Jewelry and Trinkets.* London, 1912.

Phillips, Henry, *Flora Historica: or the three Seasons of the British Parterre*. 2 vols. London, 1824

——, *History of Cultivated Vegetables*. 2 vols. London, 1827.

——, *Pomarium Britannicum: an Historical and Botanical Account of Fruits known in Great Britain*. London, 1827.

Pike, Luke Owen, *A History of Crime in England*. 2 vols. London, 1876.

Poor, Charles L., *Nautical Science*. New York, 1910.

Price, William H., *The English Patents of Monopoly* (Harvard Economic Studies). Boston and New York, 1906.

Prime, William C., *Pottery and Porcelain of all Times and Nations*. New York, 1878.

Proceedings of the Massachusetts Historical Society, vol. xvii. Boston, 1880.

Prowse, D. W., *A History of Newfoundland*. London and New York, 1895.

Pulteney, Richard, *Historical and Biographical Sketches of the Progress of Botany in England from its Origin to the Introduction of the Linnaean System*. London, 1790.

Raynal, G. T. F., *A Philosophical and Political History of the Settlements and Trade of Europeans in the East and West Indies*. 6 vols. London, 1798.

Reed, William, *The History of Sugar*. London, 1866.

Reinhardt, Ludwig, *Kulturgeschichte der Nusspflanzen*. Bd. iv. Munich, 1911.

Rimmel, Eugene, *The Book of Perfumes*. London, 1865.

Roberts, George, *The Social History of the People of the Southern Counties of England*. London, 1856.

Robinson, Edward Forbes, *The Early History of Coffee-houses in England*. London, 1893.

Rodway, James, *The West Indies*. London, 1896.

Rogers, J. E. Thorold, *History of Agriculture and Prices in England*. 6 vols. London, 1866-87.

Roze, Ernest, *Histoire de la Pomme de Terre*. Paris, 1898.

Sachs, Julius von, *History of Botany, 1530-60;* translated by H. E. F. Garnsey. Oxford, 1890.

Salamon, Malcolm C., *The Old Engravers of England in Their Relation to Contemporary Life and Art, 1540-1800*. Philadelphia, 1907.

Sawer, John C., *Odorographia; A Natural History of Raw Materials and Drugs used in the Perfume Industry*. 2 vols. London, 1892.

Scharf, John T., *History of Maryland from the Earliest Period to the Present Day*. 3 vols. Baltimore, 1879.

Scherer, H., *Histoire de commerce de toutes les nations*. 2 vols. Paris, 1857.

Scott, William R., *The Constitution and Finance of English, Scottish and Irish Joint Stock Companies to 1720.* 3 vols. Cambridge, 1912.

Seeley, J. R., *The Expansion of England.* Boston, 1900.

Skeat, W. W., *An Etymological Dictionary of the English Language.* Oxford, 1910.

Skipton, H. P. K., *The Life and Times of Nicholas Ferrar.* London, 1907.

Smith, H. Clifford, *Jewelry.* London, 1908.

Southey, Thomas, *Chronological History of the West Indies.* 2 vols. London, 1827.

Stith, William, *The History of the First Discovery and Settlement of Virginia.* London, 1753.

Sydney, William C., *Social Life in England from the Restoration to the Revolution, 1660-1690.* New York, 1892.

Thomson, W. R., *A History of Tapestry from the Earliest Times until the Present Day.* London, 1906.

Thurber, Francis B., *Coffee from Plantation to Cup.* New York, 1881.

Tiedemann, Friedrich, *Geschichte des Tabaks.* Frankfurt, 1854.

Tilby, A. Wyatt, *The English People Overseas.* 6 vols. London, 1911-12.

Tipping, H. Avery, *Grindley Gibbons and the Woodwork of His Age, 1648-1720.* London, 1914.

Traill, H. D., *Social England.* 6 vols. New York and London, 1895.

Trench, Richard C., *English Past and Present.* New York, 1868.

Trevelyan, George M., *England under the Stuarts.* New York and London, 1904.

Walpole, Charles George, *A Short History of the Kingdom of Ireland from the Earliest Times to the Union with Great Britain.* New York, 1882.

Walsh, Joseph M., *Coffee, its History, Classification and Description.* Philadelphia, 1894.

——, *Tea, its History and Mystery.* Philadelphia, 1892.

Walsh, Robert, *Account of the Levant Company.* London, 1825.

Weare, G. E., *Cabot's Discovery of North America.* London, 1897.

Weaver, Lawrence, *English Leadwork, its Art and History.* London, 1909.

Weeden, William B., *Economic and Social History of New England.* 2 vols. Boston and New York, 1890.

Weitenkampf, Frank, *American Graphic Art.* New York, 1859.

Whewell, William, *History of the Inductive Sciences from the Earliest to the Present Time.* 2 vols. New York, 1859.

Whitworth, Charles, *State of the Trade of Great Britain.* London, 1776.

Wilson, Daniel, *Caliban: The Missing Link.* London, 1873.

Willson, Beckles, *Ledger and Sword, or the Honourable Company of*

Merchants of England trading to the East Indies. London, New York and Bombay, 1903.

——, *The Great Company, being a history of the Honourable Company of Merchant-Adventurers trading to Hudson's Bay.* Toronto, 1899.

Winsor, Justin, *Narrative and Critical History of America.* 8 vols. Boston and New York, 1889.

Woodward, W. H., *A Short History of the Expansion of the British Empire.* Cambridge, 1899.